THE VICTORIAN CHURCHES OF KENT

The Victorian Churches of Kent

Roger Homan

Phillimore

1984

Published by
PHILLIMORE & CO. LTD.
Shopwyke Hall, Chichester, Sussex

© Roger Homan, 1984

ISBN 0 85033 466 7

Printed and bound in Great Britain by
BILLING & SONS LTD.
Worcester, England

For my god-children
Howard, Barry, Sinead,
Adrian and Martin,
and Cesca.

CONTENTS

LIST OF ILLUSTRATIONS
(between pages 32 and 33)

ACKNOWLEDGEMENTS

The completion of a book of this kind attests to the longsuffering of one's family, the patience of a publisher, the allowance of time and opportunity for research within one's professional commitments and the support and guidance of numerous informants. For the first I owe thanks to my wife Caroline, for the second to Noel Osborne and Dr. Frances Condick of Phillimore, for the third to my colleagues at Brighton Polytechnic and the Centre for the Study of Religion and Society at Canterbury, and for the last to a host of people with local knowledge or denominational expertise who led me to others of their kind or pointed the way to sites in fields where chapels once stood and recalled happy times in Sunday schools that had long since disappeared. In many cases their names appear as sources in the Gazetteer and I am unspeakably grateful to them all. In other cases I never knew their names but am thankful none the less: of these I recall especially the man sweeping the road at Tenterden of whom the local policeman whom I first approached advised me 'if he's not heard of it, it wasn't there: in fact if it was in the 19th century they probably had to get his permission to build it'. In the preparation of this volume I made over 700 visits and was for ever obliged to passers-by and impressed by their local knowledge, memories and longevity.

At the invidious risk of conspicuous omission, some of my guides deserve special mention and I must recognise my particular dependence upon Mr. Ronald Baldwin of the Gillingham and Rainham local history group; Mr. Legh Banfield of the Gospel Standard Library in Hove; the Library of the Baptist Union; Major David Blackwell, RIBA, staff architect of the Salvation Army; Dr. C. P. Burnham of Wye College, for his detailed knowledge of Methodist heritage; Mr. L. M. Chowns of Shadoxhurst, Methodist circuit archivist; Mr. Ronald Cooper of Greenwich; Mr. Geoffrey Copus of Tunbridge Wells; the Council for the Care of Churches on London Wall; Mr. Brian Davies of Sittingbourne; the diocesan offices of Canterbury and Rochester; Mr. L. L. Fox of Maidstone who navigated my research on the buildings of the Christian Brethren; the Home Missions division of the Methodist church, a little-known depository of valuable sources; Kent county libraries, especially the local history librarians and staff at Ashford, Dartford, Folkestone, Gillingham, Margate, Ramsgate, Rochester, Springfield, Tonbridge and Tunbridge Wells and at the London Borough Library of Bromley; Fr. Jarlath McDonagh of the Franciscan Study Centre at Canterbury who tutored my first researches on Roman Catholic churches; Richard-Hugh Perks for architectural wisdom; Mark Power, photographer; Dr. Doreen Rosman of the University of Kent; Canon N. Rothon of the Roman Catholic diocese of Southwark; the library of the Royal Institute of British Architects; Seraphim, Metropolitan of Glastonbury and student of the Catholic Apostolic Church; Miss Mary K. Smith of Elham; Mr. Mark Sorrell of Thundersley, historian of the Peculiar People; Dr. Christopher Stell of the Royal Commission on

Historical Monuments, who is recognised as a national mentor to students of chapels; Mr. Roger Thorne of Topsham, student of Bible Christians; Mr. John Vickers of the World Methodist Historical Society; the late Fr. Leonard Whatmore; Mr. Anthony Whimble, county architect; Revd. Duncan Whyte at the London City Mission; Dr. Williams's library and its staff; Mr. Nigel Yates, county archivist, for the facilities of the archives office at Maidstone, for permission to reproduce material from his book on Kent and the Oxford Movement and for astute advice on an earlier version of the text.

1

BUILDING

Sponsorship

THE ERA of church building identifiable as Victorian commenced some seventeen years before the Queen's accession and concluded abruptly with her death and a change of national mood in 1901.

The Act of 1818 by which parliament voted one million pounds to the building of churches was a timely response to decadence and decay. Many churches had long since fallen down: Newenden lay in 'ruines' from the late 17th century until its rebuilding in 1859 and the desecrated chapel at Elmley so remained until 1827. Even where the building stood intact, the behaviour within it often fell short of normal religious standards of propriety: habits like standing on the altar to open a window or of leaving upon it one's hat and gloves were not unknown in the early 19th century (White 1962: 4). At Cliffe-at-Hoo, the *Ecclesiologist* reported, 'the north aisle is used as a day school with all the accompanying juvenile nastiness; the west end of the same aisle is a rubbish hole, and is now filled with a store of brambles, coals and cinders: the transepts are falling and the tower is shored up with a gigantic buttress of brick' (Clarke 1938: 228); St Aubyn came to the rescue in 1864. These were signs of the times, if not typical. A vignette of ungodliness at Meopham is provided by the righteous historian of Zion chapel:

> In no one instance of the national *outward* reformation, is the pleasing change more apparent, than in the comparative sacred observance of the *sabbath-day*. Fifty years ago, and there were but few cities, towns, or villages, in England, in which the 'sabbath-day' was not openly dese-crated; and among the latter, MEOPHAM was not behind hand in these scenes of ungodliness. Here, on *Meopham Green*, were to be seen on the Lord's-day, both men and boys engaging in all kinds of games, such as quoits, football, cricket, &c, &c. Truly this was a dark village, a moral 'wilderness', abounding with 'thorns and briers' of ungodly men. Oh! how little could they have regarded those fearful words, — 'The wicked shall be turned into HELL, and all the nations that FORGET God'. But thanks be unto God, through the abounding of his *tender mercy*, a truly *gracious* change has succeeded.
>
> If it were possible for many of the past generation, whose silent dust yet remains beneath the dark sod in the graveyard, to re-visit their former abodes, and listen to the ascending *prayers* and *praises*, of the 'morning and evening' *sacrifices* (Psa. li. 17), as they fall from the lips of their own surviving offspring, how great would be their surprise and astonishment! (Stallworthy, 1866).

But religious reform was not the only motive of the 1818 Act. There was also a political factor; since 1789 revolutionary ideas of liberty, equality and fraternity had been current within 21 miles of Dover beach. The proliferation of pulpits was a strategy intended to combat continental Socialism (Goodhart-Rendel 1853: 50).

Out of the 'Million Act' were born the Commissioners whose contribution to Kent was to sponsor the erection of stately churches in the centres of many of the county's developing towns. The Commissioners' churches were distinctive as a group: the model was Gothic; square west towers and pinnacles were standard and it was made a requirement that all pews should be within sight and audience of the pulpit. For the Commissioners even Decimus Burton designed in Gothic, producing Holy Trinity Tunbridge Wells at the same time as his Regency developments of Calverley Park in the same town and the St Leonard's estate at Hastings; but Holy Trinity was so true to the Commissioners' style that it could be anywhere and it is understandable that in 1829 the publisher George Virtue should have produced an engraving of it entitled 'The New Church at Maidstone'. In fact Holy Trinity Maidstone was the one local exception to the Gothic rule, being done by Whichcord in the Classical style.

The more spectacular examples of the Commissioners' sponsorship include St George Ramsgate which soars from the crown of the hill and lends its distinctive lantern turret as a landmark in that town, and the Kentish needle, St Michael Blackheath, with its exciting display of slender spire and numerous pinnacles. The Commissioners thought of £10,000 as the budget for any one building and exceeded it on occasion, most notably in the case of Holy Trinity Margate (£25,000), Holy Trinity (it was a fashionable dedication) Maidstone and St Mary Greenwich, none of which survives in religious use.

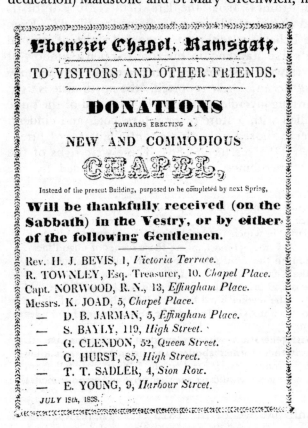

Nonconformity derived nothing from the benefaction of parliament in 1818 and the ensuing years. Indeed, while the 'Million Act' was in part seen as a thank offering for deliverance from Napoleon and continental rationalism, it was also enacted as an antidote to burgeoning dissent. Notwithstanding, the period to 1901 is the heyday of nonconformist building in Kent. In 1818 there were but a few chapels in the county: of particular note among these are the old General Baptist chapel at Bessels Green in vernacular red and blue brick (1716), the galleried Unitarian meeting house at Tenterden (1746), the Gospel Standard chapels at Cranbrook, the Baptist chapel at Eythorne and St Peter's Wesleyan church at Canterbury which barely precedes our period: all of these survive.

The majority of dissenting congregations, however, were in improvised premises in the early 19th century. At Sutton Valence the Baptists occupied a malthouse and

1. *The nonconformists had no benefaction from parliament and were compelled to appeal to their friends*

used a vat as a baptistry (Young 1972: 177). The Independents at Penshurst rented a skittle-alley and the text chosen at the opening service of their new chapel in 1866 was Luke 17. 17, 'Where are the nine?' (Strange 1949: 25). It was in the Victorian period that such communities as these established themselves for the first time in purpose-built chapels of their own. The Wesleyans, who were to build over two hundred chapels in Kent before 1901, were thin on the ground in 1821 when James Gill wrote from Maidstone to Jabez Bunting in a style appropriate for the report of a constituency association to its party headquarters:

> I wish to introduce to your consideration the County of Kent as an important country for home missionary exertion, if the finances of the Connexion should be in a condition to engage in so good a work. In 1811 the population of Kent was 373,095, and agreeably to the increase of population in several places, already published from the late Census, and the ratio of increase of population from the year 1801, which was then 307,624, at present the population of Kent must be upwards of 400,000.
>
> Last Conference the number in our Societies in Kent, including the Deptford circuit, was 5,149, and the number of members among all the Dissenters, does not amount I think to above 10,000 . . . So that Methodists have only, according to this statement, last year about 16,000 in a population of 400,000 . . .
>
> Evangelical ministers in this county are but few. Infidelity abounds. The people generally speaking are astonishingly ignorant of Divine things. Multitudes in the country places cannot read, such appears to be [the] deplorable state of the county. (Ward 1972: 85).

This good man then goes on to speculate on eligible settlements for a mission station, discounting 'Town Malling' as it already has 'two pious ministers in the Church' and preferring Wrotham.

James Gill's appeal paid dividends. In the decades that followed the munificence of the Wesleyans in Kent was unparalleled by any other denomination and surpassed that of all the Baptist sects put together. They were tireless missionaries and were systematic in supplying every centre of population with a place of Wesleyan worship. In only a minority of cases were these professionally designed: like the Congregationalists they generally adopted the Gothic style, if only signifying this preference by the odd mean lancet but in the south-east, at Elham and Dover, Classical conventions prevailed. For their part, the Baptists steadfastly resisted the Gothic taste as they eschewed the religious establishment.

Simultaneously, but without the advantage of such scientific research of the mission field, the Bible Christians arrived in Kent from the west country. The contact was a personal one with their founder William O'Bryan who opened chapels at Hartlip and Sheerness in 1821. The Bible Christians were particularly successful in rural areas in an age of rick-burning and the smashing of threshing-machines and the surviving Methodist churches at Warehorne Leacon and Luton are among those which originated as O'Bryanite causes.

Having no Lords Commissioner the nonconformists found their own benefactors, the most munificent of whom in Kent was perhaps Samuel Morley, Esq., who was to be found laying foundation stones and contributing principal donations from Forest Hill to Tunbridge. At Erith it was Sir Culling Eardley who provided pulpits for every faithful minister with an evangelical complexion: one of these was attached to his house at Lessness Heath and another passed into the Church of England in 1856 and survives as All Saints Nuxley Road. The laying of the Victorian foundation stone was a dramatic and lucrative event: a leading donor whose name had been duly engraved would place on the stone his £100 or £500 and additions were deposited with it.

Anonymity was not a virtue that appealed to Victorian benefactors and a tablet bearing one's name and placed on the front wall was the reward of generous donors: lesser contributors have their names on the side walls and the humblest of all have just their initials inscribed on bricks: the Baptist church at Canterbury has as extensive a collection of these as any.

In rural areas congregations were indebted to local farmers for the gift of a plot of land: this dependence, along with the banishment of dissenters by certain clergy of the established church, accounts for the remoteness of many chapels such as the Primitive Methodist at Ash, the Wesleyan at Pluckley and Ebenezer on the Minnis at Stelling. Wesleyans were on the whole the more successful at securing high street sites even if it meant a squeeze, as it did at Sissinghurst.

Like the Lords Commissioners, private benefactors had mixed motives. Employers looked to religion to improve the sobriety and punctuality of their workers and thought the erection of churches a good investment: in such a cause George 'Bargebrick' Smead provided All Saints Murston (Richard–Hugh Perks) and All Saints Galley Hill was aimed at the employees of the Bazley White cement works. A still more exceptional case of self-interest in church patronage concerned the building of St Michael and All Angels Lower Sydenham at the sole expense of a Hyde Park prospector who owned adjoining land and knew that an attractive church in its midst would facilitate the selling of building leases (Clarke, MSS). For others, however, the sponsorship of church buildings was a duty inherited with wealth. So it was for good Mayow Adams, the squire of Sydenham when it was but a village, who survived as its recognised leader and benefactor when it became populous and fashionable (McLeod 1974: 171–2): Mr. Adams promoted the building of Christ Church Forest Hill and his first name has been adopted, albeit indirectly, as the name of Brethren Hall at Sydenham.

Style

Augustus Welby Northmore Pugin was a convert to Roman Catholicism who shared with the Lords Commissioners a spirited resistance to the influence of ideas from the continent of Europe. This he applied to architectural taste in the way that they did not. He rejected outrightly the 'neo-Grecian' style which the Commissioners had sponsored, for example, at Southborough and Maidstone. For Pugin 'Pointed' and 'Christian' were one and the same and Classical was pagan. The compelling quality of Pugin's writings did much to advance the cause of Gothic:

> England is rapidly losing its venerable garb; all places are becoming alike; every good old gabled inn is turned into an ugly hotel with a stuccoed portico, and a vulgar coffee-room lined with staring paper, with imitation scagliola columns, composition glass frames, an obsequious cheat of a waiter, and twenty per cent. added to the bill on the score of the modern and elegant arrangements. Our good old St Martin's, St John's, St Peter's, and St Mary's streets are becoming Bell-vue Places, Adelaide Rows, Apollo Terraces, Regent Squares, and Royal Circuses. Factory chimneys disfigure our most beautiful vales; Government preaching-houses, called Churches, start up at the cost of a few hundreds each, by the side of Zion chapels, Bethel Meetings, New Connections, and Socialist Halls. Timbered fronts of curious and ingenious design are swept away before the resistless torrent of Roman-cement men, who buy their ornaments by the yard, and their capitals by the ton. (Pugin 1853: 47–8).

The contributions which Pugin and Kent made to each other are outstanding. It was at Rochester that the 14-year-old student sketched the castle and carried 'his researches so far as to take an accurate survey of the foundations. In the prosecution of this work he was 'more ardent than discreet, and twice narrowly escaped with life the consequences of his temerity' (Eastlake 1872: vii). In later life Pugin worked on the Roman Catholic churches at Greenwich (Our Ladye Star of the Sea) and Woolwich; and his son Edward Welby Pugin designed those at Ashford, Dover and Sheerness and the Anglican church of St Catherine Kingsdown. Of Pugin's disciples Benjamin Ferrey was responsible for All Saints Blackheath and Talbot Bury for St Mary Kingsdown, St James Dover and Tonbridge cemetery chapels.

But the great man's crowning achievement was his project at Ramsgate. Throughout his short life Pugin had worked to synthesize religious and architectural principles, but such were the constraints of ecclesiastical commissions that his ideas were more articulated in his teaching than executed in his designs. Crockets and pinnacles by the score for Barry's Palace of Westminster brought him pocket money if not satisfaction and in due time afforded him the opportunity to sponsor his own work and test his ideals. As Pugin explained, 'I have lately nothing but Protestant business, but that pays, and by erecting my church I turn it to Catholic purposes' (Trappes–Lomax 1932: 111). The Ramsgate project was monumental. He supervised the building himself. Neither propor-

2. *Pugin at his drawing board (reproduced by permission of* The Illustrated London News).

tions nor materials needed to be mean. He was able to avoid the features he most despised – sham, façade and non-functional ornament. Above all he could pursue the symbols of paganism which he noticed with such disapproval in the Classical styles. Authenticity, truth to materials and Christian conviction expressed through the devices of Gothic were the doctrines which Pugin strove to realise. Sadly, at Ramsgate the device in which Pugin most delighted and which he regarded above all others to assert the faith, the spire, was not executed.

What began as the building of a humble home on an edge of the cliff dear to Pugin from boyhood acquaintance became at the suggestion of his second wife a grander project. The Grange (1844) was but a part of the plan. The church dedicated to St Augustine, who brought Christianity to Kent in 597, is the realisation of Pugin's 'true principles' within the limits of annual resources and the brevity of his life. In a tribute that Pugin would perhaps have valued above all other – in view not only of the speaker but of the sentiment – Benjamin Ferrey commented 'Everything about it is truthful' (Ferrey 1861: 173). Pugin's pathetic dissatisfaction with his previous works, which in his own view fell so far short of his published ideals, is expressed in the thankfulness that he was spared to produce Ramsgate:

> I can truly say that I have been compelled to commit suicide with every building in which I have been engaged, and I have good proof that they are built little better than ghosts of what they were designed; indeed, had I not been permitted by the providence of God to have raised the church at St Augustine's, I must have appeared as a man whose principles and works were strangely at variance. (Ferrey 1861: 422).

The monument perches still on the west cliff. It is now the abbatial church where in Pugin's dim religious light the Benedictine monks sing their Latin vespers nightly at six, when the public are welcome, then trip through the traffic of St Augustine's Road to the seclusion of E. W. Pugin's abbey. Here worked and worshipped from six in the morning until compline the architect and paymaster: and here, on 14 September 1852, after his third wife Mary had rescued him from Bedlam, he died aged 40 and left his work unfinished but durable. Purcell quotes an appreciation of uncertain source:

> Tower and temple – built not in a day
> And built to fall, but when the sea-rocks fall,
> With jealous ivy on the garden wall
> To bar the envious outer world away,
> And turret-flag high o'er the dashing spray
> Music of waters – beauty of the night –
> Here Art and Nature in one work unite,
> Rear the white cliff, and crown the rock-hewn way.   (Ferrey 1961: 423)

3. The Rt. Hon. A. J. Beresford-Hope, M.P., ecclesiologist and patron of Kilndown and the missionary college at Canterbury (rep. by permission of Illustrated London News)

Within the established church, the pursuit of truth and beauty – that is, of Gothic – was the purpose of of the Cambridge Camden Society which was founded in 1839 by the hymnologist J. M. Neale and was later known as the Ecclesiological Society. Its president Alexander James Beresford-Hope, sometime M.P. for Maidstone, had a home in Kent and was responsible for two major ecclesiological projects in the county. Christ Church Kilndown was originally commissioned by Beresford-Hope's stepfather, the Viscount Beresford, who lived at Bedgebury Park. By the time of the stepson's intervention the project was already well-developed without heed to ecclesiological principles. Some say that Viscount Beresford had engaged Anthony Salvin, others that there was no original architect: in either event, Beresford-Hope rescued the work and transformed what would have been a commonplace country church into what Betjeman calls 'a museum of the Camden Society'.

The Ecclesiologist, which had described the original design as 'mean and bad', warmly acclaimed the outcome of the President's instructions to Salvin. It was indeed spectacular, not least in the rich colours of its interior traces of which can today be seen beneath this century's whitewash: but some of the initial defects remained, notably the low-pitched roof which Beresford-Hope concealed behind a parapet — a solution that might have disturbed Pugin as much as the object of offence.

Mr. Beresford-Hope's strategy was compensatory. He employed the best approved designers of his day and the most truthful of available materials. He ordered stained glass for the lancets from the royal works at Munich. For the altar, he had a copy of William of Wykeham's tomb in Winchester Cathedral, which was of stone, not marble. The chancel screen and stalls were by R. C. Carpenter, who was to become one of the darlings of the Ecclesiological Society: the lectern and distinctive brass candelabra were by Butterfield who was to become the other. And so in a remote village church a way was found to test the theory and exemplify the ideals. Overnight Kilndown became an object of national interest. Its interior was ablaze with colour and there was not a fitting that did not excite. So porous is sandstone and so problematic is damp, however, that mural paintwork and gilding could not without enormous expense have been maintained and they are now washed over, but the furnishings remain intact. When the first paymaster died in 1854, Butterfield was engaged to direct the funeral

4. *Butterfield's arrangements for the funeral of the Viscount Beresford at Kilndown (reproduced by permission of the* Illustrated London News).

arrangements which were reported and depicted in the *Illustrated London News*. And in 1882, some five years in advance of need, Carpenter and Ingelow designed Beresford-Hope's tomb.

Beresford-Hope's other Kent project was at Canterbury where in 1844 he purchased the remains of St Augustine's abbey which had been dissolved and destroyed after the Reformation. Again liaising with Butterfield — a partnership that in the 1850s was to produce All Saints Margaret Street — they reconstructed the ruins as a training college for missionary clergy. The buildings here occupied three sides of a spacious quadrangle, entered through the ancient gateway: cloisters, student rooms, library, refectory and a workroom for the teaching of such practical skills as carpentry which might be found useful in the mission field. Eastlake's classic *History of the Gothic Revival in England* carries an appreciative description of the chapel:

> The west side of the quadrangle is occupied by the chapel and refectory, standing at right angles to each other, the former having been recently rebuilt, and the latter partly restored from the old Guesten Hall. The chapel is fitted with stalls to the whole length of both sides, each stall having its 'miserere' seat carved after a different design. Every detail in this chapel, from the encaustic tiles with which the floor is paved to the braced roof overhead, exhibits evidence of careful study. The proportions of part to part are excellent, the mouldings graceful and refined in character, and the decorative features — which are but few — skilfully and effectively introduced. (Eastlake 1872: 227).

St Augustine's college has in recent years been superseded by the Canterbury School of Ministry and its buildings are now occupied by the King's School.

The college at Canterbury was Butterfield's first major commission: one of his later works — considered by Paul Thompson to be his best (Ferriday 1964: 171) was St Mary Langley, commissioned by Pusey's brother to replace a victim of fire.

For all that he courted the approval of the *Ecclesiologist*, the prolific Victorian architect (later Sir) George Gilbert Scott never secured the *nihil obstat* of the Camden Society or the patronage of its friends. He blotted his copybook in 1844 by furnishing the winning design for a Lutheran church in Hamburg (White 1962: 125-7). In Kent, however, he found plenty of work, little of which ranks as outstanding. Scott's churches survive at Ramsgate (Christ Church), Hawkhurst, Langton Green and Underriver. His St Gregory Canterbury is currently converting to an arts centre for Christ Church College, and his dockyard church at Woolwich has been bodily removed to Eltham where it serves as St Stephen Rochester Way.

Scott also carried out a number of restorations, additions and subtractions beginning at Canterbury (St Margaret 1850 and St Paul 1856) and going on to Hayes, Bridge, Cobham, Ditton, Dover (St Mary-in-Castro), Penshurst, Frinsted, Rochester cathedral, Chillenden, Faversham parish church and the St Bartholomew hospital chapels at Sandwich and Chatham. He sometimes lacked the reverence for the heritage of past ages that marked Butterfield's St Augustine's abbey: far from enhancing the existing building he occasionally removed or obscured it, as at Ditton and Frinsted. Newman describes as 'crushing' Scott's blow to Hayes parish church and his work at Bridge as 'grotesque insensitivity'.

None of Scott's works in Kent were major, either in the moment of commission or in the act of execution. Few here believed in him as a great architect, but he compensated by so esteeming himself throughout his *Recollections*. He reckoned that all odds had been heavily loaded against him, regarded his own designs as superior, resented the patronage of Butterfield and Carpenter and was baffled by the *Ecclesiologist*'s boycott of his work:

> Amongst Anglican architects, Carpenter and Butterfield were the apostles of the high church school — I of the multitude. I had begun earlier than they . . . but as they became the mouthpieces — or hand-pieces — of the Cambridge Camden Society, while I took an independent course, it followed that they were chiefly employed by men of advanced views, who placed no difficulties in their way, but the reverse; while I, deemed to deal with the promiscuous herd, had to battle over and over again the first prejudices, and had to be content with such success as I could get. (Scott 1879: 112-3).

While the works of the Pugins and Scotts have been the most frequently noticed, however, they were not typical of the bulk of Victorian church and chapel building. The established church produced only half as many buildings in Kent during our period as the Baptists, Congregationalists and Methodists. Yet on the whole nonconformity and its architecture failed to engage the compilers of fashionable almanacks and visitors' guides. Of the parish churches *Kelly's Directory* was wont to record dates, architects, style, fabric, cost, principal features, the names of benefactors and to add 'there are also Baptist and Wesleyan chapels and a room for the Brethren'. The *British Almanac and Companion* which annually noticed 'Public Improvements' gave its space for religious buildings almost exclusively to the Church of England and variously commented 'The Roman Catholic and Dissenting churches we must dismiss with the briefest reference' (1878: 134) and 'The churches and chapels of the Wesleyan Methodists do not usually possess much architectural character, but collectively they are of some importance' (1874: 180). As if this perennial neglect were not frustrating enough for the latter-day student — not to say for the dissenting architects whose achievements were unnoticed — the Pevsner series, the resources of provincial reference libraries and the Council for the Care of Churches share its preoccupation with the grand and mainstream. So does Canon Basil Clarke in his published works, although his manuscripts include careful details on many a desecrated mission church and disused chapel, especially in London. Victorian engravers and Edwardian postcard publishers did nothing to correct the imbalance. But perhaps the guiltiest culprit of all is the photographic collection of the National Monuments Record in which villages are often 'done' by views of the medieval parish church alone.

Yet the smaller Victorian chapels were justly prized by those who built and used them and it was not with condescension that they were appreciated as 'neat', 'graceful' and 'elegant' in the denominational yearbooks. Such are the compelling virtues of the vernacular chapels at, for examples, Biddenden (Ebenezer) and Chislet (Marsh Side Wesleyan), both of which survive in religious use. Other more demonstrative buildings include J. K. Cole's Bible Christian chapels at Chatham and Plumstead which have in recent years been adopted by the established and Roman Catholic churches respectively: thus they more effectively command the kind of attention that stands a building in good stead when development plans loom.

The various fellowships of Baptist were between them prolific. The Strict, Particular and Gospel Standard communions normally used cottages and hired rooms in their early days but by the end of the century had scores of their own purpose-built chapels, typically small, plain, neat, porched and with a Hebrew name. Mount Zion at Ramsgate and Priory Chapel at Maidstone were among the very few Strict Baptist chapels with Gothic pretence: the town chapels of the Strict Baptists were normally lightly classical, those of the Baptist Union more full-bloodedly so. But the natural habitat of those who loved the doctrines of grace being the countryside, the vernacular chapel style predominated, Hadlow, Brabourne, Ryarsh and Tenterden (Jireh) providing good examples. Among the most curious was Zoar at Canterbury, built in 1845 in the outward form of a water-tower in the city wall: it is a case of unwonted conformity to the way of the world. James Wilson's Cavendish chapel at Ramsgate was also Strict and Particular when it was built in 1840 but under the ministry of a Mr. Etheridge the communion table was declared open: a suit in Chancery in 1860 failed to retrieve the building for adherents to the Strict communion and Cavendish is today Baptist Union (Chambers 1957: 32-3): modern aesthetes call it ugly, tasteless and dreadful and there is a certain indelicacy about the Prince of Wales' feathers that are intended as a finial but its well-appointed interior provides a classic example of Victorian nonconformist arrangements.

The Baptists of the open communion were always in the better positions, both economically within the class system and geographically within the towns. Before he left the Baptist Union in 1887, the magnetic preacher Charles Haddon Spurgeon persistently inspired Baptist munificence and attended in person the foundations or openings of many a chapel in Kent. The comparative pretension of the open Baptists was instanced in their commissions of recognized architects, either local men like Grant of Sittingbourne or Gardner of Folkestone or designers who were by belief or practice especially committed to Baptist ideals: John Wills of Derby was pre-eminent among these, and for all the distance of his practice was the most frequently engaged by the Baptists of Kent, both for town churches as grand as those at Deal and Sevenoaks and for modest village chapels like Brasted.

While the Baptists had Wills of Derby, the Congregationalists had John Sulman and, though in Kent they made less use of him, W. F. Poulton. At Milton, Bromley and Westgate-on-Sea Sulman had some formidable projects into which were built lecture rooms, Sunday schools, catering facilities and toilets. Like Cavendish chapel at Ramsgate these were complexes rather than mere chapels: the function of worship, which was exclusive in the design of the episcopal church, was but a prior purpose for nonconformists. By contrast, the Church of England, for reasons on which it is instructive to speculate, did not provide toilets: for one thing its sermons were shorter and for another its equivalents to the anniversary tea were held in a separate building, the parish hall.

As far as building new premises was concerned, the Victorian period was a quiet time for the Quakers of Kent who produced their only new meeting house at Tunbridge Wells, as ever in a contemporary domestic style. The Friends have always eschewed architectural pretence in their own places of worship. Curiously, however, Thomas Rickman, the great architect of the Gothic Revival to whom we owe the very terms 'EE', 'Dec' and 'Perp', was a Quaker: but his own kind had no place for his skills in design and Hubert Lidbetter comments that 'it is perhaps fortunate for the Society that he exercised his medieval proclivities in quarters more sympathetic thereto than a Friends' Meeting House could be' (1961: 8). There were such quarters in Kent: with R. C. Hussey Rickman rebuilt Goodnestone parish church and St Mary Lower Hardres was by Rickman and Hutchinson.

Of the new denominations of the 13th century the Salvation Army was the most conspicuous. The early corps buildings — 'barracks' as they were called from 1879 —

were invariably premises leased or purchased from other organisations. In 1882 the resolution expressed in *The Salvation War* was 'We never build unless it is impossible to rent buildings'. But the insecurities that attended the hiring of premises and the subsequent availability of the architectural skills of Major E. J. Sherwood, the self-styled 'Commissioner for Property', effected a revision of this policy. Purpose-built halls in the citadel style appeared in various towns before the end of the century, including Sherwood's fortress at Tunbridge Wells (Blackwell 1956).

Among Brethren a sentimental attachment to makeshift premises and the ubiquitous pre-fabricated hut or iron room coincided with a purposeful indifference to any form of pretension, whether in the adoption of names or in architectural style. They called their meeting-places merely 'halls', either simply 'Gospel hall' or naming the chapel after the neighbourhood, as Mayow Hall at Sydenham. The appearance of these places is often as studiously inconspicuous as their names and the resistance on principle of denominational descriptions is complemented by the avoidance of a recognisable ecclesiastical style (Coad 1968: 184).

The Catholic Apostolic church was established in Sheerness and Chatham but its provincial buildings were unremarkable beside the church in Gordon Square now serving the University of London. The Church of the New Jerusalem (Swedenborg) set up at Bromley, Deptford and Chatham, with a most dramatic and surviving edifice at Snodland: its quaintly entitled journal of the Victorian times, *The Intellectual Repository*, reports persistent missions to the Medway towns but seldom did the seed germinate.

The category of chapels that is most distinctive of the Victorian period, however, is the cemetery. The Victorian way of death was without precedent and the 20th century way of cremation has rendered the cemetery a thing of the architectural past. The advent of municipal cemeteries, though barely documented in parish histories and Victorian visitors' guides, provides useful insights of the period, not least of the exclusiveness of the established church. At Tunbridge Wells, for example, the churchyard of Holy Trinity was already bursting at the seams in 1849 when a supplementary burial ground was opened with a simple mortuary chapel; but this soon filled and in 1873 a site was cleared in Frant Forest under the direction of a joint burial board constituted of the different churches in the town. So it was throughout the county, from Thanet to Thamesside.

The standard arrangement was to construct two chapels, one for the use of the established church and the other for nonconformists. In some cemeteries (Ashford, Charlton, Maidstone, St James Dover, St Nicholas Rochester and Lee among them) there was an unfriendly distance between the two buildings but elsewhere the two chapels were separated only by a *porte cochère*, invariably surmounted by a spire (Canterbury, Tunbridge Wells and Sittingbourne, for examples). The bell, flèche or spire was a device which distinguished the episcopal chapel from its poorer neighbour and there were also variations in tracery and glass. In most of Kent's Victorian cemeteries, only one chapel (if that) survives for its original purpose, the other having been adapted as a workshop and shed or demolished.

Not only for last respects but also in subsequent repose members of the established church had a place of their own. At Tunbridge Wells 13 acres were allocated to the Church of England, seven acres to nonconformists and half an acre to Roman Catholics, thus providing an intriguing measure of religious allegiance in the town (*Sussex Weekly Advertiser*, 12 August 1873).

Burial boards adopted various procedures for selecting designs for cemetery chapels. At Canterbury and Faversham the task was assigned to the borough surveyor while elsewhere competitions were held and architects submitted designs which were considered as from 'Fido' or 'Lucifer'. The burial boards took their deliberations seriously and these were always reported prominently in the local press. A cemetery with a good prospect and imposing chapel and lodge was a feature that enhanced a town and the residents would readily contribute shrubs and plants as the grounds were laid out. However, there is a startling exception at Gravesend of all places where the cemetery chapel is a former dance-hall by the Regency architect Amon Henry Wilds.

Chronology

The accompanying table demonstrates the extraordinary munifence of the religious people of Kent. Their 327 Anglican churches are to be compared with 207 built in Sussex in the same period, their 765 nonconformist chapels with only 244 in Sussex (Elleray 1981: 42). The building effort of the established church was normative: having lagged behind that of the Wesleyans in the early part of the period, it peaked at 1880 and declined in the closing years of the century when ground was yielded to the late Victorian sects. A quarter of all church buildings in Kent were episcopal, another quarter were Methodist. The fate of this stock is detailed in Chapter 4.

THE DISTRIBUTION OF VICTORIAN CHURCHES IN KENT

Church etc.	1818-31	1832-41	1842-51	1852-61	1862-71	1872-81	1882-91	1892-1901	Total
Church of England	19	20	32	35	53	77	54	37	327
Roman Catholic	–	1	6	2	7	9	11	15	51
Baptist	19	21	17	11	28	23	32	27	178
Ind. Cong.	20	19	15	19	24	18	23	16	154
Wesleyan	26	29	28	12	27	36	37	19	214
Prim. Methodist	1	1	5	2	16	16	7	6	54
Bible Christian	12	4	7	2	3	5	9	4	46
Other Methodist	--	–	1	1	2	–	3	1	8
Jewish	–	2	1	–	1	–	–	–	4
Cemetery	–	1	1	16	6	10	4	8	46
Other Public	2	1	2	5	3	5	3	5	26
Brethren	–	–	–	–	2	2	6	4	14
Salvation Army	–	–	–	–	–	–	4	2	6
Other Christian	1	6	6	5	14	19	17	23	91
Totals ..	100	105	121	110	186	220	210	167	1,219

2

MISSION

THE VICTORIAN county of Kent was vast and heterogeneous. Until the Local Government Act of 1888 it was inclusive — as is the gazetteer in this volume — of Woolwich, Plumstead, Greenwich, Blackheath, Lewisham, Forest Hill, Sydenham and parts of Deptford. Anerley and Penge, however, were then in Surrey. In the early Victorian period these places were small detached settlements; the village atmosphere survives most recognizably at Blackheath. When a suburban site was sought for the Crystal Palace, Sydenham had fields enough to spare. Though now absorbed by the dense development of the late Victorian period and early 20th century, metropolitan Kent had in its day its leafy commuter suburbs: Lewisham has long since been deserted by the rich but Blackheath Park, a development of the 1820s, remains intact. There are further signs of a now fading glory on Sydenham Hill, Forest Hill and at Lee.

In these places the habit of worship was assured and comfortably accommodated: the commodious churches of the Lords Commissioner were maintained throughout the century and here the established religion prospered. But these were not the communities that at the end of Victoria's reign were to engage students of London life, labour, poverty and religiosity like Charles Booth and Richard Mudie-Smith: their concerns were rather the approaches of the churches to the casualties of urban and industrial development at Bell Green, the 'dust-hole' at Woolwich and the more squalid reaches of Deptford. In all these places the churches were persistent in missionary activity:

> The poorer parts of Deptford are, indeed, a veritable 'Tom Tiddlers ground' for missions, and we hear of one woman busy at the wash-tub calling out, 'You are the fifth this morning'. (Booth 1902, 5: 14).

By the end of the century, Deptford was like many places thick with churches and missions of all kinds:

> on either side, as one walks up or down the High Street, are churches of various denominations — Wesleyans and Congregationalists, Roman Catholics and the Society of Friends, with various mission buildings in the side streets and a Baptist church hard by in Octavius Street (Booth 1902, 5: 15)

In every circumstance the faithless or merely non-attending are pursued and we read of the London City missioner there that 'he finds the people specially amenable at a time of death' (Booth 1902, 5: 23). But the wash-tub witness was an approach to the preoccupied, and the death-bed testimony ill-timed if supposed to produce an increment of attendance at Sunday worship.

Mission consisted not only in the knocking of doors and bearing of tracts but in the taking of church buildings to the people. Mission buildings were squeezed between

13

terraces and suddenly appeared on vacant corners: Mr. Kent's iron rooms could be ordered and delivered within weeks and removed to another mission district at will. Whether of wood, iron or brick the missions were designed to be hospitable but to lack the grandeur and formality that might intimidate the humbler worshipper. The poor on whose doorsteps these buildings appeared were not allowed to think they were un-wanted or that worship was a high vocation to which one responded grandly dressed and in a carriage. Notwithstanding, the mission hall strategy was widely unsuccessful and Charles Masterman added a critical comment to Booth's:

> Mr. Booth brought a sweeping indictment against the whole collection of shabby, dilapidated mission-halls, of tin or drab-brick, which he found offered as homes for the spiritual nourish-ment of the poor. And in practically every borough the attendance of adults at these lamentable erections is found to be approaching the vanishing point ... 34, 43, 16 in the Anglican, 8 in the Baptist, 41, 41 in the Congregational, I find the mission-hall attendance in one district. In another are ten Baptist missions with an average morning adult attendance of 7 ... in another five Anglican with a morning average of 13 ... Not on such lines, it may safely be asserted, will the good news of the kingdom of God come to the working population of South London (Mudie-Smith 1904: 202).

The failure of the mission system is partly attributable to an absence of the habit of Sunday worship among working people — Roman Catholics excepted: they had other occupations in their only free time such as unaccustomed rest and shopping for a late Sunday lunch with wages that were only paid on Saturday evening (Homan 1970). But there were other factors too: the mission hall was the concrete expression of a patronising view of the working class by which its members were excluded from the worship of the respectable chapel or parish church. Not even the liberal distribution of meat, clothing and coals lured the humble poor to ministrations and hymn-singing that were by design 'popular and breezy' (Mudie-Smith 1904: 202). Indeed, charity was at its worst part of a desperate strategy of soul-winning; of Holy Trinity, Charlton Booth made a penetrating comment:

> Solace has to be sought in caring for the individual and letting the mass go by, but it may be that the individual proves hardly less elusive than the crowd. In the pursuit of the individual the parish is visited from house to house, and this church has a bad name for making relief dependent on religious response. (Booth 1902, 5: 82).

One of the exceptional missionary spirits of metropolitan Kent and a favourable contrast to the practices which Booth observed was that of Catherine Marsh, a clergy-man's daughter who came from Leamington Spa to the rectory at Beckenham in 1850. Neither place at that time might have been thought an obvious base for outreach to the dispossessed and disaffected, but in 1853 the removal of the Crystal Palace from Hyde Park to Sydenham brought some three thousand railway excavators to the area, nearly two hundred of whom lodged in the village of Beckenham. Catherine Marsh's mission to the navvies commenced forthwith. She gained entry to their lodgings on a Sunday evening and finding that none of them had been to church reported the sermon to them. She conducted Bible classes for the navvies three times a week and there was an evident dividend in terms of social control, for she wrote:

> During the winter, the attendance of the navvies at church continued to be large and regular: and the cottages where 'readings' were given were thronged. On the last day of 1853 the sergeant of the police, stationed at Beckenham, called to return thanks for the interest that had been taken in these noble fellows. He said that his duty had never been so easy before in

Beckenham, for their example had restrained the wilder young men of the place, and had even shamed a few into attendance at public worship. So we wrote at the close of our first year's intercourse with the navvies, 'Hitherto hath the Lord helped us'. (O'Rorke 1917: 88–9).

When the Crimean war came Catherine Marsh and her beloved navvies set about earnest prayers for the soldiers and fortified them with Testaments to go in their kits: and when peace was declared and the surviving soldiers returned there was open-house for them at Beckenham rectory. Captain Anstruther, turning his back on the world's allurements following a prayer meeting at Elmer's End testified 'I have found peace, or the way to it, at Beckenham' (O'Rorke 1917: 135). Catherine Marsh wrote and published the story of this work in 1857 under the title *English Hearts and English Hands* and out of that book the Navvy Mission was formed. The Archbishop of Canterbury wrote to her, 'If the navvies are to be deacons, I think you should be the Archbishop'. (O'Rorke 1917: 157).

The Navvy Mission was not the only effort addressing a particular occupational group. There was a Mission to Coalies and a Barmaids' Mission. The Congregationalists had a mission at Deptford for railway workers. In the provinces there were missions for sailors and fishermen, as at Ramsgate, always with their own place of worship; and there were dormitories for the smack boys among whom delinquency was high. St Andrew's waterside mission at Gravesend began as a 'floating parish' on a Thames barge before Street's church was built in 1871. Brickmakers at Murston and cement workers at Galley Hill had places of worship built by their employers which subsequently became parish churches. One of the most active centres of missionary organisation was the Bible Mission hall at Tunbridge Wells where under Pastor John McAuliffe were directed The Gospel Tents Mission in Villages and Rural Towns, The Wayside Bible Carriage Mission, The Bible Hand-cart Mission, The Lime-light Protestant and Bible Instruction Mission, The 'Wayside Words' Gospel Leaflet Mission and Mrs. Bingham's Memorial Fund for Poor Women. (Pearce 1904).

5. *The Clifton Castle mission hall at Plumstead, a converted pub testifying to the conversion of its landlord (reproduced from Vincent, 1830).*

The special relationship which rural Kent has long had with the metropolis was developed annually by migrations to the hop-fields. Booth depicted the poor of Bell Green, Sydenham as 'gas-workers of all kinds, carmen, porters, painters, jobbing gardeners, roadmen, costermongers, laundresses and a very large population of casual labourers' (Booth 1902, 6: 145). Of such sorts and others — though so much the worse for the wear of a long journey — were the processions of hoppers as the residents of the Weald watched their arrival:

Towards the end of August, or beginning of September, the long, white, dusty highways and bye-ways leading from the great Metropolis, become plentifully studded with groups of dingy-looking, sun-burnt, foot-sore men, women and children. So large is the number, so continuous the stream, that a stranger might well be forgiven for assuming that a general exodus of the

> poverty-stricken and miserable was taking place from some poor district of the English capital, or that the London workhouses were being emptied of their living human contents. Nothing more squalid can be imagined than the appearance of these wretched hordes. They often appear one seething mass of rags and tatters ... Old and young, whole and maimed, coster-monger and 'reduced gent', newsboy and shoeblack, flower girl and fruit seller, together with a host of others. (Shindler n.d.: 98–9).

The history of hopping is told by legends of squalor, disease, suffering and tragedy. In 1849 cholera broke out in East and West Farleigh. In 1853 a wagon carrying 30 hoppers ditched into the Medway over Hart Lake Bridge: the victims' grave in Hadlow churchyard was subsequently marked by an obelisk.

But for the woman at the Deptford washtub, the hop-fields offered no escape from missioners. The principal organisation of these was the Hop-pickers' Mission initiated in 1862 by J. J. Kendon of Goudhurst, a disciple of Spurgeon whose efforts in circumstances adverse to Christian proselytizing were appreciated by conformist and nonconformist alike. The greater the perceived depravity, the more zealous was Kendon's Christian response, and the missioners to hop-pickers were indeed capable of observing their field in an unfavourable light:

> Barns, sheds, stables and other buildings are converted into sleeping berths, a small heap of straw serving as a bed. Sometimes the overcrowding leads to much indecency. Some of the scenes frequent among the hop-pickers during the season are a grave scandal to our boasted civilization. It is as if the whole moral sewage of London had been suddenly disgorged upon the rural districts, spreading contagion wherever it flows. Among this class we have been seeking to labour year after year . (Shindler n.d.; 99).

With the familiar inducements of food, clothing and free teas, Mr. Kendon's followers went out two at a time to read the scriptures, distribute tracts, sow the seed and pray for germination. Meetings were often held in fields and open places and chapels – particularly but not exclusively Baptist ones – were used if appropriately situated as were Curtisden Green, Yalding, Horsmonden, Lamberhurst and Hadlow. Shindler remembers one of the earliest crusades in 1849 which started with a service in the Baptist chapel at Hadlow and was followed by a mission to Golden Green:

> I don't remember that there was anything 'golden' about the place or time, unless it was the 'golden' opportunity of preaching Christ to a company of poor, neglected, destitute sinners. (Shindler n.d.: 35).

The prescription, like the diagnosis, was formulated in absolute terms:

> The Gospel is, distinctly, and emphatically, the weapon of the warfare of the agents of the Hop-pickers' Mission; it is the message they bear to the sin-sick, the sorrowful, the guilty and the perishing among whom they labour. They seek to awaken and convert, to soothe, comfort and save the men and women and children who come from the slums of London and elsewhere to gather in the hop-harvest amid the hills and in the valleys of the Weald of Kent ... It would be absurd to deal with the poor degraded hoppers on the humanitarian system, which has taken the place of the Gospel of Jesus Christ in so many pulpits and churches. They are 'ready to perish', and nothing but the glorious Gospel of full and free salvation in and through Jesus Christ, to every one that believeth in Him can reach their case. (Shindler n.d.: 6 and 24).

For some of Mr. Kendon's hearers, however, it was he who was lost: the story is told of an Irish woman who fell on her knees before him and prayed, 'Oh God, convert his soul, and bring him over to the true Church, by the Holy Virgin and all the saints, Amen'. (Shindler n.d.: 135).

The established church was active too though its profile was lower. The Church of England Missionary Association for Hop-pickers was formed at Maidstone in 1877 as a co-ordinating organisation (Harland 1981): one of the legendary figures of the Church among the hoppers was Father Richard Wilson of Stepney who at the end of the century was to be found accompanying the East Enders on their annual migrations, ministering to their physical sores from a bottle of Pond's extract and to their spiritual needs from an orange-box in a small marquee. (Farley 1962: 18-19).

The Salvation Army, Victorian mission *par excellence*, waged its war at two levels: it opened fire with the Gospel upon summer visitors to the seaside resort and there were battles on the streets with those who resented the disturbance on a Sunday of their accustomed peace or else seized the opportunity for the expresssion of base instincts legitimised by middle-class opinion. So it was at Folkestone, while elsewhere the Salvation Army was an accepted feature of the seaside atmosphere: the *Visitor's Guide to the Isle of Thanet* in 1888 gave a picture of Ramsgate in summer:

> We have life in earnest — the wandering black minstrels are in full feather, accompanied by the hymning Salvationists, the cocoa-nut sportsmen, the ranting preachers, the acrobats, street conjurers, performing cats and birds, itinerant photographers, bathing machines, 'Arries and 'Arriets, brass bands, children and spades, dirt and heat, beer and baskets, love and litter, goat chaises, donkey riders and donkey boys, pleasure boats, excursions, steam to Boulogne, 3s. a head, and time no object.

But as we see in this vignette, there was a measure of indifference in the toleration of beach missions: of the Army's progress in Folkestone, Dover and Ramsgate, General Booth reflected:

> It is still in the painful truth, that during the busy summer months, religion is almost forgotten by multitudes of persons residing in health resorts unless when it is absolutely forced upon their attention (*Kentish Gazette*, 3 December 1887).

From Ramsgate to Deptford, absolute force was the order of the day.

3

RELIGIOUS DEVIATIONS

BY ANY STANDARDS religious activity in Victorian Kent was feverish and diverse and a number of religious movements celebrated for their eccentricity were based in the county. In addition to the purpose-built places of worship listed in the gazetteer there were countless hired rooms, adapted premises and open-air meetings. In non-metropolitan Kent, particularly in the countryside, Calvinism had its strength: the budding Strict and Particular Baptist preachers were often young men and they readily made pulpits of their own. Their theology sanctified traditional rural values such as humility and honest work, was emphatic in offering a hope of salvation to the under-privileged of this world and provided a domain of intellectual activity for those whose daily work occupied only the hands.

Calvinism was and is the characteristic religion of rural Kent, not only in its theology and social teachings but in its organisation. The Baptists, above all denominations active in the county, were highly fissiparous. For a young agricultural labourer who had no subordinates at work, the prospect of an audience was a compelling factor in the claim to vocation: subject to the criteria of competence in preaching and ortho-doxy in doctrine, aspirants to the ministry were engaged as itinerant preachers and subsequently as settled pastors in particular chapels.

The hopes and frustrations, the poverty and persecution, the endless dependence of self and family upon the charity of fellows are the dominant themes of the testi-mony of James Weller, 'born in sin in the parish of Headcorn, Kent, Dec. 30, 1806, of poor yet honest parents; but very ignorant of the power of godliness' (Weller 1844: 5). After various preaching engagements throughout the county and frequent indisposition in hospital and workhouse, he came again to his native village:

> Another door opened to me . . . at a house in the Church Yard at Headcorn, where, after the friends had raised a few subscriptions to furnish seats, and had obtained a licence, I preached the Word of Life to a company of poor perishing sinners . . .

> I continued to travel with tea, &c., but was much troubled to make my way as I could wish. The prospect before me was one rapidly multiplying my fears, for . . . my family had increased, my clothes were becoming too scanty and too much worn to appear decent in, and many enemies were surrounding me watching for my halting, who said, 'Ah, Ah, he is only a mushroom preacher, that is up today and gone to-morrow'.

> As it was needful to appear decent when speaking to the people, I sighed and groaned to the Lord to send me some more clothes; and one evening, as I sat by the side of my fire, an impression crossed my mind that the Lord had heard my prayer . . . Accordingly, when I went the next day to Ulcomb to see my brother, he told me that the same gentleman that allowed me the ten shillings per week during my illness at Margate Infirmary, desired me to go down and call upon him. I attended according to request, when the gentleman, after inquiring very kindly respecting my welfare, &c., entered into conversation with me on eternal things, and truly we sucked sweetness therefrom. When I was about to leave, he asked me if the loan

of five pounds for two months would be of any service to me in my trade, and I said it would, at the same time thanking him for his kind offer. He then gave me a check to take the money either at Maidstone or at Ashford; and then said, 'Stay, I have got some clothes I think will fit you', and ran up stairs and fetched down a large bundle, which contained a very good black cloth suit, together with braces, collars, and ankle boots. (Weller 1844: 83–4).;

But for plain believers like James Weller Kentish Baptism was full of hazards: his faith was honest but uninformed, for by his own admission he knew less of 'parties' than a baby knew of letters. In consequence his preaching was not always steered clear of the pitfalls of simple faith:

One Lord's Day as I walked down the street in company with a Mr. P——, he asked in a friendly way if I knew what people called me. I answered, 'no'. 'Why, some say you are an *Arminian*, some a *Baxterian*, some call you a *Calvinist*, some an *Antinomian*, and some say you are a *Huntingtonian*'. I declare I knew no more of the names or creeds these different men professed than I knew of another language at that time. I remember saying to my friend, '*Huntingtonian*, why what doth it mean?' He then asked if I had ever heard of a man by the name of Huntington, who was brought up a poor man in the Weald of Kent, and became a very great preacher and writer. I replied that I never had. (Weller 1844: 71–2).

It was often the case that ministers would withdraw from the churches they served, ostensibly on points of doctrine: this would have been exceptional in the Methodist sects but among Baptists and Congregationalists it was common, and it happened too in the Church of England — Christ Church at Tonbridge was erected for a former curate of the parish church. Whether leaving of their own accord or by the verdict of the church, seceding ministers invariably took with them the nucleus of a new congregation who, where appropriate, obtained 'dismission' from their former church. Such were the origins, for example, of Salem at Tunbridge Wells, of John Fraser's short-lived presbyterian mission at Canterbury, of Providence and Priory chapels at Maidstone, and Enon at Chatham which set up under a Mr. Jones with 41 members dismissed from Zion where they believed the minister was preaching 'another gospel' (Chambers 1957: 93–4). To an outsider at least, the nuances of doctrines about grace and baptism appear too slight to justify the breaking of fellowship, and it is likely that there were in many cases accompanying factors not committed to the minute books. In particular, a Baptist chapel was too small a place with too few meetings to occupy more than one or two aspiring pastors and there were doubtless power struggles within the churches disguised as conflicts of doctrine. That a pastor needs his own pulpit as a priest needs an altar is evidence when he moves home: in the 1820s Charles Smith came from Rye to Tenterden and Salem was built for him even though there was already a like-minded cause in Honey Lane (Chambers 1957: 56–60). The durability of these separations is itself remarkable: most notably at Cranbrook there survive two ancient Baptist chapels within a stone's throw of each other, both of them within the exclusive Gospel Standard Strict Baptist Connexion.

But for outstanding cases of religious movements based around personalities of leaders, Victorian Kent has examples to offer much more colourful than Smith and Jones, the further eccentric in their style, the more outrageous in their conduct and the more dangerous in their charisma. The legendary figures of Sir William Courtenay (pseud.) and James Jershom Jezreel (pseud.) are well documented by 'Canterburiensis' (1838), and by Philip Rogers (1961 and 1963) but warrant a further place in this account. Sir William Courtenay was, as only he knew, a humble Truro maltster called John Tom who had gone missing after a successful sale of malt in Liverpool. Under the soubriquet of Count Rothschild he presented himself in Canterbury during the September of 1832. At that time feelings were running high against the introduction of threshing machines and east Kent had become known as a centre of incendiary fires, tithe-riots and machine-breaking. The first threshing-machine had been destroyed on the night of 28 August 1830 at Lower Hardres; the second attack was at Newington the next day, the assailants being a party of men from Elham, Lyminge and Stelling.

6. John Tom the maltster presenting himself at Canterbury as Sir William Courtenay, Knight of Malta (reproduced from 'Canterburiensis', 1838)

By October nearly a hundred machines had been destroyed in the area south of Canterbury while at Orpington and in the neighbourhood of Bromley and Sevenoaks protests took the form of burning rick-barns (Hobsbawm and Rudé 1969: 97–9).

If the *soi disant* Count Rothschild wanted a second cause, there was the question of the franchise in which the Goliath of Canterbury, Archbishop Howley, opposed reform. The occasion for assault came when the Archbishop visited Canterbury to consecrate St Mary Northgate and attend a sumptuous civil banquet at a time when public funds were running low. A demonstration was staged in which 'one individual, named Olieve, was charged with throwing a pocket handkerchief into the carriage, and using opprobrious epithets' (*The Times*, 11 August 1832). The Archbishop was much taken aback by these disturbances and complained afterwards that he had not been afforded adequate protection.

It was as Sir William Courtenay that John Tom then became known and under this name he became committed to history. He appeared in Canterbury as a spectacle, dressed in an exotic style like Vanbrugh's Lord Foppington and held forth to the crowds. He stood for Canterbury in the parliamentary election of December 1832 and again in the East Kent election: in the latter, 9,450 votes were cast of which only three went to Courtenay. Undeterred in his as yet inchoate campaign in Kent, he launched a weekly newspaper, *The Lion*, in 1833 which carried numerous biblical quotations reflecting Courtenay's sense of divine mission and always insisted on strict religious principles. He saw himself as a kind of messiah, though it later transpired that certain aspects of his behaviour ill became that role. With an eye to publicity he gave evidence in a smuggling case of which he knew little and found himself tried for perjury. He was sentenced at Canterbury for swindling a waiter and as the mob stood poised to storm the Westgate and release him, the mayor had to send to Dover for military support.

At the eleventh hour of his rejection by men, as he was awaiting transportation from Maidstone gaol, his wife arrived from Truro and on the basis of her pleas and assurances he was transferred to the lunatic asylum. At length, in 1837, Queen Victoria granted him a free pardon and he returned forthwith to his former ways and former haunts. The final and fatal battle of his crusade was an armed uprising in which he rallied around himself a group of agricultural workers from the neighbourhood of Hernhill, Dunkirk and Boughton-under-Blean. A warrant was issued for his capture and, as a tablet on the north nave wall of Canterbury cathedral bears witness, one Lieut. Bennett was killed in his attempt to execute it. But in the same affray Sir William Courtenay, the failed messiah, and his immediate disciples were also killed, and they now lie in an unmarked but identifiable grave in Hernhill churchyard.

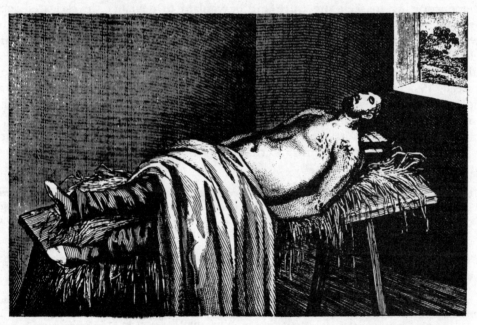

7. *Sir William Courtenay at his post mortem following the battle in Bossenden Wood (reproduced from 'Canterburiensis' 1838)*

James Jershom Jezreel, the Sixth Messenger, was formerly and simultaneously Private James White serving at Chatham. Once he discovered his place in late 19th-century revelation, he commanded a following, chiefly of shopkeepers, and drove around the streets with liveried coachmen (Montgomery 1962). There was already in existence in New Brompton a 'New House of Israel' to which White gravitated in 1875: it met in the home of one of the members under the leadership of a Mr. and Mrs. Head. White's self-realisation was more than the New House of Israel could take and he was expelled, only to be followed by all 18 ordinary members: in the case of one of these, 15-year-old Clarissa Rogers, the attraction was mutual and he later understated his own age and married her.

Jezreel and his wife conducted missionary campaigns in Australia and the United States and returned to New Brompton — which was to their Israel what Mecca is to Islam — to establish in 1884 'Israel's International College' and a number of trading concerns including a German bakery, restaurant, carpentry shop, grocery, and a boot and shoemakers: they were proud to announce a patent furniture cream called 'Jezreel's Magic Polish'. But Jezreel is best remembered for his magic tower, Israel's sanctuary on Chatham Hill which was built to his eccentric specifications after his death, was for want of funds never finished, was claimed by the builders and remained a gigantic white elephant until its demolition in 1960.

After Jezreel's death his wife Clarissa became Queen Esther, the Seventh Messenger, Jezreel having been the Sixth, the 18th-century prophetess Joanna Southcott having been the Second. In 1888 Queen Esther died and an American follower under the assumed name of Prince Michael became the Eighth. Like many of its kind the sect was the subject of rumours and scandals of variable substance and the provincial press, as ever purporting to seek the truth and be vigilant of deviance, investigated reports that young girls were stripped and whipped for indiscipline, that Jezreel had confined his wife to a dark room as punishment and that various frauds had been committed and debts undischarged. (Rogers 1963).

Public outrage and an intolerance of deviant moral principles distinguished too the Plumstead Peculiars. The Revd. C. Maurice Davies, a keen student of marginal religiosity who visited and documented a number of metropolitan sects including the Walworth Jumpers, commented that 'If unpopularity be a test of saintliness, the "Peculiars" are certainly at the head of modern hagiology' (1873: 295). So notorious were they at that time that Blunt's international *Dictionary of Sects* included an entry, if not a charitable assessment:

> PECULIAR PEOPLE. A quite recent sect of very ignorant people, found chiefly in Kent, whose principles are very similar to those of the American Tunkers. The characteristic which has been most prominently brought forward is their refusal to adopt any material means of recovery from sickness; their dependence being placed entirely on prayer. (Blunt 1874: 415).

So were their dependants, and it was this that engendered public concern. In 1899 a man accused of the manslaughter of his child by refusing medical care affirmed:

> 'I have an honest belief in the power of prayer. When the King was Prince of Wales and had typhoid, prayers were offered up throughout the land, and he recovered'.
> The Judge observed: 'My recollection is that Sir William Gull had something to do with recovery . . . It is wicked that these people should let their children die, when by taking ordinary precautions which God has placed in their power they could save them'. (Montgomery 1962: 124).

In fact, the Peculiars were natives not of Kent but of Essex and a fascinating history of them has recently been provided by Mark Sorrell (1979). But they had four stations south of the river, at Upchurch, New Brompton, Gravesend and Plumstead.

It was following the inquest on a small child held at the *Windsor Castle* public house that the Revd. Maurice Davies was to be found 'perambulating the essentially slummy regions of Plumstead most affected by the Peculiar People', some of whom he found to be away at Newgate Prison visiting Brother Hurry whose two little ones had died of small-pox. He found the men hard-working, the women sombrely dressed in distinctive saintly bonnets, and all much concerned with the fate of their incarcerated Brother: it was a concern unshared by the non-Peculiars:

> The neighbourhood was literally up in arms against them — a fact on which I found the 'Peculiars' greatly prided themselves, as going to prove them in the coveted minority of the saints as opposed to the world. Were I to quote half the hard sayings I gathered by diligent inquiry among the small shopkeepers and citizens in general, I should convert this article into a series of vituperations. (Davies 1873: 295).

In the extreme and notorious instances in which the Plumstead Peculiars allowed their children to languish and die, their principles had only a sectarian appeal, and even within the Peculiar community some members had misgivings. But at the more general level of trust in divine providence, the Peculiars had the respect of a wider company. Davies tells:

> Rumour brought to my ears tidings of a certain coloured gentleman who was a bright and shining light among the Peculiar People. To this apostle's humble store I accordingly betook myself, and unearthed him easily, for, sooth to say, the Peculiars are not a retiring sect. He was airing himself at his shop door, and on my inquiry whether he belonged to the Peculiar People, seemed at first inclined to put in a modest disclaimer. He worshipped with the Peculiar People. He thought them good consistent Christian folk. He believed, however, that everything came 'from de Lord', even — wonderful to relate! — doctors. He did not believe the doctor cured. It was 'de Lord'. But he had a supreme conviction that 'de Lord' could use all means, even doctors, if there was faith in the recipient . . . He liked the Peculiar People's literal acceptance of 'de Lord', but he was inclined to throw in 'de doctor' too . . . As he left me on the platform of Plumstead station I heard the little street-boys calling 'Peculiar' after him, and saw him stride over the bridge amongst his tiny persecutors with an air of contempt that was simply superb. (Davies 1873: 299-300).

The Peculiar People are no more, having in 1956 forsaken their name and affiliated to the Fellowship of Independent Evangelical Churches (Sorrell 1979: 60). And the 'little grimy chapel' at Plumstead to which they came from miles around to spend all Sunday long 'making a sort of pious picnic of their devotions' (Davies 1873: 300) is now occupied by Air Scouts.

So much for Protestants. Moderate and evangelical though the towns of Kent were in the majority of cases, there were among them several certres of the Catholic Revival which was itself the object of animosity and disturbances. The practices that were condemned by the early Victorians as 'advanced' or 'ritualist', however, are such as are now general in the Church of England, like the wearing of a surplice in the place of black Geneva gown, the decoration of the altar table by flowers and the celebration of holy communion on a monthly instead of quarterly basis (Cooke 1942: 67-70). There was even a hostile reaction when in 1860 the vicar of Northfleet Frederic Southgate introduced the service of harvest thanksgiving, as he recalled 15 years later in his parish magazine:

> There was a large attendance, and the outcry afterwards was considerable. Did you ever see such doings? Popery, rank Popery. And those flowers too. Disgraceful. Why, the church looked like a garden thrown into a cornfield. Yes, shameful. And those men in surplices? Ridiculous.
> And the Vicar too preaching in his surplice? Ah why is it that I never heard of such a thing. And those churchwardents going round with bags from pew to pew in that way? Why can't we chuck in our money at the door as we always have done? Oh it's all of a piece, popery, popery, from beginning to end. However, that can't last — it must be put down. No one will go

to Northfleet Church on another Harvest Thanksgiving. Nevertheless it has lasted and Northfleet Church is still thronged on such occasions, and more than this. For other churches in the neighbourhood began to do likewise and at last even Swanscombe has followed suit. (Cooke 1942: 67).

The social conscience of churches relating to the Oxford Movement was invariably keen and they were often placed in areas of material need. At Northfleet, for example, good works included the distribution of coal (or 'coals', as the Victorians called it) to the poor, a soup kitchen, clothing clubs, maternity charities and a Dorcas Society in which ladies of the church made clothes for the poor while the curate read to them from some appropriately edifying work. The vicar initiated a literacy campaign which involved the establishment of a lending library, night schools and a reading room and the organisation of spelling bees. (Cooke 1942: 72).

At Tunbridge Wells too the first mission of the Catholic party, St Stephen, came about when the Revd. Harry William Hitchcock was 'painfully struck' by the conditions of the poor inhabitants of the Camden Road and its neighbourhood. Mr. Hitchcock proposed the mission and took charge when it was established in 1870 as a chapel-of-ease to the evangelical parish of St James, the vicar of which appears seldom to have visited the mission. When he did so in 1872 he too was painfully struck but on a different count, for he was alarmed to discover tippets, birettas and coloured stoles, incense and candlelight. On the pastoral side Mr. Hitchcock established an orphanage in the parish. Nevertheless, when the incense invaded the vicar's nostrils Mr. Hitchcock was charged with having neglected his pastoral duties, the judgement went against him, St. Stephen's mission was boarded up and his licence was withdrawn. Mr. Hitchcock was banished to the wilderness from where he maintained an interest in the orphanage and mission, even in his will: for the closure was only temporary and the Catholic faith has survived in the later church of St Barnabas (Copus 1970).

At Folkestone, by contrast, the High Church was the dominant party. Canon Matthew Woodward introduced a riot of decoration to the parish church of SS Mary and Eanswythe and affirmed the catholic faith until his death in 1898. St Peter Folkestone was and still is a shrine of that faith and was in 1877 at the centre of the Folkestone ritual case in which the Revd. C. J. Ridsdale was prosecuted under the Public Worship Regulation Act of 1874 (Yates 1983: 81) for use of vestments and wafer bread. *Punch* joined the protestors:

> O Ridsdale, Reverend Gent., desist
> From antics Ritualistic.
> Are you determined to persist
> In aping rites Papistic?
> What, is it really your intent
> To disregard 'monition'?
> On that wild course if you are bent
> Consider your position.
>> In the face of the Law no longer fly
>> At Popery cease to play, Sir.
>> You had better cave in and knuckle down,
>> And act the Vicar of Bray, Sir.

Ridsdale eventually reached an agreement with Archbishop Tait on the form of worship to be followed at St Peter's and at once lost to Rome several of the community of sisters associated with the church. At St Michael Folkestone too the catholic faith prevailed: the famous Father Tooth, who was imprisoned for wearing vestments, had been curate here in the 1860s.

AT THE CATTLE SHOW.

8. An 1877 cartoon from Punch *which conducted a lively campaign against contemporary ritualism; the farms to which the poster refers are the parishes of St Peter Folkestone and St James Hatcham (Deptford) where the famous Father Tooth served.*

Barely ten years elapsed between Northfleet's first Harvest Thanksgiving and the creation of St Stephen's mission, Tunbridge Wells: but in terms of the advancement of churchmanship there is a generation of difference. What might be regarded as the second generation of Catholic doctrine in the established church was distinguished by more extreme forms of liturgical arrangement and practice. Its shrines throughout the county were managed by committed priests for the benefit of a local, often poor, congregation: but in due course they found themselves attracting the faithful from farther afield. In addition to St Barnabas Tunbridge Wells and the Folkestone churches, St Stephen Lewisham was of the catholic party under its vicar, the prominent ritualist Rhodes Bristow. There were anti-ritualistic disturbances at Holy Trinity Charlton and at St Luke Deptford where the trustees intervened to restore order and compromise with 'an ornate, but Evangelical service' (Booth 1902, 5: 82, 22), whatever that might mean. The parishioners of East Farleigh petitioned the Archbishop as early as 1844 when they noticed an 'unprotestantising' tendency in the practices of their vicar Henry Wilberforce 'such as turning the back on the people in reading the Creed, frequent bowings, sitting within the communion rails in the surplice when not reading the prayers, preaching sometimes (which is not a liturgical act) in the surplice' and so on (quoted in Yates 1983: 29). In due course the Archbishop advised Mr. Wilberforce:

> My experience tells me, that if you persevere in the faithful and diligent discharge of your duties with kindness and gentleness to all, preaching sound Christian doctrine in plain and simple language, not suffering your temper to be ruffled by any provocation, and not appearing over-anxious even in the refutation of calumny, you will in the course of time find the advantage of such forbearance and patience, and with the blessing of God, will probably see the end of all your troubles (quoted in Yates 1983: 49).

But Mr. Wilberforce did not stay the course of time which Archbishop Howley had in mind: he resigned his living and became a Roman Catholic.

4

CHANGE AND DECAY

DURING THE seven hundred and more field visits made during the course of preparing this book, I three times had the experience of approaching a site marked by a cross on a recent street map only to hear the rumbling of contractors and the crashing of stonework. In many more cases the buildings have disappeared since my first visits to them: the red brick and Bath stone steeple of St John's Presbyterian church, on which I became accustomed to gaze as the London Bridge train pulled out of Forest Hill, was one day there and gone the next. Visiting and recording Victorian churches is a race against time.

But there was an incident in the field that in its way was more ominous still and just as disturbing. A visit to a disused chapel bearing a Victorian date on the exterior wall met with the insistence of current occupiers that the building had 'always been Air Scouts'. This conviction not only signified an ignorance of the history of science and of the Air Scout movement but showed a blindness in vision of the past and an indifference to inheritance. Being for ever lost or frustrated by changes in street names – Gas Street, I found, had become Honey Lane on the advice of estate agents – I was frequently dependent upon passers-by, among the younger generation of whom the very word 'chapel' often failed to communicate; they knew no functional differences between the Baptist church and the British Legion and the association of pointed windows and religious usage had evidently eluded them. Not so the older people I approached who had invariably worshipped in the buildings I sought, knew Bible Christian from Primitive Methodist and told me when and why they closed: buildings had enjoyed a prominent place and commanded an affection among those who were young 50 years ago whereas among the young of today there is perhaps less attention to locality, certainly less allegiance to it, and apparently an indifferent consumerism that portends ill for the future preservation of buildings of historical or architectural interest.

Such a consumerism is to be found also among some but happily not all of those into whose possession yesterday's chapels have now passed for residential or commercial use. On the whole those who have converted chapels for private use cherish their history, and are happy to preserve principal architectural features: there are, for example, most sensitive conversions at Horsmonden and Waltham. In commercial use, however, the tendency for value to be estimated in terms of utility means that several former chapels have been 'improved' or disposed of in the cause of business interest. However, some fine exteriors have been well preserved while the interior space has been adapted for business purposes: among these are a number of formerly Primitive Methodist chapels at Chatham (now Southern Sheds), Dover and Tunbridge Wells (now antiques salerooms), Ramsgate (now a furniture showroom) and Maidstone (now Peter Preedy's dance school).

For the great number of humble chapels, however, closure heralds demolition. In this century some 282 of Kent's Victorian churches have been closed, half of them since 1960: and in addition to the 63 victims of World War II, 135 have been demolished. The rate of demolition has increased in each of the last three decades. These statistics and the following table account only for those demolitions and closures since 1900 which it is possible to date with accuracy. Demolitions of buildings by accident or enemy action are not listed as closures since they do not reflect the condition of the occupying congregation. Dates of closure are interpreted as those on which religious use ceased: transfers of property between denominations are not counted as closures.

Years	Closure	Demolition	Bombed	Years	Closure	Demolition	Bombed
1901–10	16	8	—	1951–60	25	15	—
1911–20	18	2	—	1961–70	62	39	—
1921–30	24	5	—	1971–83	75	47	—
1931–40	39	11	63				
1941–50	23	8		1901–83	282	135	63

Of the 1,200 religious buildings listed in the Gazetteer, just over seven hundred survive, whether in their intended or in secular use. They have proven resilient to war — for many of them were hit and recovered — but vulnerable to urban development. The fate of the Victorian churches of Kent is epitomised by the Wesleyan chapel at Grace Hill, Folkestone, which endured the Blitz only to be demolished after the war for a traffic scheme. Others, like St Lawrence at Catford and the Wincheap Presbyterian church at Canterbury were razed in the cause of development plans that never transpired: so it is that the monuments of the last century become the car parks of this. These illustrate the peculiar vulnerability of Victorian religious buildings. Their original sponsors sought central locations in developing towns and villages, and their descendants now find themselves occupying prestigious and valuable sites, the sale of which to covetous neighbours is a compelling prospect for a diminishing congregation with the burden of a heavy financial commitment. The reluctance to surrender one's chapel for a road, car park or supermarket seldom withstands the economic inducements and the offer of an alternative site: thus the Baptists of Tonbridge and Dover found themselves surrounded by High Street stores and moved out, to be replaced by the International Stores and Boots respectively. The last vestiges of Victorian taste and character are bought up and dismantled and the shopping precinct is fully streamlined.

Further threats arise within the Christian community itself: many chapels have been rendered redundant by denominational unions. Of these, the union of the Methodists in the early 1930s left a number of buildings surplus to requirements, not only in towns like Canterbury, Tunbridge Wells, Whitstable, Sheerness, Faversham and Maidstone, but also in villages like Minster and Elham. In Shorne and Stelling, peculiarly, both Primitive and Wesleyan chapels survived in use, but the common practice was to use the major building for worship and the other for some auxiliary purpose such as youth work or Sunday School. A generation and more later, when residual allegiances to the earlier sects had waned, the maintenance of additional buildings was increasingly regarded as an extravagance and so by the 1960s these former chapels were being put up for sale. In the 1970s a similar pattern followed the union of Congregational and Presbyterian churches, although the Presbyterians were never as thick on the ground in Kent as the minor Methodist denominations. The policy of centralisation of denominational worship, afforded by the sufficient possession of the motor car, has been adopted by Methodists in the Folkestone area and — as a consequence of the expiry of outlying causes — in Faversham. And in Ashford a local union of Methodists and Congregationalists has involved a rationalisation of property arrangements.

As regards conservation, a Victorian building loses its security when it passes from religious to secular use. Not being designed as factories or shops, chapels are often purchased cheaply and adapted as such by individuals who are in the early stages of establishing a business and who in due time will look for better premises, perhaps on the same site. Sentiment does not attend commercial as it does religious use: the lady who looked at a tin hut in the corner of a field at Ash and said 'We used to have some lovely services in that mission' was expressing an affection and attachment to a simple building that are never as developed in the secular domain.

Residential use is another matter. Scores of little chapels have been converted as private dwellings and are lovingly preserved and maintained. Partly because of the number available in recent years, and partly because of the suitability of their size, the majority of these are former Wesleyan chapels in rural areas. Stanford offers an example of early conversion; Brookland, Mersham and Wickhambreaux are all worth a view and at Bromley a Wesleyan chapel has recently been converted to flats. At Chislet is to be found a rare example of an Anglican church having become a private house: as the rate of redundancies increases, and as the alternative uses for rural churches are limited, we may expect others to follow.

But conversions to changed needs are undertaken not only by secular proprietors: one of the most enduring of threats to Christian architectural heritage is posed by liturgical fashion. This was so in the 19th century as it is now. The desirability expressed by the Lords Commissioner of rendering the sermon visible and audible throughout the church was justification enough to remove time-honoured pillars or close off remote aisles. In Canon Basil Clarke's view, 'the most dangerous type of nineteenth-century restoration was that which was animated by a theory: the ecclesiological theory of pure style and correct arrangement' (1938: 230). On this basis attempts were made to recover what was supposed to be original style and the architectural testimony of the Reformation was removed: or else the ecclesiologists disliked Perpendicular and commended the restorations which eradicated it. Clarke's *Church Builders of the Nineteenth Century* (1938) was not the first 'plea for the faithful restoration of our ancient churches', however: indeed, George Gilbert Scott had written a treatise under that title in 1850, though in his own practice at Hayes and Bridge he failed to demonstrate the sensitivity he counselled.

In our own times liturgical fashion constitutes a comparable threat to the architectural inheritance and testimony of the English church. There is today an eclectic interest in the practice and doctrines of the Early Church: our religious buildings are invariably suited to acts of worship in which clergy and congregations are symbolically directed to a God that is beyond their own domain, but the modern emphasis is increasingly upon the immanence of God and the faithful are urged to face inward upon themselves and exchange greetings with each other. In many Anglican and Roman Catholic churches — if not in most — the altar has now been pulled away from the east wall, or else a new altar has been set up in the nave, rendering the chancel a kind of backwater. The trend from eastward to inward has implications for the location and usefulness of fittings: memorials are pushed into corners and the pulpit is rendered redundant by a less formal style of address. The great east windows of Burne-Jones, Morris & Co., Kempe and Clayton & Bell will no longer engage the inevitably vagrant minds of the faithful who have only themselves and their President on whom to gaze. The charge of conservation is no better expressed than in the words of St Paul's exhortation to the Philippians:

> Whatsoever things are pure, whatsoever things are lovely,
> whatsoever things are of good report, if there be any virtue
> and if there be any praise, think on these things.
>
> (*Philippians 4.8*)

GAZETTEER OF VICTORIAN CHURCH BUILDINGS IN KENT

This Gazetteer is intended to be comprehensive of all places of worship purpose-built between 1818 and 1901 within the boundaries of Kent that obtained before the Local Government Act of 1888. Inevitably, however, there will be omissions. There will also be disagreement over locations, which have on the whole been classified according to *Kelly's Directory of Kent*. The Gazetteer is arranged alphabetically under towns. Each church building is then listed separately under the town heading. An asterisk denotes a building illustrated in the plates.

Each entry follows a standard pattern, but, of course, the full range of information is not available in every case. These items included are as follows:

DENOMINATION responsible for the erection of the building, and any NAME given to the building (for example, St Mildred's, Zion Chapel). Any special functions (for example, school chapel, cemetery chapel, mission hall) are also noted.

The original ADDRESS is given, and any subsequent change in the street name noted, for example, Barrow Hill (New St.).

Abbreviations used throughout Gazetteer to the
Victorian Churches of Kent

Bapt.	=	Baptist
Bapt. M.	=	Baptist Mission
Bapt. M.H.	=	Baptist Mission Hall
Bapt. Sch.	=	Baptist School
Beaver Cong.	=	Beaver Congregational.
Bible Ch.	=	Bible Christian
Breth.	=	Brethren
Cath. Apos.	=	Catholic Apostolic
C.C.	=	Cemetery Chapel
C. of E.	=	Church of England
Cong.	=	Congregational(ist)
Cong. Sch.	=	Congregational School
C. of Hunt.	=	Countess of Huntingdon's Connexion
Ev.	=	Evangelical
F.C. of E.	=	Free Church of England
Gen. Bapt.	=	General Baptist
H.C.	=	Hospital Chapel
Indep.	=	Independent
L.C.	=	Lunatic Asylum Chapel
M.C.	=	Mission Church
M.H.	=	Mission Hall
Op. Breth.	=	Open Brethren
Part. Bapt.	=	Particular Baptist
Ply. Breth.	=	Plymouth Brethren

Presb.	=	Presbyterian
Prim. M.	=	Primitive Methodist
Priv.	=	Private
R.C.	=	Roman Catholic
S.A.H.	=	Salvation Army Hall
St. Bapt.	=	Strict Baptist
St. B. and Part. B.	=	Strict Baptist and Particular Baptist
St. Cal.	=	Strict Calvinistic
Trin. Bapt.	=	Trinity Baptist
Unden.	=	Undenominational (in places spelt in full, depending on context)
Trin. Presb.	=	Trinity Presbyterian
Un. Bapt.	=	Union Baptist
W.	=	Wesleyan
W.M.	=	Wesleyan Methodist

The DATE OF CONSTRUCTION of the main part of the original building is noted next.

The name of the ARCHITECT responsible for the original construction, if known, is given. Architects responsible for later features are noted later in the entry.

The COST of the original construction, exclusive of that of later additions, is shown to the nearest £.

REFERENCE SOURCES (shown within brackets) include: names followed by dates, which are citations of published works listed by author in the Bibliography; personal communications, acknowledged by name; and certain standard referenves, represented by the following abbreviations:

B	*Baptist Handbook*		K	Kelly's various *Directories*
BA	*British Almanack & Companion*		KAO	Kent Archives Office
Basil	Canon Basil Clarke's MSS		MAC	Methodist Circuit Archives
Betj	John Betjeman, *English Parish Churches*		MCSR	Methodist Church Statistical Returns
BPO	Borough Planning Office		Min	The minister or pastor
C	*Congregational Yearbook*		Mins	Minutes
CCC	Council for the Care of Church records		Occ	Current occupants of building
CD	*Catholic Directory*		OS	Ordnance Survey maps or reports
Cent	A centenary history of the church or congregation		Pev	Pevsner's *Buildings of England* series: *Kent* volumes, ed. John Newman
chap	A chapel of parish history		RC	Religious Census of 1851.
Dioc	Diocesan Secretary's Office		RFC	Ralph Chambers, *Strict Baptist Chapels of Kent*
E	*The Ecclesiologist*			
Gdbk	Guidebook of church or chapel		SD	Street directories, town guides
GPO	A Post Office Directory		Sec	Secretary of church or chapel
Inc	The incumbent concerned		WCC	Annual report of the Wesleyan Chapel Committee
ILN	*The Illustrated London News*			
Jub	A jubilee history of the church or chapel		WA	Tindall's *Wesleyan Atlas*
			WW	World War (I or II)

The final section of each entry (on a separate line and indented) consists of DESCRIPTIVE REMARKS, covering such information as is available relating to the architecture and history of each building. Where known the original architect's description of the style he employed has been given; hence more than one system of classification is represented in this Gazetteer.

Drawn by Geo. Shepherd.   Engraved by John Clghom.

1. Holy Trinity, Margate, a design by a local architect in accordance with the early pattern of the Church Commissioners, and latterly a victim of enemy action.

2. An Edwardian postcard of the Commissioners' church at Sydenham, Vulliamy's St Bartholomew.

3. George Virtue's 1829 engraving of the new church at Tunbridge Wells which is now the new arts centre.

4. Trinity Church, Sissinghurst, a monument to the bankruptcy of local builder James Reed who exceeded but honoured the contract price. (*Photograph: Mark Power*)

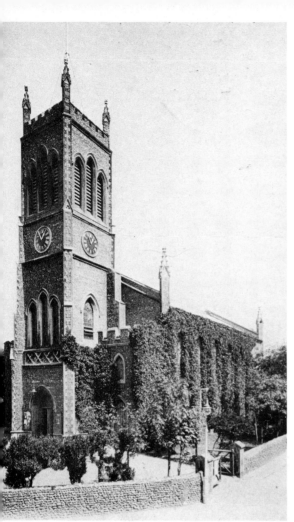

5. (*Left*) A 1910 view of Holy Trinity, Broadstairs which Dickens described as 'a hideous temple of flint, like a petrified haystack'.

6. (*Above*) The 1829 engraving of St George's, the Commissioners' church at Ramsgate.

7. (*Below*) 'The Kentish needle': a contemporary engraving of St Michael's, Blackheath, built in 1830 to the design of George Smith.

8. The distinctive octagonal steeple of St Mary's Lower Hardres, by Rickman & Hutchinson.

9. Christ Church in Tunbridge Wells High Street, providing a contrast to local churches of the period both in fabric and in style. (*Photograph: Mark Power*)

10. Salvin's Christ Church, Kilndown, wherein were patronized the favoured artists of the Ecclesiological Society. (*Photograph: Mark Power*)

11. John Brown's St Margaret's, Lee, approved by the *British Almanac* of 1841 as being 'free from that offensive baldness and that crudity of design which stamp so many of our lately erected churches, and which bespeak unbecoming, tasteless, niggardliness rather than simple or sound economy'.

12. Christ Church, Dover, as seen in 1977. (*Courtesy of The Dover Express*)

13. Hezekiah Marshall's St Alphege's, Whitstable a more conventional project than his Canterbury synagogue.

14. The new church of St Peter at Pembury, given by the Marquess Camden in 1846: an elegant building of local sandstone. (*Photograph: Mark Power*)

15. The imposing parish church of Fordcombe anonymously designed in 1847.

16. Salvin's neo-Norman St Mary's, Betteshanger.

17. (*Left*) Here at Kilndown lies the president of the Ec
lesiological Society, Alexander James Beresford-Hope, wh
died in 1854. (*Photograph: Mark Power*)

18. (*Above*) The now demolished church of St James,
Gravesend as it was in 1904.

19. St John's, Deptford, designed by P.C. Hardwick in 1855 and here seen in 1904.

20. All Saints', Blackheath: in Nairn's words, 'Ferrey's preposterous church gives just the kind of hilarious *bonne-bouche* that Blackheath needs. Prickly, sit-up-and-beg Gothic, stuck down on a corner of the grass like a postage stamp as if to say: if I weren't here it would all blow away'.

21.   St John's, Tunbridge Wells enjoys a prominent position above the town: the beacon turret on Cronk's tower is a feature distinctive of many ancient Kentish churches. (*Photograph: Mark Power*)

22.   Ebony Church, now at Reading Street. It proved inaccessible at its previous site one mile away and was therefore pulled down in 1858 and rebuilt here under the direction of S.S. Teulon. (*Photograph: Mark Power*)

23. An unusual view of the interior of St Andrew's, Paddock Wood, hit by a bomb in 1940. (*Photograph by courtesy of* Kent Messenger)

24. G.G. Scott's All Saints, Hawkhurst, built and endowed by its first vicar in 1861. (*Photograph: Mark Power*)

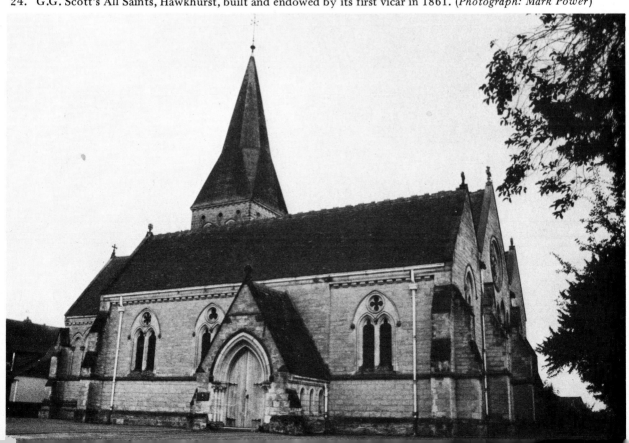

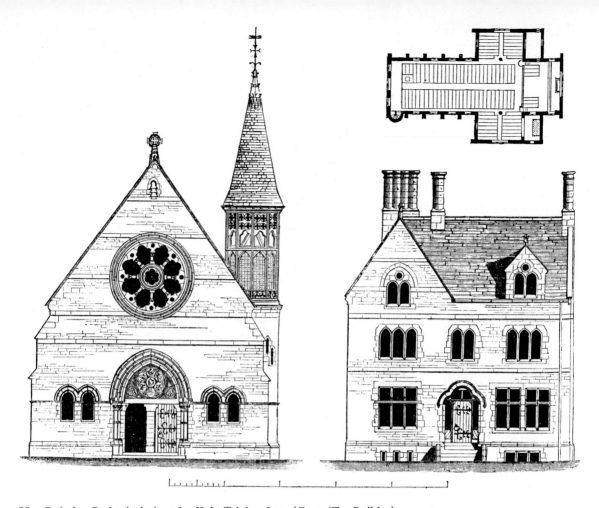

25. Swinden Barber's designs for Holy Trinity, Lee. (*From* The Builder)

26. The garrison church at Woolwich which was destroyed by a flying bomb in 1944: the ruined walls now enclose a memorial garden.

27. Roumieu's gracious St Mark's, Broadwater Down, built of local sandstone in 1864-6 and given by the earl of Abergavenny. (*Photograph: Mark Power*)

28. St Michael's, Tenterden as it was in 1920: some of the trees and the fashion for overgrown churchyards have now gone.

29. The cover picture from the parish magazine of St Bartholomew's, Dover which was demolished in the mid-1970s.

30. Carved capitals and gas fittings at St James's, Kidbrooke. (*From* The Builder)

31. Christ Church, South Ashford, built as a chapel-of-ease in 1867 following the arrival of the railway works: a typical example of facing with Kentish rag. (*Photograph: Mark Power*)

32. G. E. Street's Holy Trinity, Eltham, before the removal of the flèche.

33.   Reginald Beale's 1896 sketch of Arthur Blomfield's St Mary's, Strood.
(*Smetham, 1899*)

34.   Robert Wheeler's All Saints,
Horsmonden in Edwardian cladding.

35. (*Left*) An Edwardian view of Trinity Church at Charing Heath.

36. (*Below*) St Faith's, Maidstone by local architect E. W. Stephens: the pinnacles have since been dismantled for safety reasons.

37. (*Below*) Victorian EE: Robert Wheeler's church at Swalecliffe.

38. St Mildred's, Acol, by the Westgate architect C. N. Beazley, built on to the ruins of an ancient chapel.

39. Interior of St Alban's, Dartford, an inconspicuous building of 1880. (*Courtesy of Dartford Reference Library*)

40. Interior of W. C. Banks' St George's, Catford. (*From* The Builder)

41. (*Right*) The mission church of St Paul's, built in Forge Lane, Ashford in 1881 and celebrating its centenary in the hands of the boy scouts. (*Photograph: Mark Power*)

42. (*Below*) A vanished monument: H. R. Gough's St Lawrence's, Catford which was cleared in 1966 for a traffic scheme that was never executed.

43. The iron rooms of the 1890s survive in great numbers, though seldom in religious use. Few are as well maintained as the mission church of St Michael and All Angels at Hythe.

44. James Brooks' soaring SS Peter & Paul at Charlton-in-Dover.

45. St Peter's, Woolwich (front row second from right) illustrated by Pugin alongside other of his contributions to 'the present revival of Christian architecture'. (*Pugin, 1843*)

46. An Edwardian view of SS Henry and Elizabeth, Sheerness built in 1863 to the design of Pugin's son, Edward.

47. (*Above*) One of E. W. Pugin's less exciting projects, St Teresa of Avila at Ashford, constructed around its predecessor which was subsequently removed. (*Photograph: Mark Power*)

48. (*Left*) St Thomas's at Canterbury 'wherein may be seen the martyr's finger': both the architect, John Green Hall, and the patron saint lived locally. (*Photograph: Mark Power*)

49. The sanctuary of St Francis, Maidstone, as arranged in the Edwardian period.

50. The Sacred Heart at Goudhurst, an unpretentious village chapel built in 1882. (*Photograph: Mark Power*)

51. (*Above*) A grander project at Folkestone: Our Lady Help of Christians and St Aloysius by Leonard Stokes. (*From* The Builder)

52. (*Right*) Darkness thickens on St Anselm's, Dartford, in April 1975. (*Courtesy of Dartford Reference Library*)

53. (*Above*) Bethel, the original Baptist chapel at Brabourne built in 1818.

54. (*Left*) Hanover Chapel, the plain but elegant home of Strict and Particular Baptists at Tunbridge Wells. The chapel was built in 1834 but enlarged in 1892 as it only accommodated 450 persons. (*Photograph: Mark Power*)

BAPTIST, *including* STRICT BAPTIST

55. Zion Chapel at Brabourne, testifying to a schism from Bethel in the same village in 1838 and surviving as a separate fellowship.

56. Zoar, the Strict Baptist chapel at Canterbury built into the city wall in 1845 to masquerade as a water tower—an uncharacteristic adaptation of the church to the world. (*Photograph: Mark Power*)

57. (*Below*) The Strict Baptist chapel at Dacre Park, Lee, which has served for 65 years as the parish hall of St Margaret.

58. R. H. Moore's Early Christian design (renovated in 1877) for the Baptists of Bromley, a congregation that owed much to the work of C. H. Spurgeon.

59. The opening of Jireh Chapel at Tenterden in 1869. (*Photograph by courtesy of Jireh Chapel*)

60. Salem Baptist Church at Folkestone, a studiously Classical project by the local nonconformist architect, Joseph Gardner. (*Mackie, 1883*)

61. Parson's Hill Chapel at Woolwich as enlarged in 1881 and before sale to the Co-op. (*Vincent, 1890*)

62. (*Right*) The conscientiously Classical facade of Marsh Street (now Station Road) Baptist Church at Ashford, built in 1881 and now painted in blues and whites. (*Photograph: Mark Power*)

63. (*Below*) Appleton & Mountford's magnificent Elm Road Baptist Church of 1884 which survives as a Beckenham landmark. (*From* The Architect)

64. (*Above*) The modest vernacular Baptist chapel at Tyler Hill which cost only £210 when it was built in 1885. (*Photograph: Mark Power*)

65. (*Right*) The Derby architect, John Wills was the G. G. Scott of 19th-century Baptist chapel building: the chapel at Brasted was one of his diminutive works. (*From* The Baptist Handbook)

66. (*Below*) Zion Baptist Church at Tenterden, erected in 1835 and rebuilt in 1887. (*Photograph: Mark Power*)

67. John Wills's Baptist church at Sevenoaks: space was often reserved for extensions according to need and in this case schools were built at the rear of the chapel two years later. (*From* The Baptist Handbook)

68. John Wills's drawing for his Tabernacle at New Brompton which bears striking resemblances to his Sevenoaks chapel (67) and typifies the Gothic style he pioneered amongst Baptists. (*From* The Baptist Handbook)

69. (*Above*) 'The meeting house of
the Baptist church' at Hawkhurst:
the painting of the tracery and dressings suits some tastes more than others.
(*Photograph: Mark Power*)

70. (*Left*) Perhaps the smallest of all
Kent chapels, the mission room at
Hastingleigh, built in 1895, surviving
in use and best approached in Wellington boots.

71. W. H. Woodroffe's design for the expensive Baptist Tabernacle at Woolwich which has now been and gone. (*From* The Baptist Handbook)

72. St John's Free Church on Mount Ephraim at Tunbridge Wells: an extensive complex by Councillor Caley, sometime Mayor, and built in 1899 for £7,560. Nowadays United Reformed. (*Photograph: Mark Power*)

73. The Congregational chapel built in 1853-4 on a rural site that has since become the centre of Bexley Heath. (*Courtesy of* Congregational Year Book)

74. Vine's Congregational Church at Rochester, built for 600 worshippers but, like many of its period, with optimistic provision for galleries at a later stage. (*Courtesy of* Congregational Year Book)

75. Zion Church at Whitstable, here seen in April 1982 when it opened as Whitstable Playhouse. (*Courtesy of* Kentish Gazette)

76. The interior of Poulton & Woodman's Congregational chapel for Margate, giving an unrivalled place for the preaching of the Word. (*Courtesy of* Congregational Year Book)

77. Moffat Smith's bold Congregational church at Erith which was closed and demolished in 1973. (*Courtesy of* Congregational Year Book)

78. The galleried interior of Francis Pouget's Congregational chapel at Deptford. (*Courtesy of* Congregational Year Book)

79. The former Congregational chapel in Queen's Road, Forest Hill which is now St Paul's, Taymount Rise, accommodating an Anglican congregation bombed out of Waldenshaw Road.

80. Habershon & Pite's grandly Classical design for Week Street, Maidstone which is now secluded behind shops. (*Courtesy of* Congregational Year Book)

81. (*Above*) Tunbridge Wells Congregational Church on Mount Pleasant, built in 1848 and rendered a Tuscan temple in 1866: the building is now occupied by 'Habitat'. (*Photograph: Mark Power*)

82. (*Below*) Habershon & Brock's New Brompton Congregational Chapel which is now a shoe shop. (*Courtesy of* Congregational Year Book)

83. (*Right*) John Sulman was a prolific designer of Congregational churches: this imposing building at Milton-on-Thames is now a Sikh temple. (*Courtesy of* Congregational Year Book)

84. (*Above*) The Cage Green mission room at Tonbridge was demolished for road widening in 1970. (*Courtesy of Tonbridge Reference Library*)

85. (*Left*) A bold project by a local architect: Joseph Gardner's bicentenary Congregational church in Deal High Street. (*Courtesy of* Congregational Year Book)

86. The congregational chapel at West Hill, Dartford, built in 1882 and seen here eight years later. (*Courtesy of Dartford Reference Library*)

87. Sulman's Congregational church at Westgate-on-Sea, amongst the most ambitious of his projects. (*Courtesy of* Congregational Year Book)

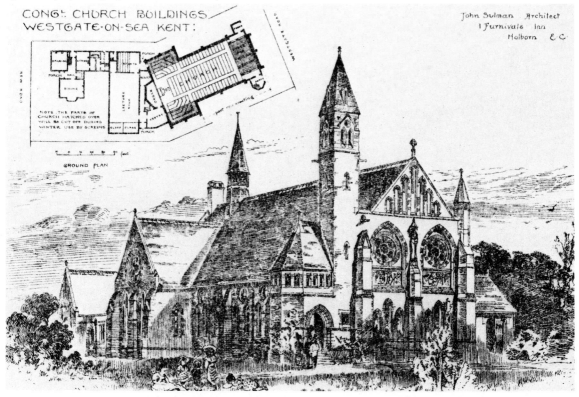

88.   The mid-20th century concept of a 'Christian centre' with facilities for worship, teaching, weekday meetings, offices and catering was often anticipated in the building projects of the nonconformists: this example is the Congregational church at Hawkenbury (Tunbridge Wells) designed by Potts, Sulman & Hennings and built in 1889. (*Courtesy of* Congregational Year Book)

89.   John Gordon served Congregationalists on the Isle of Sheppey as minister and historian. In the case of Bethel Chapel on the Isle of Grain, he served as architect. (*Gordon, 1898*)

90. St Andrew's Presbyterian church at Canterbury, designed by John Green Hall, demolished in 1973 for a development project that did not materialize. (*Courtesy of* Kentish Gazette)

91. St John's Presbyterian church at Forest Hill, built in 1883 and demolished in its centenary year.

UNITARIAN

92. A rare surviving octagon: Thomas Read's Unitarian chapel at Adrian Street, Dover, built in 1820.

COUNTESS OF HUNTINGDON'S CONNEXION

93. (*Left*) Poulton's Union chapel at Canterbury, a casualty of the Second World War. (*Courtesy of Congregational Year Book*)

94. (*Below*) Emmanuel, the Countess of Huntingdon's graceful chapel on Mount Ephraim, Tunbridge Wells, built in 1867 and demolished in 1974.

WESLEYAN

95. (*Right*) Appledore's neat and functional Wesleyan chapel built in 1836. (*Photograph: Mark Power*)

96. (*Below*) The Wesleyan chapel at Barham, in Classical proportions but plainly executed.

97. (*Above*) The unpretentious village chapel at Ruckinge built in 1839 and surviving in Methodist use.

98. (*Left*) The Wesleyan Centenary Chapel of 1839 in Elham which survives in use while the humbler chapel of the Bible Christians is now a garage.

99. An early photograph of W. W. Pocock's Wesleyan church at Dartford built in 1844 and lately denuded of its pinnacles and creepers. (*Courtesy of Dartford Reference Library*)

100. Chapel House at Brookland: a Wesleyan chapel of 1849 now converted to residential use.

101. Local building materials combined to good effect in the facade of the Wesleyan chapel at Stelling.

102. A cheerful and early use of polychromatic brickwork at Wye.

103. The Wesleyan chapel at St Peter's which after a lapse into secular hands is now the property of Elim.

104. 'The Shared Church' of the Methodists and Anglicans of Ham Street (Orlestone) which was built as a Wesleyan chapel in 1872.

105. (*Left*) Charles Bell's rag-faced Wesleyan church in Vale Royal, Tunbridge Wells built in 1873 in the style of Early French Gothic. (*Photograph: Mark Power*)

106. (*Below*) The simple village chapel erected by the Wesleyans of Bethersden in 1875 when they moved from a smaller building across the lane. (*Photograph: Mark Power*)

107. (*Right*) Bank Street Wesleyan Church at Ashford which opened in 1875: the great Gothic window required a higher-pitched roof which cost an extra £1,000. Perceptive observers will notice recent 'improvements'. (*Photograph: Mark Power*)

108. (*Below*) An Edwardian view of two Cliftonville churches of the 1870s: in the foreground the Early French Wesleyan Church and behind the Early English Episcopal Church of St Paul.

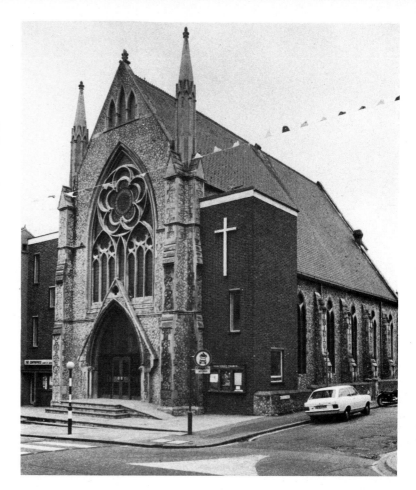

109.   The simple Wesleyan chapel at Ivychurch which now serves boy scouts.

110.   Goudhurst Wesleyan Chapel built in the 1870s on ground that cost £50 40 years earlier: elegant rat-trap brick-work in red and yellow. (*Photograph: Mark Power*)

111. (*Above*) The Wesleyan chapel at Blean built of red and yellow brick in 1879, now in the custody of Elim. (*Photograph: Mark Power*)

112. (*Above right*) The Wesleyan chapel at Pembury awaiting sale for private use in 1981. (*Photograph: Mark Power*)

113. (*Right*) James Weir's Wesleyan chapel at Tenterden built in 1884. (*Photograph: Mark Power*)

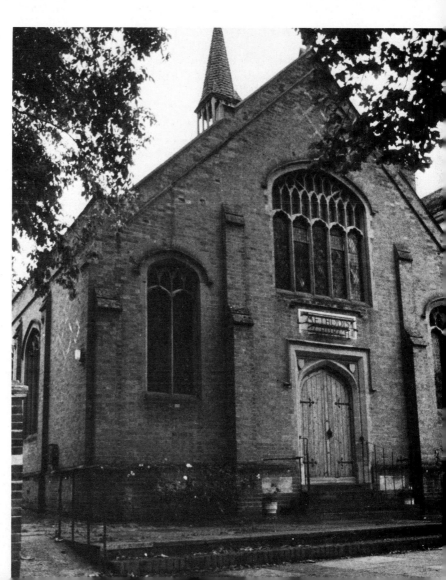

114. Wesley House at Bromley, converted to a block of six flats from a chapel built in 1884.

115. The flint chapel at Waltham built in 1887, here seen in the process of conversion to a dwelling.

116. Charles Bell's 1891 design for the Wesleyan chapel at Catford, done to a budget of £4,000. (*Courtesy of Wesleyan Chapel Committee*)

117. Albert Smith's drawings for his Wesleyan garrison chapel at Old Brompton, recently demolished. (*Courtesy of Wesleyan Chapel Committee*)

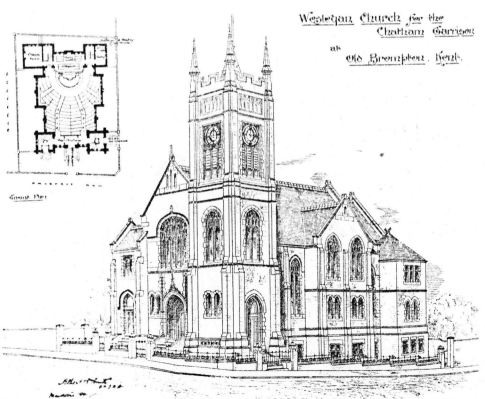

118. A standard John Wills design, favoured by the Baptists but here commissioned by the Wesleyans of St Lawrence. (*Courtesy of Wesleyan Chapel Committee*)

119. Rampart Road Wesleyan chapel at Hythe built in 1897.

120. Hawkhurst, for all its smallness, acquired a chapel of every kind: the Wesleyans built theirs in 1898. (*Photograph: Mark Power*)

PRIMITIVE METHODIST

121. The vernacular chapel of the Primitive Methodists at Goudhurst: like many of its size, it gave way after Methodist union to a larger Wesleyan chapel in the locality and is now a private dwelling. (*Photograph: Mark Power*)

122. The plain Primitive Methodist chapel in the fields of Petham.

123. Dartford Primitive Methodist Church as it was in 1900: the building is now occupied as Emmanuel Pentecostal Church and the entrance has been modernized. (*Courtesy of Dartford Reference Library*)

124. (*Left*) Religious conversion: the pointed windows of the Bible Christian Chapel at Woodchurch still visible in September 1981 as the building is adapted for private use. (*Photograph: Mark Power*)

125. (*Below*) Providence Chapel at Warehorne Leacon, one of a cluster of early Bible Christian causes in the area south of Ashford and Canterbury.

126. (*Right*) The Bible Christian chapel at Union Street, Chatham as enlarged in 1890. (*Bourne, 1905*).

127. (*Below*)Beulah, South Ashford, built for nonconformist railway workers, taken by the Bible Christians and now serving as a mortuary chapel. (*Courtesy of Dr C. P. Burnham*)

128. The Friends have invariably favoured contemporary domestic styles: the 1894 meeting house at Tunbridge Wells was the only building by Kent Quakers in the 19th century. (*Photograph: Mark Power*)

FREE CHURCH

129. Though now a parish church in the established order, Christ Church, Bromley was built independently by the generosity of Samuel Cawston, a converted Jew.

SALVATION ARMY

130. The Tonbridge quarters of the Salvation Army designed in 1898 in the citadel style favoured by that denomination.

NEW HOUSE OF ISRAEL OR JEZREELITE

131. Jezreel's Tower at New Brompton, here pictured during the white elephant period of its unhappy career: intended as the Temple of the New and Latter House of Israel, the building was projected beyond the resources of its sponsors, and was abandoned in 1892 before it reached the scheduled destination of heaven and remained incomplete until its demolition in 1960.

132. (*Above*) Hezekiah Marshall's Canterbury Synagogue of 1847 as it stood for sale in 1982.

133. (*Below*) The interior of Chatham Memorial Synagogue at Rochester, designed in 1865 by H. H. Collins. (*From* The Builder)

134. The precursor to the municipal cemetery was the overflow to the parish churchyard, often detached from the parish where land was available. Dover has a cemetery campus at Charlton of which this photograph of c. 1900 shows the cemeteries and chapels of St James (left) and St Mary. (*Courtesy of* Dover Express)

135. The Tunbridge Wells cemetery chapel model: one chapel was designated for Anglicans, for whom 13 acres of burial ground were set aside in 1873, and the other for nonconformists, for whom seven acres were allowed. Roman Catholics were expected to occupy half an acre. (*Photograph: Mark Power*)

136. The cemetery chapels of 1877 at Canterbury. Again we find a *porte cochère* surmounted by a spire. To the left of the path is the grave of John Green Hall, the architect. (*Photograph: Mark Power*)

137. Chartham cemetery chapel designed by Mr. Bromley of Folkestone. The entrance door was widened after the first burial in 1899 at which it was found necessary to tilt the coffin. (*Photograph: Mark Power*)

138. Butterfield's chapel for St Augustine's missionary college at Canterbury, built on to the remains of a monastery at the initiative of Beresford-Hope: now occupied by the King's School.

139. P. C. Hardwick's clergy orphan school and chapel (left) which is now St Edmund's School and has the University of Kent as its immediate neighbour. (*From* The Builder)

140. The 'old chapel' of Tonbridge School which stands on the Shipbourne Road and was designed by Wadmore & Baker: the school has found other uses for it since the building of Campbell-Jones's new chapel at the turn of the century.

HOSPITAL CHAPEL

141. The hospital chapel at Etchinghill by Joseph Gardner of Folkestone.

GAZETTEER

ACOL C. of E., St Mildred, Plumstone Rd. 1876. C. N. Beazley.
EE. Flint with stone dressing and tiled roof. Bellcote. Porch. (A. T. Walker).

— W., Plumstone Rd. 1866. £107.
Vernacular. Brick with slate roof. Used as chapel of rest since 1966. (W, 1868; K; W. S. Cole, funeral director).

ADISHAM Bapt., Adisham St. 1886. £211 7s. 0d. Mr. Stiff of Dover.
Plain. Brick. Porch. (B, 1888; Clark, 1981).

— W., Adisham St. 1840.
Long since disappeared. (RFC).

ALDINGTON M.H., Bonnington Rd. 1896.
Plain. Red brick with slate roof. Now Aldington Evangelical Mission.

ALKHAM W., Slip Lane. 1835.
Flint. Sold 1962 for £600 and now a dwelling. (RFC; MCA; Mrs. M. Preston, churchwarden).

APPLEDORE W., The Street. 1836.
Vernacular. Red brick with slate roof. Porch. (K).

ASH (near Canterbury) C. of E., M.H., Richborough. 1888. £120.
Iron. Dismantled 1973. (K; Mr. and Mrs. L. Foat of Goldstone).

— C. of E., Goldstone M.H., Lower Goldstone. 1892.
Plain. Iron. Last service 1978, now on the market. (K; Mrs. Lewis Foat).

— Cong., Sandwich Rd. 1849. W. R. King.
Lancet style. Polychromatic brick with slate roof. School chapel in style 1882. (C, 1850; Timpson, 1859; Turner, 1950).

— P.M., Cooper St. 1870.
Lancet style. Yellow brick with red brick dressings. Closed, now a barn.

ASH (near Dartford) Part. Bapt. 1843.
Affiliated to Meopham, becoming independent post-1900. Surviving 1926. (RC; Whitley, 1928).

ASHFORD C. of E., Christ Church, Beaver Rd., South Ashford. 1867. H. J. Austin. £4,500.
EE. Kentish rag with slated roof. Lancets; S porch; spirelet. Built as chapel-of-ease following the arrival of the railway works and remained dependent until 1959. (SD; Pev.).

— C. of E. M.H., St Paul's, Forge Lane. 1881.
Pointed. Red brick with white brick dressings. Now used by 7th Ashford Scouts. (K).

— R.C., St Teresa of Avila, Barrow Hill (New St.) 1865. Edward Pugin.
Altar added 1892, Dec. Brick and stone dressings; slated roof. Its predecessor, a temporary structure of 1862, remained within its walls during building. (K; Ashford, 1970).

— Bapt., Marsh St. (Station Rd.). 1881.
Classical. Red and white brick. Pediment. Ionic capitals. Doorway recently modernised. (B; 1895; K).

— Part. Bapt., St John's Lane. 1829.
Brick. Superseded by Marsh St. following merger 1881. (Bagshot's 1847 *Directory*).

— St. B. and Part. B., Ebenezer, Norwood St. 1863. James Wood.
Vernacular. Brick. Built by James Wood, one of the deacons. Demolished for new police station and rebuilt in Albert Rd. 1968. (RFC; Cent. 1963).

ASHFORD (*continued*)   Cong., Back Lane (Tufton St.).   1821.
    In Countess of Huntingdon's Connexion 1823 to 1862. Replaced 1866. (Timpson, 1859; Watson, 1979).

—   Beaver Cong., Kingsnorth Rd.   1863.   £145,
    Plain. Brick with slated roof. Renovated 1907. Replaced in merger with Ashford Methodists 1970, now electricians' workshop. (Cent. 1963; Watson, 1979; Dr. C. P. Burnham).

—   Cong., Church Rd.   1866.   W. F. Poulton.   £2,202 inc. schools.
    Gothic. Rag and Bath stone. Spire. Plate tracery. Demolished 1972. (C, 1865. Watson, 1979).

—   W., Hempstead Place.   1846.   Wm. Betts.
    Built by Wm. Betts to follow farmhouse converted 1810. Superseded 1874. (Bagshot's *Kent*, 1847; RC).

—*   W., Bank St.   1874.   £4,394.
    Dec. Rag. United with Congregationalists 1970 and is now Methodist/U.R.C. (GPO, 1874).

—*   Bib. Ch., Beulah, Denmark Rd.   1868.   H. J. Austin.
    Roundheaded windows. Rag faced brick with slated roof. Built by S.E. Railway Co. Closed 1972 after merger with Ashford Congregationalists, sold to F. C. Wood, undertaker and since serving as chapel of rest. (Dr. C. P. Burnham).

—   C.C., Canterbury Rd.   1860.
    Gothic. Rag. Two separate buildings, the C. of E. chapel having a spire. Demolished *c.* 1969. (PO Directory 1862; Peter Runciman, BPO).

ASHLEY   Bapt.   1871.   £180.
    Plain. Brick. Extended 1933. (B, 1872; Clark, 1981; W. Philip Clark).

AYLESFORD   W., Rochester Rd.   1851.
    EE. Rag and slated roof. Design based on book of models by Revd. F. J. Jobson. Land given by E. L. Betts, Esq. of Preston Hall. Gallery 1859. Schoolroom and enlargement 1864. (Mr. Don McKay).

BAPCHILD   Bapt. M.H., The Street.   1895.
    Domestic. Brick with tiled roof. Built on to a dwelling house of 1761 at the expense of a local farmer, Mr. Doubleday. Closed *c.* 1952 and sold. (B; neighbours).

BARHAM*   W., Derringstone.   1836.
    Classical. Flint and RB dressings, façade rendered. Now also used as doctors' surgery.

BARMING   L.C., Queen's Rd.   1869.
    County lunatic asylum (Oakwood hospital). Lancet style. Rag. Spire. Later dedicated to St Saviour. (Revd. J. Cossins, chap; Mrs. Geraldine Proctor, librarian).

—   C.C., Queen's Rd.   1872.
    County lunatic asylum (Oakwood hospital),. Pointed. Rag. Closed 1980. (Mr. Fenner, superintendent gardener).

BAYHAM   Priv., Bayham Park.   1870.   David Brandon (but BA says Raphael Brandon).
    EE. Sandstone. SE tower and spirelet. For Marquis Camden. Vandalised ante-1977 and boarded. Converting to dwelling 1983. (*Builder* 22 January 1870; BA, 1872; Pev; NMR).

BEARSTED   W., Ware St.   1877.   £201.
    Lancet style. Polychromatic brick. Polygonal end. Succeeds chapel of 1817. (W. 1878; K; Dr. Felix Hull).

BECKENHAM   C. of E., St Barnabas, Oakhill.   1878 and 1884,   A. Stenning and H. Hall.
    EE. Red brick. Clerestory; lancets. Replaced iron church, on to which the chancel was built; enlarged 1912 and 1933. Bombed 1944 and restored 1948. (SD; K. Pev).

—   C. of E., Christ Church, Fairfield Rd.   1876.   Thos. Blashill and Chas. Forster Hayward.
    EE. Suffolk brick and Bath stone dressings; pillars of shap granite. SW tower and spire 117 ft. Lancets. Largely the gift of C. Lea Wilson. Bombed and reconstructed. (BA, 1877; K; Pev).

BECKENHAM (*continued*)   C. of E.. Christ Church M.H., The Avenue. 1873.
Iron. Transported 1907 to Eden Park Ave., until present church built and consecrated 1938. (Copeland, 1970).

—   C. of. E., St George, High St. 1885-7. W. Gibbs Bartleet. £25,000.
Dec. Rag. Built on site of old parish church. Pinnacled SW tower added 1902-3. (SD; Pev; Bushell, 1976).

—   C. of E., St George's mission, Arthur Rd. (Churchfields Rd.) 1893.
Iron. (K; SD; Copeland, 1970).

—   C. of E., St James, Elmers End. 1879. A. R. Stenning.
EE. Red brick. Lancets. Gables. Built as mission church for St George. Now hidden behind Sworder Powell's 1934 extension. (SD; Pev).

—   C. of E., The Blessed Virgin Mary, Shortlands. 1867-8. John Whichcord, the younger.
EE. Rag and Bath stone. Spire. Given by family of W. A. Wilkinson, built by Dore of Islington, constructed 1870, enlarged 1888, demolished by enemy action 1944 and replaced by new church in Kingswood Rd. 1953. (SD; Knight and Duffield, 1926).

—   C. of E., St Michael and All Angels, Birkbeck Estate (Ravenscroft Rd.) 1899-1906. Arnold H. Hoole.
EE. Brick. Succeeds iron church of 1877. Destroyed by enemy action March 1944 and rebuilt 1955-6. (K; Borrowman, 1910).

—   C. of E., St. Paul, Brackley Rd. 1872. Smith and Williams.
Dec. Rag. faced. W. spire. (SD).

—   R.C., Transfiguration and St Benedict, Overbury Ave. 1891-2.
Simple. Brick. Last mass 1969, sold 1970 and demolished. (SD; St Edmund's Presbytery, Beckenham).

—*   Bapt., Elm Rd. 1884. Herbert D. Appleton and Edward W. Mountford. £5,100.
EE. Stock brick and Doulton stone dressings. Spirelet. (B, 1883 and 1884).

—   Cong., Crescent Rd. 1887. J. W. and R. F. Beaumont. £11,500.
Dec. Rag and Portland stone dressings. Spire 120 ft. Jas. Holloway, builder. Superseded school chapel. (SD; C).

—   Cong., Langley Rd., Elmers End. 1884. E. W. Whitaker.
Lancets. Brick. Succeeds iron mission in Eden Rd. 1872, removed to Ancaster Rd. 1975 and thence to the present site 1884 where it was demolished 1979. Extension 1931. Now Elmers End Free Church, URC since 1972. (SD; Borrowman, 1910).

—   Cong. Sch., Oakhill (Crescent Rd.). 1878. John Sulman. £2,350 incl. site.
EE. Red brick and Bath stone, with polychromatic tiled roof. (C, 1877; *Beckenham Journal*, August 1878).

—   Cong. M.H., Shortlands. 1891.
Iron. Superseded 1908 by building in Martins Rd. (Horsburgh, 1929; C. Grubb, treasurer).

—   W., Bromley Rd. 1887. Jas. Weir.
Perp. Rag and Bath stone dressings. Spire. (SD; Copeland, 1970).

—   Old Beckenham M.H., Bromley Rd. 1880-1.
Tudor. Brick. Founded by B. A. Heywood and Capt. P. W. Stephens. Converted to flats 1937. (K; SD; Borrowman, 1910; Copeland, 1970).

—   M.H., Arthur Rd. (Churchfields Rd.) *c.* 1890.
Plain. Brick with red brick quoining and slated roof. Established 1876, variously used by London City Mission and by Brethren as girls' club. Commandeered on the outbreak of war 1939 but since returned to religious use. (K; Mrs. Molly Newton).

BELVEDERE, *see* Erith.

BENENDEN   C. of E., St Margaret, East End.   1892.
    EE. Red brick patterned with grey brick; tile roof. W porch and bellcote. Built by Lord Cranbrook, passing to the parish church in 1926 and being used since the early 1930s as chapel to the Benenden Chest Hospital. (Gdbk).

BETHERSDEN   W., Forge Hill.   1834.
    Plain. Brick. Succeeded across the road 1875 and surviving as a dwelling. (RC; Leslie M. Chowns, CA).

—*   W., Forge Hill.   1875.   £476.
    Lancet style. Red and burnt brick and slated roof. (W, 1877).

BETTESHANGER*   C. of E., St. Mary.   1853–4.   Anthony Salvin.
    Neo-Norman. Byzantine porch 1868. (Pev; Revd. J. C. Brooks).

BEXLEY   C. of E., St John the Evangelist, Park Hill Rd.   1881–2.   Geo. Low.   £4,000.
    Vaguely early French. Rag. Tall NE spire. Apsidal chancel. Bldr: J. G. Naylor of Rochester. Chapel-of-ease until 1937. (Vincent, 1890).

—   C. of E., St John B., Bourne Rd.   1850s.
    Iron. Removed c. 1880 to Albert Rd. where it became Free Church. Purchased 1916 by Rochester diocese and removed to Barn's Cray as All Saints. Unused 1942, then vandalised and demolished. (K; Carr, 1951).

—   Bapt., Bourne Rd.   1846.
    Roundheaded windows. Rendered. Congregation removed to Trinity, New Bexley 1868. Demolished c. 1893. (RC; K, 1891: Whitley, 1928; RFC).

—   Cong. Sch., Hurst Rd.   1890.   Geo. Baines.
    Dec. and Geom. Rag with slate roof. NW pinnacle developed to a spire. Built by J. G. Naylor of Rochester. Now URC. (C, 1891).

—   H.C., Dartford Road.   1899.   Geo. T. Hine.
    Georgian. Brick. Unconsecrated. (Pev; chaplain).

BEXLEY HEATH (or New Bexley)   C. of E., Christ Church, The Broadway.   1872–7.   Wm. Knight of Nottingham.   Cost £10,000 by 1890.
    Early French Gothic. Rag. Supersedes 1841 brick building with tall spire. (Vincent, 1890; Betj; Pev).

—   Part. Bapt., The Broadway.   1827.
    Neo-classical. Rendered. Porch. Demolished 1956 for Co-op stores; congregation removed to Townley Rd. and thence in 1975 to Grace chapel, Albion Rd. (RC; Timpson, 1859; RFC).

—   Trin. B., The Broadway.   1868.   Habershon and Pite.   £1,650.
    Classical. Brick and stucco. Pediment. Schoolroom added 1878 for £800. (B, 1869 and 1879; RFC; Pev).

—*   Cong., Chapel Rd.   1853–4.   Joseph James.   £1,800 incl. schoolrooms.
    Dec. Rag with Caen stone dressings. Built by Joseph Amos to succeed adapted Athenæum. (C, 1891; Timpson, 1859).

—   W., North St.   1860.
    Pointed windows, classical proportions. Brick. Porch. Given by Thos. Banks of Hurst. Succeeded by Broadway chapel 1925 surviving as Bethany hall, Pentecostal. (Castells, 1910; Mrs. E. Standhaft).

—   C.C., Banks Lane.   1880.   E. Hodgkinson.
    Dec. (K; Meller, 1981).

BICKLEY   C. of E., St George, Bickley Park Rd.   1863–5.   F. Barnes.
    Dec. Rag. Original Caen stone. Spire of 175 ft. was replaced by Sir E. Newton 1905–6. (Horsburgh, 1929).

BIDDENDEN   Bapt. M.H., Sissinghurst Rd.   1872.
    Plain. Brick. Porch. Closed post-1909. (OS).

BIDDENDEN (*continued*)   St. B. and Part. B., Ebenezer, Bounds Cross.   1879.   Jas. Hickmott.
Neat vernacular. Alternating red and grey brick with tiled roof. Roundheaded windows. School chapel added 1907. (Jub, 1930; RFC).

BIRCHINGTON   W.M., Chapel Place.   1830.
Perp. and Dec. Yellow brick. Castellated. Schoolroom added 1928.

BLACKHEATH*   C. of E., All Saints, Blackheath Vale.   1857–8.   Benjamin Ferrey.
Transitional. Rag. Plate tracery. Open timber roofs. W porch 1893. (BA, 1859).

—   C. of E., Church of the Ascension, Dartmouth Row.   1697.
1834 nave and W gallery on to 1697 apse. Classical. Brick with stone dressings. Built as a chapel by Lord Dartmouth, became parish church 1883, bombed 1940, restored 1950. (Baker, 1961; Clarke, 1966).

—   C. of E., St George, Kirkside Rd., Westcombe Park.   1890–1.   Newman and Newman.
EE. Red brick with stone dressings and slate roofs. Lancets. Clerestory. Balaam Bros. bldrs. (Clarke, 1966).

—   C. of E., St German, St German's Place.   1822.
Renaissance. Brick and stucco. Name altered to St Germain during WW I for patriotic reasons. Extended 1929, bombed 1940, re-opened 1942, bombed 1944 and cleared 1952. (Basil; leaflet 'St German's church, Blackheath', 20 pp. illus., 1952).

—   C. of E., Holy Trinity, Blackheath Hill.   1838–9.   Jas. Wm. Wild.   £4,598 7s.
EE. Yellow brick with stone mouldings. Two spires. Galleries. Polygonal apse. Commissioners church. Capacity 1,200. Bldrs: Pain and Dixey. Bomb damaged 1941, repaired, damaged again, parish merged with St Paul 1951, demolished 1954. (BA, 1840; Howarth 1885; Basil; Port, 1961; Binney and Burman, 1977).

—   C. of E., St John the Evangelist, Stratheden Rd.   1852–3.   Arthur Ashpitel.   £6,500.
Perp. Rag. W tower and spire. Gallery by Dru Drury 1898. (*Builder*, 19 March 1898; Port, 1961).

—*   C. of E., St Michael and All Angels, Blackheath Park.   1829–30.   Geo. Smith.   £4,000.
Perp. White brick and stone. Pinnacles, clerestoried nave and 172 ft. spire known locally as 'the Kentish needle'. W. B. Moore, bldr., the gift of John Cator, Esq. (Bushell, 1976).

—   R.C., St Mary's O.C., Cresswell Park.   1872.
Brick. Galleries. Orphanage founded by Canon Todd and chapel open to public. Closed 1904, bombed WW II and reconstructed as parish hall 1955. (Bernard Kelly, 1907; Cent., 1973).

—   R.C., Our Lady Help of Christians, Cresswell Park.   1890–1.   A. E. Purdie.   £4,147.
Dec. Rag. Octagonal tower and spire. Cost defrayed by Chas. Butler, Esq. Smith and Son of Norwood, bldrs. (Bernard Kelly, 1907; Cent., 1973).

—   Bapt., Sunfields Place.   1863?
Brick. Stood to rear of *Sun-in-the-sands* inn. Purchased by Wesleyans 1869. Enlarged 1876–7. Served as Sunday School from 1892. Demolished. (Whitley, 1928; Baker, 1961; Mr. R. M. Jermey).

—   Bapt., Shooter's Hill Rd.   1869.   £1,400.
Plain. Brick. Enlarged 1896. Superseded 1905 and subsequently used as school hall. Demolished 1978. (B, 1870, 1896; Baker, 1961; Mr. Ronald Cooper).

—   Cong., Lawn Terrace.   1853–4.   Richie and Brandon.
Gothic, Glen of Islington, bldr. Schoolrooms and vestries 1884 by P. L. Banks Townsend, John Outhwaite, bldr. Bombed 1940, new church built on to ruins 1956. (C, 1855; Timpson, 1859; Duncan, 1908; Baker, 1961).

—   W., Tranquil Vale.   1847.
Land given by Thos. Allen (his own back garden). Superseded by The Avenue 1863 and demolished 1866. (Timpson, 1859; Rhind, 1976).

BLACKHEATH (*continued*)   W., The Avenue (Blackheath Grove). 1863-4. Jas. Wilson. £6,500.
    Dec. Rag and Bath stone. Tower 120 ft. 1,000 sittings. Built by a Mr. Streeter who consequently
    went bankrupt. Schoolroom and extension 1884, W. Dunk & J. M. Geden, Kennard Bros. of Lewis-
    ham, bldrs. Bombed by V2 1945 and demolished 1960. (W, 1884: Baker, 1961; Rhind, 1976).

—   W., Sunfields, Banchory Rd. 1896.
    Iron. Superseded by permanent building 1902 and then removed to Eltham Pk. (Mr. R. M. Jermy).

—   Breth., Gospel Hall, Bennett Park. 1872.
    Demolished and replaced by modern residence. (SD; Baker, 1961).

—   Presb., Vanbrugh Park. 1887. Thos. Arnold.
    Gothic. Rag. Spire (until 1973). Demolished 1982. (*Presbyterian Yearbook*, 1959-60; church
    records, vi, Mrs. D. Baker).

BLADBEAN Prim. M. 1864.
    Plain. Brick. Porch. Geo. Boughton, Bldr. Sold to Bible Christians 1884 for £60. Now residen-
    tially occupied as 'La Chapelle'. (Elham *Circuit Messenger*, May 1912: Mr. Derek Boughton).

BLEAN* W., Chapel Lane. 1879.
    Vernacular. Brick; façade of yellow brick with red dressings; slate roof. Pointed windows.
    Follows chapel of 1836. Now Elim. (RC).

BORDEN W., Oad St. 1858.
    Plain. Brick with slated roof. Porch. Façade now rendered.

—   W., Key St. 1869. £641.
    Condemned and demolished *c.* 1960. (W, 1869; Dr. C. P. Burnham).

BORSTAL C. of E., St Matthew, Borstal St. 1878. Chas. Lock Luck. £1,285.
    Pointed. Rag. Bell turret. J. Naylar, bldr. Sanctuary 1904. (CCC).

BOUGHTON MALHERBE Part. Bapt., Jehovah Jireh, Grafty Green. *c.* 1833.
    Plain. Red brick. First trust deed 1821. (RC; Mr. V. Oliver, min.)

BOUGHTON-UNDER-BLEAN C. of E., St Barnabas, Boughton St. 1895-6. W. M. Fawcett.
    Lancet style. Brick with tiled roof. Bellcote. Barge-boards. (K; Basil).

—   W., Boughton St. 1844.
    Dec. Red brick. Flying buttresses. Lancets. Spire, dismantled during last war. Sold 1981;
    consent being sought 1982 for conversion as studio and gallery. (K).

—   W., Oversland, South St. 1870.
    Plain vernacular. Brick with tiled roof. Porch. Closed and for sale 1982. (K: Dr. Doreen
    Rosman, University of Kent).

BRABOURNE* Bapt., Bethel, Plain Rd. 1818.
    Vernacular. Brick (now partly rendered) and hung tiles. Roundheaded windows. (RFC).

—*   St. Bapt., Zion, Canterbury Rd. 1838.
    Vernacular. Stone with brick quoining. Wooden porch.

BRASTED C. of E., St Martin, Church Rd. 1864-5. Waterhouse.
    Dec. Local sandstone with tiled roof. Victorian rebuilding on old foundations. Tower restored
    1882. (Glynne, 1877; K; Pev).

—*   Bapt., High St. 1886. John Wills. £750.
    'Old English'. Red brick dressed with white. Porch. Bldr. R. Durtnell. School and lecture room
    built previously for £400. (B, 1886).

BREDGAR W., Silver St. 1868. Carey.
    Gothic. Follows chapel of 1811. (RC; BA, 1870: MCSR, 1980).

—   W., Sch., Silver St. 1872.
    Wood. Sold 1930. (Mr. Brian Davies).

BREDHURST Ind., The Street. 1827.
    Plain. Long since closed and now used as a store. (Timpson, 1859. Belsey and Dunstall, 1899;
    Revd. John King).

BRENCHLEY   W., Hill Top.   1839.
     Brick. Enlarged 1846. (Later?) chapel closed 1964 and converted to flats. (RC; Igglesden, 1936; Tonbridge jub. 1964; Mrs. Gladys Mercer, former member).

BRIDGE   W., Patrixbourne Rd.   1894.   £194.
     Iron. Survives in use. (W, 1895; K).

BROAD OAK   C. of Hunt., Broad Oak chapel, Shalloak Rd.   1867.
     Plain. Brick (now rendered) and slated roof. Enlarged 1869, used WW I as sickbay for East Kent Yeomanry and surviving in the Connexion 1982. (McIntosh, 1972).

BROADSTAIRS*   C. of E., Most Holy Trinity, Nelson Place.   1829.   David Barnes.
     EE. Flint with stone facings. Built by Messrs. Raine as chapel-of-ease to St Peter. Tower 1862. Parish church of Broadstairs from 1866. Enlarged 1914–15 and 1924–5. (Grayling, 1913; Basil; Bird, 1974. Gdbk).

—   R.C., Our Lady Star of the Sea, St Peter's Park Rd.   1888.
     Corrugated iron. Plain. Succeeded by Scott's church in Broadstairs Rd. and survives as parish hall. (Bernard Kelly, 1907; Basil; Bird, 1974).

—   Bapt. Sch., Queen's Rd.   1899.   A. H. Clarke of Broadstairs.   £1,100.
     Pointed. Red brick with stone dressings. Built by R. Price. Chapel adjoining built 1907. (B, 1900).

—   Cong., The Vale.   1870–1.   Hinds & Son.   £1,250.
     Gothic. Polychromatic brick with slated roof. Dec. and Geom. tracery. Spire. Land given by Thos. Henson. Classroom and vestry 1890. (C, 1871; architect's drawings in KAO; tricent, 1951; Mrs. Valerie J. Hughes, sec.).

—   W., York St.   1883.   £2,557 estim.
     Lancets and Geom. Rag. faced brick. NW tower. Following Wesleyan chapel in Harbour St. from 1823. (RC; W, 1883; MCSR, 1980).

BROADWATER DOWN, *see* Tunbridge Wells.

BROCKLEY   C. of E., St Cyprian, Adelaide Rd.   1900.   Sir Arthur Blomfield.   £10,650.
     Gothic. Red brick and Bath stone dressings. Fleche. Built by J. Dorey and Co. of Brentford to succeed temporary brick mission church of 1881–2. Bombing 6 September 1940 left a ruin which was subsequently removed. (*Builder*, 78, 1900; K; Dews, 1884; Basil).

—   C. of E., St George's mission, Foxberry Rd.   1893.   W. Gilbert Scott.
     Dec. Red brick. Spirelet. Balaam bldrs. Succeeding earlier church of 1887. (Baker, 1961).

—   C. of E., St Hilda, Courtrai Rd., Crofton Park.   1900.
     Domestic. Red brick and hung tiles. Bellcote. To succeed temporary iron church of 1899. Used as St Hilda's hall since the building of the present church in 1908. (Baker, 1961).

—   C. of E., St Peter, Wickham Rd.   1866–70.   Frederick Marrable.
     Geom. Rag. Tower by A. W. Blomfield. (Dews, 1884).

—   R.C., St Mary Magdalene, Howson Rd.   1899.
     Romanesque. Red brick, interior rendered. Bombed 1940 and restored 1943 and 1947–8. (Bernard Kelly, 1907; CD; Baker, 1961).

—   M.Ch., Brockley Rd.   1881–2.   G. Finlay of Clapham Junct.   £950.
     W triplet. C. Wade of Deptford, bldr. Precursor to St Stephen. Served again as church when St Cyprian was bombed. Closed 1960. (Basil).

—   Bapt. M., Brockley Rd. (corner Rokeby Rd.).   1867.
     Gothic. Often damaged WW II. (K; Baker, 1961).

—   Presb., Brockley Rd.   1876.
     Iron. Superseded 1883. (Dews, 1884).

—   Presb., St Andrew, Brockley Rd.   1883.
     Gothic. Rag and Bath stone. Spire 170 ft. W door based on Jedburgh Abbey. (Dews, 1884; K).

BROCKLEY (*continued*)   W., Brockley Rd.   1872.
    Iron. Removed to Windmill Lane. 1876. (Dews, 1884).

—   W., Brockley Rd. and Harefield Rd.   1876–7.   Banister Fletcher.
    Dec. Rag and Bath stone. Spire 100 ft. Job Bishop of Reading, bldr. Superseding chapel of
    1872. Destroyed 1945. (W, 1877; Dews, 1884; Baker, 1961).

BROMLEY   C. of E., Holy Trinity, Bromley Common. 1839 and 1842.   Thos. Hopper.   £3,148.
    Dec. Knapped flint and stone dressings. Tower. Restored and extended by C. Pemberton
    Leach 1884. (SD; Horsburgh, 1929; Pev).

—   C. of E., St John Ev., Park Rd.   1879–80.   Geo. Truefitt.   £5,400.
    Perp. Kentish rag and brick. Spire. Built by T. Crossley of Bromley. Succeeds iron church of
    1872, bought for £450 from Ryde, Isle of Wight. (SD; Horsburgh, 1929; Betj; Pev).

—   C. of E., St Luke, Bromley Common.   1886.   Arthur Cawston.   £8,500.
    EE. Red brick. Spire and fleche. Clerestoried nave. (Horsburgh, 1929).

—   C. of E., St Mark, Mason's Hill.   1887.   Evelyn Hellicar.   £2,600.
    EE. Brick. Tower 1903. South chapel 1911. Succeeds iron church of 1884. Bombed and
    gutted 1941 and rebuilt 1953. (SD; K; Horsburgh, 1929).

—   C. of E., St Mary Plaistow, College Rd.   1863–4.   Waring & Blake.
    Dec. Flint with Bath stone. Flèche. Nave extended by W. R. Mallett's chancel 1881, S. transept
    and narthex 1891, and N. transept 1899–1900 by Wadmore, Wadmore & Mallett. Nave £4,000,
    chancel £2,000. (K; Pev).

—   Widmore M., Nightingale Lane.   1888.
    Dec. Brick with stone dressings. Now occupied by Boy Scouts.

—   R.C., St Joseph, Freelands.   1892.   Harbour of London.   £460 excl. furnishings.
    Iron. Succeeded 1911 by the Romanesque church in Plaistow Lane. (*Bromley Record*. 1 March
    1892; Strong's *Directory*, 1897; Horsburgh, 1929).

—* Bapt., Widmore Rd.   1864–5.   R. H. Moore.   £1,200.
    Early Christian. Brick with slate roof. Contract price exceeded by £800. Renovated 1877. (B,
    1866; Horsburgh, 1929; Pev).

—   Un. Bapt., Sherman Rd.   1886.
    Iron. Formed by seceders from Bromley Baptist church, who reunited 1891. Sunday school
    1891–1906 and Salvation Army 1906–1934, then site acquired by GPO. (SD; 'Salvation Army
    in Bromley', leaflet in Bromley Ref. Lib.).

—   Bapt., Sherman's Rd. (Sherman Rd.).   1887.
    Iron. Affiliated to Park Rd. Gospel Hall ('Ravenite' Brethren) from 1892. Closed WW I.
    Reopened as mission room 1923 and surviving 1962; since removed. (SD; Whitley, 1928).

—   Bapt. M., Southborough, Salisbury Rd.   1898.
    Follows activity at Turpington Farm. Survived until WW II. (Bush's *Directory* 1900, 1904; SD).

—   Cong., Widmore Lane.   1881.   John Sulman.   £15,000.
    Gothic. Red brick and Bath stone. Built on site of previous chapel. Tower 1889 by Potts.
    Sulman and Hennings. Bombed and destroyed 16 April 1941. (C, 1880 and 1889; SD;
    Horsburgh, 1929).

—   Indep., Bethel, Centenary Place.   1835.
    'Gothic Tudor'. Lancets. Galleries. Sometime United Methodist. Superseded 1881. (C, 1855;
    Timpson, 1859; OS, 1863; Bush's *Directory*, 1892).

—   Cong. Sch., chapel, Cage Field.   1867.   £300.
    Iron. Superseded 1881. (Bush's *Directory*, 1892).

—   C. of Hunt., Bromley. Widmore Lane.   1835.   W. Tress.   £1,870.
    Gothic. Built at controversial extravagance on land given by John Bromley (hence in part the
    name). Demolished. (Bromley, 1837; SD; Timpson, 1859: Horsburgh, 1929; dedication
    service 1948).

BROMLEY (*continued*)   W., Zion, Upper High St.   1825.
  Classical. Stucco. Pediment. Superseded by larger building 1876. (Worship certificate in KAO; chap).

—   W., Zion.   1841.
  Formed by defection from Upper High St. Disappeared. (RC; Horsburgh, 1929).

—   W., off High St.   1873–4.   Land £1,100, building £815.
  Plain. Brick with tiled roof. Roundheaded windows. Adapted as meeting rooms 1899. ('Milestones: the story of Bromley High St. Methodist church').

—   W., High St.   1875–6.   W. W. Pocock.
  Gothic. Rag. Spire. School and meeting rooms added 1893. Chancel destroyed 16 April 1941. Closed 1964 and demolished for access road 1965. (SD; Horsburgh, 1929; Bromley Ref. Lib.).

—* W., Widmore, Tylney Rd.   1884–5.   E. E. Hollis.
  EE. Brick. Lancets, spirelet, side porch. W. A. Grubb, bldr. Closed 1975, sold for £18,000 and converted 1981 to Wesley House, a block of six flats. (*Bromley Times*, 24 July 1980; SD; Horsburgh, 1929).

—   W., Zion chapel mission, Farwig Lane.   1883.
  Plain. Iron. Enlarged 1887, 1888, 1890, 1891. Succeeded 1905 by the Central Hall then used as laundry and commercial premises. (SD; Horsburgh, 1929; 'Bromley Circuit', typescript in Bromley Ref. Lib.).

—   Prim. M., Bloomfield Rd., Bromley Common.   1877.   A. J. Rowse.
  Pointed vernacular. Brick. Bldr. Geo. S. Copping. Extended by Childs Porritt's adjacent Perpendicular building of 1907. Survives as Bromley Common Methodist church.

—   Swedenborgian, West St.   1867.
  Iron. (K).

—   Unden., Cherry Orchard Rd.   1870.
  Plain. Brick. Baptist from 1892. Superseded by modern building and now serves as church hall. (Horsburgh, 1929).

—   Ply. Breth., 'Darbyite', Gospel hall, Grove Rd. (Freelands Grove).   1871.
  Plain. Brick with slated roof. Porch. (SD; Mr. H. W. Moss).

—   Op. Breth. Gospel hall, East St.   1871.
  Plain. Brick. Front extended between wars. (SD; Mr. E. Reynolds of Hayes).

—   Bromley Common iron room, Great Elm Rd.   1873.
  Established by Matthew Henry Hodder. 'Elms hall' from 1928. Rendered. (SD; Horsburgh, 1929).

—   F.C. of E., Christ church, Highland Rd.   1887.   Walter A. Williams.   £2,600.
  EE. Brick with red dressings and tile roof. Lancets. Flèche. The gift of S. Cawston, Esq. Joined established church 1889. (*Bromley Record*, Feb. 1887 and Nov. 1889; Strong's *Directory* 1897; Horsburgh, 1929).

—   F.C. of E., Christ church children's chapel, Highland Rd.   1892.
  Plain. Brick with red dressings beneath a tiled roof. Sam Cawston, benefactor. Sold *c.* 1920, used for residential purposes and from 1968 as a reform synagogue for which purpose — perhaps because Cawston was a converted Jew — the original non-representational stained-glass has been kept. (SD; *Bromley Record*, 1 May 1892; Rabbi and Mrs. David L. Freeman; Mr. Mervyn Elliott).

—   Trin. Presb., Freelands (Upper Park Rd).   1895.   John. C. T. Murray.
  Mainly EE. Red brick and stone. Steeple 118 ft. Rebuilt after destruction by lightning 1936. Now URC. (SD; Horsburgh, 1929; Pev).

—   London City Mission, Chatterton Rd.   1898.
  Possibly converted from working men's institute. Sold, cleared and replaced by Glad Tidings hall 1982. (SD; LCM head office).

BROMLEY (*continued*)   C.C., London Rd.   1876-7.   Geo. Truefitt.   £3,320.
Dec. Rag and stone dressings under tiled roof. Two gabled chapels separated by porte cochère. Contract to G. S. Copping of Bromley. (*Bromley Record*, 1 October 1876 and 1 December 1876).

—   C.C., St Luke's, Magpie Hall Lane.   1894.   P. V. Strudwick.
Gothic. Red brick under tile roof. Mr. Harmer's contract to build two chapels and caretaker's house was £955.   (*Bromley Record*, 1 March 1894, 1 May 1894 and 1 September 1894).

—   Bromley college, London Rd.   1875.   Waring and Blake.
Dec. Red brick with diapers. Surviving in use. (K; Horsburgh, 1929; Pev; chaplain).

BROOKLAND*   W, Salters Lane.   1849.
Plain. Stock brick with slated roof. Porch. Part demolished and converted to dwelling 1971. (RC; K; Mr. A. Wimble, county architect).

BROOMFIELD   Cong., Bog's Hole Lane.   1868.
Lancets. Brick. Closed 1934 and used sometime as bakery. (Mrs. L. Baker, former member).

BUCKLAND, *see* Dover.

BURHAM   C. of E., St Mary, Church St.   1881.   E. W. Stephens of Maidstone.   £4,500.
Early Dec. Rag. Central tower. J. G. Naylar and Sons, bldrs. Demolished 1979. (CCC).

—   W., Church St.   1847.
Pointed. Stock brick. Porch. School chapel added 1873. (RC; MCSR, 1980).

CANTERBURY   C. of E., St Alban (Garrison), Military Rd.   1844.
EE. Ragfaced. Bellcote. Purchased by diocese 1975 for £44,000 and opened 1976 as All Saints. (K; *Kentish Observer*, 5 February 1963; *Kent Herald*, 16 September 1975; *Kentish Gazette*, 12 November 1976; Revd. David Matthiae, inc; City archivist, cathedral library).

—   C. of E., All Saints, East Bridge (High St corner of Best's Lane).   1827-8.
Dec. tracery. Yellow brick and stucco. Castellated tower. Interior walls ornamented with Corinthian pilasters. Demolished 1938 for street widening. (K; Oyler, 1910; Kaehler, 1939).

—   C. of E., St Gregory, Old Ruttington Lane.   1848.   Geo. Gilbert Scott.   £2,069.
Dec. Knapped flint with stone dressings. Built in memory of Archbishop Howley. Closed 1976, sold 1981 and April 1982 conversions commenced to a theatre for Christ Church college. (Basil; *Kentish Gazette*, 31 December 1976; Richard Hugh-Perks).

—   C. of E., St Mary Bredin, Rose Lane.   1868.   F. Wallen.   £4,000.
EE. Flint with Bath stone dressings. Octagonal tower and spire. Succeeded Norman church. Destroyed by fire and then dismantled. (BA, 1868; Glynne, 1877; Oyler, 1910; Kaehler, 1939).

—   C. of E., St Mary, Northgate.   1830.
Lancet style. Brick. Bald pinnacles. Incorporates Norman N wall. Converted to a hall 1913, declared redundant 1970 and now used for educational purposes. (Oyler, 1910, SD; Pev; Dioc).

—*   R.C., St Thomas, Burgate.   1874-5.   John Green Hall.   £3,000.
Gothic. Brick with rag façade. Extended 1962 by J. C. Clague. Pinnacled buttress. Consecrated 1931. (BA, 1876; Gdbk).

—   Bapt., St George's Place.   1864.
Italianate. Polychromatic bricks. Alterations 1889-90 by J. D. Smith. Turret and porch added 1914. Began as Particular Baptist, affiliated to Eythorne. (B, 1865; Cantacuzino. 1970).

—*   Part. Bapt., Zoar, Burgate Lane.   1845.
Vernacular. Brick and stone dressings; boarded interior. Rounded and castellated W end, being a water tower in the city wall. Church formed by dismission from Eythorne 1825, and survives as a Gospel Standard cause (RFC).

CANTERBURY (*continued*)   Cong., Guildhall St.   1876-7.   John Green Hall.   £5,000.
EE. Brig and rag faced. Spires. Gallery. Built by James G. Naylor of Rochester. Declared unsafe and closed 1948. Sold to Lefevres and converted to a shop, as which it is now occupied by Debenhams. (*Kentish Gazette*, 27 February 1877; Taylor, 1926; *Kent Herald*, 15 February 1972).

—*   Presb., St Andrew, Wincheap Green.   1880-1.   John Green Hall.   £5,000.
EE. Red brick with Bath stone dressings. SW tower and spire. Lancets. Demolished March 1973 for redevelopment, but the site is still vacant 1982. (SD; Taylor, 1926; *Presbyterian Handbook*, 1959-60; *Kent Herald*, 20 March 1973).

—   Presb. M.H., Gas St.   1876.
Built by John Fraser, formerly of Guildhall St. Independents, who demolished his house for the site. Recognised preaching station 1877. Cause usurped 1881 by St Andrew. (Taylor, 1926; Watson, 1967).

—*   C. of Hunt., Union, Watling St.   1863.   W. F. Poulton.   £2,100.
Dec. Rag, dressed and banded with Bath stone. Pinnacles. Plate tracery. Blitzed 1942. Connexion united with Guildhall St. Congregationalists 1942 and started rebuilding together 1954. (C, 1864: *Kent Messenger*, 22 August 1958).

—   Prim. M., The Borough.   1876.
Pointed. Red brick. Pinnacled. United with St Peter's St. Wesleyans 1936 then used as youth centre. Assemblies of God Pentecostal since 1969. (*Methodist Recorder*, 8 June 1961; Vickers, 1961; *Kentish Gazette*, 7 March 1969).

—*   Synagogue, King St.   1847-8.   Hezekiah Marshall.   Overall cost £1,253.
Classical. Brick with rendered façade of Portland cement. Built by Thomas French Cousins. Acquired by Church Commissioners 1937, used as St Alphege church hall, sold 1981 and converted to music room for the King's School. Canterbury is said to be the second oldest Jewish community in England: its former synagogue in St Dunstan's Rd. was built in 1763 and expropriated for the railway station approach in 1846. (Roth, 1950; Rabbi Dan Cohn-Sherbok, University of Kent).

—*   C.C., Westgate Court Ave.   1877.   John Green Hall of Canterbury.   £9,000 all in.
14th-cent. Gothic. Twin chapels separated by archway beneath tall spire. H. B. Wilson, bldr. Carving by Candy. Architect was city surveyor; now reposes five graves from the gate. (Mrs. J. Beeching, Cemetery office; Cantacuzino, 1970).

—*   St Augustine's college, Monastery St.   1845-8.   Wm. Butterfield.   £4,544.
Early Dec. Caen stone, knapped flint and rag. Glass by Willement. Bellcote. Incorporates EE structure acquired by Beresford Hope. Now occupied by King's School. (E, 1848; Boggis, 1907; Hugh Perks, surveyor).

—*   Clergy Orphan Sch. (St Edmund's school), St Thomas's Hill.   1857.   P. C. Hardwick.
Gothic. Rag and Bath stone. W bell gable. 'Tame', said the *Ecclesiologist*. (E, 1854; Cantacuzino, 1970).

CAPEL   Cong., Whetstead Rd, Five Oak Green.   1869.   £400.
Pointed. Brick and rendered. Succeeded cottage converted 1864. Enlarged 1876 for £160. Rail traffic eventually affected preaching so sold and new chapel built 1925. Now derelict. (SD; Bailey, 1970).

CAPEL-LE-FERNE   Prim. Meth., The Street.   1870.
Pointed. Red brick and rendered. Now Baptist Union. (K).

CATFORD   St Andrew's Mission, Sandhurst Rd.   1900.
Succeeded by permanent church 1903-4. (K; Baker, 1961).

—   C. of E., St George, Perry Hill.   1878.   Wm. C. Banks.
Dec. Rag. Tower. Clerestoried nave. The gift of George Parker, J.P., to whose taste the tower was heightened in 1887. B. E. Nightingale, bldr. Succeeds iron building of 1871, erected as mission of Christ Church. (Baker, 1961; Clarke, 1966).

CATFORD (*continued*)   St George Sch., Carholme Rd.   1899.   Tolley and Son.
Brick.

— St Lawrence Mission, Brookdale Rd.   1883.   Horace Thos. Bonner of Eastbourne.
EE. Polychromatic brick and slate roof. Spirelet. Lancets. S. J. Jerrard of Lewisham, bldrs.
Became parish hall 1887 upon opening of permanent church, which it survives. Sold to Baptists
1954: now Lewisham Baptist church. (Basil).

—* St Lawrence, Catford Rd.   1886-7.   H. Roumieu Gough.   £8,450.
EE. Bracknell brick and Corsham stone; slated pyramidal spire. Demolished for traffic scheme
which never happened and new church built on nearby site 1966. (BA, 1868; Clarke, 1966;
St Lawrence vicarage).

— Bapt., Catford Hill.   1879-8.
Perpendicular. Brick with stone facings and polychromatic slated roof.

— Bapt., St Germain's Estate.   1900.   Smee, Mence and Houchin.
Iron. Followed in 1902 by the great Gothic buildings in Brownhill Rd. Tin tabernacle replaced
by war memorial buildings 1925. (Whitley, 1928; Judge, 1973).

— Cong., Rushey Green.   1858.
Temporary. Listings cease 1890s. (K; Baker, 1961).

— Cong. Sch., Torridon Rd.   1899-1900.   Louis Jacob of New Cross Rd.   £2,283.
Dec. Red brick and Bath stone dressings. Built by C. Castle and Son of Clapton. Church added
1936. (C, 1901; Lemmy, 1949).

— W., Wildfell Rd.   1883.
EE. Brick and stone dressings. Plate tracery. Purchased 1910 by Mr. Batley as a preaching
place for Mr. Weston: now Wildfell hall (Brethren). (Baker, 1961; Mr. A. E. Goodwin of Forest
Hill; title deeds).

—* W., Rushey Green.   1891.   Chas. Bell.   £4,000.
Dec. Red brick and Bath stone. Spire. Galleries. Demolished. (W, 1891).

— Bible Ch. hall, Torridon Rd.   1900.
Dec. Brick. Succeeds tent 1898. Church built 1913. (Baker, 1961; Judge, 1973).

— Disciples of Christ, Glenfarg Rd.   1900.
Plain. Brick with red dressings and slated roof. Sometime Brethren. Now Glenfarg Evangelical
church. (Baker, 1961).

CHARING*   Holy Trinity, Charing Heath.   1872.
EE. Brick faced with rag, tiled roof. Lancets. Bellcote. Gallery. Gabled sides (Grayling, 1913).

CHARLTON-IN-DOVER, *see* Dover.

CHARLTON (by Woolwich)   Holy Trinity, Woolwich Rd, North Charlton.   1893-4.   John
Rowland of Charlton.
Lancet style. Red brick and stone dressings. Consecrated 9 April 1894. Demolished 1975.
(Vincent, 1890; Binney and Burman, 1977).

— St Paul, Fairfield Grove.   1866-7.   Wm. Wigginton.   £5,500.
Dec. Brick and stone dressings. Built by Robert Abraham of Poplar. Chapel-of-ease from 1908;
bombed 4 September 1940 and remains cleared 1941. (BA, 1868; Vincent, 1890; Basil).

— St Thomas, Maryon Rd.   1849-50.   Joseph Gwilt.   £5,169.
Romanesque. Polychromatic brick with slated roofs. Renovated by Ewan Christian 1892-3.
(Vincent, 1890; Port, 1961).

— W., Woolwich Rd.   Ante-1884.
Salvation Army purchased 1892 and sold 1910. (K; Major David Blackwell, Salvation Army).

— Sundorne M.H. (Free), Swallowfield Rd.   1895.
Congregational from 1906 and St Luke's parish hall from 1911. (SD; Baker, 1961).

— C.C., Charlton, Cemetery Lane.   1855.
Episcopalian chapel. EE and spired; Nonconformist Dec. and disused. (Vincent, 1890).

CHARTHAM   W., Bolts Hill.   1880.   £650.
   Lancet style. Supersedes chapel of 1828. Converted to dwelling, 'La Chapelle', 1965. (RC;
   W, 1880: Occ).

—   Prim. M., Town Lane, Chartham Hatch.   1840.
   Demolished ante-1968. (RC; Vickers, 1961).

—*   C.C., Canterbury Rd.   1898.   Bromley of Folkestone.
   EE. Red brick. (Mins).

—   E. Kent L.C. (St Augustine hospital), The Downs.   1875.   Gough and Gough.
   Romanesque. Outstanding brickwork. (K; Revd. M. Fulljames, chap.).

CHATHAM   C. of E., Christ Church, Luton.   1843.   Inwood and George.
   Plain. Brick. Superseded 1884, thence serving as church hall. Condemned and demolished
   c. 1970. (RC; K. Basil; Mr. L. Collins).

—   C. of E., Christ Church, Luton Rd.   1884.   E. R. Robson.   £6,000.
   Dec. Rag. Cross gabled. Glass by Kempe. Tower and spire 1926. Dismantled 1982. (K;
   Basil; CCC).

—   C. of E., St John the Divine, Railway St.   1821.   Sir R. Smirke.   £14,157.
   Doric. Ragstone. Clocktower. Apse by G. M. Hills 1863. Commissioners contributed £13,797.
   (Betj; Pev; Port, 1961).

—   C. of E., St Mary, Dock rd.   1884–7 (chancel).   Arthur Blomfield and Son.
   EE. Rag and Bath stone. Tower 1897. Nave 1901–3. Rebuilding of 1788 church. Redundant
   1974. Survived demolition plans 1977 to convert as heritage centre. (*Builder*, 1897; *Chatham
   News*, 11 February 1977; Binney and Burman, 1977; Binney, *Save Churches at Risk*).

—   C. of E., St Paul, New Rd.   1853–4;   Alex. Dick Gough.   £4,174.
   Neo-Norman and Romanesque. Rag. Restored 1890. Declared redundant 1974 and demolished.
   (Grayling, 1913; Pev; *London Gazette*, 27 September 1974, Binney and Burman, 1977; CCC).

—   R.C., St Michael, Archangel, Hills Terrace.   1862–3;   Rochester St, H. Clutton (nave) and
                           Walters (chancel)
   Romanesque. Banded brick with slate roof. (BA, 1864; B. Kelly, 1907; Whatmore, 1973).

—   Episcopal, (Garrison).   1840s.   £10,000.
   EE. Stone. Used as school. (Timpson, 1859; K; Maj. Hancock, librarian at Brompton barracks).

—   Part. Bapt., Zion, Clover St.   1821.
   Classical. Brick. Rendered. Pediment. Porch. Sabbath school 1858 demolished 1980 and rebuilt
   in sympathetic style. Latterly Baptist Union. (RFC; Pastor T. R. Harrison).

—   Part. Bapt., Enon., High St.   1843.
   Superseded 1881. (RC; *Gospel Standard*, 1881).

—   Part. Bapt., Jireh, Cannon St., Ordnance Place.   1864.
   Listings cease 1889. (*Chatham Almanac*, 1878; B, 1889–90; RFC).

—   Bapt., Luton Rd.   1864.   £533.
   Plain. Brick. Closed 1888. (B, 1866 and 1888–9).

—   St. Bapt., Enon, Nelson Rd.   1881.
   Roundheaded. Rendered façade with stone quoining. (Paul, 1966).

—   Bapt. M., Bluebell Hill.   1894.   £200.
   Plain. Brick. Surviving under Zion and said to be one of the smallest Baptist chapels in the
   country. (B, 1894; Pastor T. R. Harrison).

—   Cong. chapel and Sch., Slykate's Hill (Slicketts Hill).   1818.
   Demolished. (RC; C, 1855; Belsey and Dunstall, 1899).

—   Cong. M., Chatham Hill.   1873.   £376.
   Plain. Brick. Succeeding chapel of 1812. Listings cease 1953. (RC; Belsey and Dunstall, 1899;
   C, 1953, 1954).

CHATHAM (*continued*)　　　Cong., Ebenezer, Clover St.　1892.　G. E. Bond of Rochester.　£5,350.
Perpendicular. Red brick and Bath stone dressings. Galleries. Succeeds chapel of 1810 and survives as URC. (C, 1893; Timpson, 1859; K).

— 　Presb., New Rd.　1862.
Iron. Succeeded by St Andrew in 1903. (K; *Presbyterian Handbook*, 1959–60).

— 　Unitarian, Church of the Great Companions, Hamond Hill.　1889.
Dec. Red brick and stone dressings; tiled roof. Rebuilding of church of 1802. (Mr. Frank R. Clabburn, Unitarian information office; Mrs. J. W. Dyer, sec.).

— 　W., Ordnance Place.　1822.
Still Wesleyan 1887, then hired by Congregationalists and sold to Roman Catholics 1892. (RC; K. Ebenezer cent.).

— 　W., Salem, Rhode St.　1822.
Swedenborgian, retaining name Salem, 1866 to 1891. (RC; K).

— 　Prim. M., Fair Row, George St.　1849.
Surviving 1891, apparently superseded 1893. (RC; K).

— 　Prim. M., Mills Terrace.　1893.　G. E. Bond.
Lancet style. Brick, red facings. Spire. C. E. Skinner, bldr. Closed *c.* 1962. Southern Sheds since 1975. (Occ.).

—* 　Bible Ch., Union St.　1829.　£900.
Plain. Brick. Enlarged with Classical façade 1890. Closed 1956, used as furniture store then demolished for traffic mid-1970s. (Wright's *Topography*, 1838; Bourne, 1905; Mr. R. A. Baldwin, district archivist).

— 　Bible Ch., Luton Rd.　1884–5.　J. K. Cole.　£1,800.
EE. Red brick. Turrets. Rose window. Built by C. E. Skinner of Chatham. School 1902. Survives in Methodist and Anglican use. (K).

— 　Cath. Apos., Brook.　1836.
Congregation removed ante-1871. Thence Ebenezer mission (Congregational). (RC; Seraphim, Metropolitan of Glastonbury).

— 　Cath. Apos., New Rd.　Post-1854.
Dec. Brick, rendered. Porch. Closed 1948, paper store until 1959, dedicated Seventh Day Adventist 1961. For sale 1982. (*Chatham Observer*, 22 September 1961; Seraphim, Metropolitan of Glastonbury).

— 　S.A. H., Church St.　1890.
Citadel style. Stock brick. Young people's hall added 1913. (Cent., 1973; Major David Blackwell, Salvation Army architect).

CHELSFIELD　C. of E., M.Ch., Greenstreet (Green Rd.).　*c.* 1876.
Iron. Erected and served by Ebenezer Robinson and subsequently by clergy of Darenth. Demolished *c.* 1973 having served in later years as church hall. (K, 1874, 1878, 1891, 1903; Darenth vicarage).

— 　W.,　1872.
Renaissance. Stock brick and red dressings. Schoolroom 1875. Enlarged 1885. Superseded 1967 in Windsor Drive. Now private dwelling. (*The Cray*, 1 August 1872; Judd, 1932; Mr John Bowen).

CHERITON　C. of. E., All Souls, High St.　1894.　Ewan Christian.　£4,000.
EE. Rag and tiled roof. Apsidal chancel. W bellcote. Bequest of Mrs. C. Thompson of Seabrook. (K).

— 　Cong., Ashley Rd. (Ashley Ave.).　1883.
Pointed. Iron. Closed 1981 and now recreation centre. (Occ).

CHIDDINGSTONE　C. of E., St Luke.　1897–8.　J. F. Bentley.
Perpendicular. Bath stone, Pinnacled tower. Financed by Hills family. (K).

CHIDDINGSTONE (*continued*) C. of E., St Saviour, Causeway. *c*.1875.
  Iron. Became village hall *c.* 1902 and so remains. (K; rectory).

CHILHAM   W., Old Wives' Lees.   1869.   £450.
  Rendered with tiled roof. Follows chapel of 1840. Now a dwelling. (RC; W, 1869).

CHISLEHURST   C. of E., Annunciation of the Blessed Virgin Mary, West Chislehurst High St.
       1868-70.   Jas. Brooks.   £10,000.
  EE. Rag. Chapel and separate tower 1885, completed 1930 by E. J. May. (K; Grayling, 1913;
  Pev).

—   C. of E., Christ Church, Lower Camden (Lubbock Rd.)   1871-2.   Habershon and Pite.
  EE. Rag and Bath stone. Tower and Kentish turret. (BA, 1873; K).

—   C. of E., St John the Baptist, Mill Place.   1886.   E. Crutchloe.
  EE. Stock and red brick with tiled roof. Closed *c.* 1939, thence factory for aircraft parts,
  pharmaceuticals and since 1954 Pearce Transformers. (Pev; Mr. Northwood of Pearce
  Transformers).

—   R.C., St Mary, Hawkwood Lane.   1854.   W. W. Wardell.   £1,500.
  EE. Rag. Bellcote. N chapel by Clutton 1874; paid for by Empress Eugenie for the repose here
  of Louis Napoleon. (CD; K; Pev).

—   W., Chapel Lane (Park Rd.).   1835.
  Superseded 1870, used subsequently by other denominations. Demolished 1969. (RC; cent,
  1970; Revd. Douglas Maw, min.).

—   W., Chislehurst Common (Prince Imperial Rd.).   1868-70.   £5,800.
  EE. Rag. Plate tracery. (Webb *et al.*, 1899; cent, 1970).

CHISLET   C. of E., St John Ev., Marshside.   1879.
  Vernacular. Brick and hung tiled. Turret. Closed 1971, sold with planning permission 1975 and
  converted to private residence. (K; McIntosh, 1972).

—   W., Marshside.   1841.
  Plain. Red brick with burnt headers and slated roof. (McIntosh, 1972).

CLIFTONVILLE, *see* Margate.

COLLIER STREET   C. of E., St Margaret.   1847-9.   P. C. Hardwick.
  EE. Rag. Lancets. S porch. Tall shingled spire. (Pev).

COOLING   W., Church St.   1889.   £569.
  Brick and stone dressings. Known locally, on account of its remoteness, as 'the chapel in the
  orchard'. Demolished 1979 after period of disuse. (W, 1890; K; Macdougall, 1980; Mrs. D.
  Macrow).

COWDEN   Trin. Presb., North St.   1894.
  Vernacular. Brick. Closed and sold 1958 and now occupied as private residence, St Andrew's
  lodge. (K; Bradford, 1972).

COXHEATH   Cong., Linton Rd.   1825.
  Roundheaded. Wood. Porch. Remains Congregational. (C, 1855. Timpson, 1859).

CRANBROOK   Cong., High St.   1857.   £1,400.
  Yellow brick. Gothic façade. Two twin-light Dec. traceried windows and round window above
  gabled porch, W end. Succeeds chapel of 1831 in Crane Lane. (C, 1855; Timpson, 1859;
  chapel records).

CRAYFORD   C. of E., St Augustine, Slade Green.   1900.   £4,000.
  EE. Brick. Spirelet. Clerestory. Fridays, bldrs. (Carr, 1951; Revd. Christopher Johnson).

—   R.C., St Mary of the Crays, Old Rd.   1842.
  Cruciform. Brick rendered. N porch. Augustus Applegarth, benefactor. Demolished 1974
  following erection of new church. (RC; CD; Bernard, Kelly, 1907; Carr, 1951).

—   Bapt. Sch., Chapel Hill.   1858.
  Romanesque. Brick.

CRAYFORD (*continued*)   Bapt., Bexley Lane.   1867.   Habershon and Pite.   £1,300.
   Romanesque. Brick and stucco. Twin porches. (B, 1868; K; Carr, 1951).

CROCKENHILL   C. of E., All Souls, Church Rd.   1851.   Edwin Nash.
   EE. Rag. Bellcote. Lancets. (K; Pev).

CROCKHAM HILL   C. of E., Holy Trinity.   1842.
   Perp. Sandstone, with tiled roof. Castellated tower. Given by Chas. Warde and built by Mr.
   Horseman. (K; Basil; Pev).

CUDHAM   Bapt.,   *c*. 1871.
   Superseded post-1924. (K; Whitley, 1928).

—   W.   1846.
   Domestic. Wood. (RC; Judd, 1932).

CUXTON   Cong. M.Rm., Bush Rd.   1897.
   Plain. Corrugated iron. Porch. Given by Ald. F. Smith and erected by J. H. Durrant. Survives
   as URC. (K; Church, 1976).

DARENTH   W., Bethesda.   1844.
   Extant 1851. (RC).

—   L.C. asylum (Darenth Park hospital).   1878.   C. and A. Harston.
   Pointed. Brick. (K; Revd. C. Newman, chaplain).

DARTFORD*   C. of E., St Alban, East Hill (St Alban's Rd.)   1880.
   EE. White brick. Consec. 1902. (K; Revd. John Ansell).

—   C. of E., Christ Church, West Hill.   1872.
   Iron. Bellcote, W porch and gabled roof. Succeeded by Caröe's red brick church in 1909 and
   demolished 1932. (Keyes, 1933).

—   Episcopal chapel, Crayford Rd.   1870.
   Iron. Temporary. (K).

—*   R.C., St Anselm's, Spital St.   1900.   F. A. Walters.
   EE. Brick, built by J. Smith and Son of Norwood. The gift of E. J. Fooks of Chislehurst.
   Demolished 1975. (Bernard Kelly, 1907; Basil).

—   Bapt., Highfield Rd.   1867–8.   £1,400.
   Lancet style. Brick and red brick with high pitched slated roof. Porch. (B, 1869).

—   Indep., Lowfield St.   1819.
   Classical. Brick. Here worshipped seceders from Zion chapel (Countess of Huntingdon's).
   Later converted to office premises and demolished for new shopping parade. (Timpson, 1859;
   Keyes, 1933; Gillham, 1968).

—*   Cong. Sch., West Hill.   1882.   John Sulman.
   Pointed. Red brick with stone dressings. Plate tracery. Flèche. Built by J. G. Naylor of
   Rochester. Hampden Pratt's designs for completion were never realised so this survives as the
   URC church. (C, 1882; Keyes, 1933).

—*   W., Spital St.   1844–5.   W. W. Pocock.   £2,500.
   Yellow brick, revealed by cleaning of façade 1979. Two square initially pinnacled towers
   enclosing castellated vestibule. New galleries and vestries by Pocock, Corfe and Parker 1869;
   and enlarged along Kent Rd. 1910. (Keyes, 1933; Pev).

—*   Prim. M., East Hill.   1874.   J. C. Waller.
   Geom. Brick and Bath stone. Site given by H. Pigon. C. D. Higgins, bldr. Sunday school 1906.
   Now Emmanual Pentecostal with modern façade. (K; Keyes, 1933).

—   C.C., East Hill.   Ante-1867.
   Episcopal and nonconformist. Demolished post-WW II. (K; Porteus, 1981).

—   C.C., Watling St.   1900.
   EE. Rag with stone dressings and tiled roof. (K).

DEAL   C. of E., St Andrew, West St.   1848–50.   Ambrose Poynter.   £7,000.
EE. Rag with Caen stone dressings. Intended as a church for boatmen, hence the dedication. Chancel by Wm. White 1867. Recessed spire rebuilt 1910. (K).

— C. of E. M.H., St Andrew's, Duke St.   1881.
Roundheaded. Brick. Erected as a mission to boatmen. Old Age Pensioners' Association since 1953. (K; Mrs. Cope of O.A.P.A.).

— R.C., St Ethelburga's convent, West St.   1879.
The gift of Lady Southwell. Consec. 1902. Closed 1980 and demolished. (K; Fr. Leonard Whatmore; Sr. Veronica Kavanagh, R.N.D.M.).

— R.C., St Thomas of Canterbury, Blenheim Rd.   1885.   F. A. Walters.
Norman. Red brick. W tower with Norman cap. (K; Cd; Little, 1966).

— St. Cal., Providence, St George's Place.   1837.
(RC).

— Bapt., Victoria, Victoria Rd.   1881.   John Wills.   £3,300.
Gothic. Local bricks and Bath stone dressings. Built by Geo. Cotton and Jas. Trollope of Deal. Enlarged 1864. (B, 1882).

—* Cong., Bi-centenary Memorial, High St.   1882.   Joseph Gardner of Folkestone.
English Gothic. Yellow stock brick and Bath stone. Twin steeples. Disused 1978, congregation uniting with Trinity Methodist. (C, 1882; K; Laker, 1921).

— W., Union St.   1865.   C. L. Crowther.   £3,000.
Land given by Wm. Betts. Demolished and replaced 1966. Wesley hall, 1901, roundedheaded, brick, stet. (Laker, 1921; *East Kent Mercury*, 23 June 1966).

— Prim. M., Park St.   1852.
Closed and sold to council 1932 then used as library. Destroyed WW II. (K; Methodist circuit archives; Deal reference library).

— C.C., Cemetery Rd. (Hamilton Rd.)   1856.
Dec. Rag and slated roofs. Two chapels, one with bell spire, aside porte cochère. (K; Laker, 1921).

DEPTFORD   St Barnabas M., Evelyn St.   1882–3.
Brick with Bath stone dressings. Site given by W. Evelyn. Served until 1953 as headquarters of Royal Association in Aid of the Deaf and Dumb; then closed down and used as a boys' club. Destroyed by fire 1959. (Dews, 1884; Basil; Baker, 1961).

— C. of E., Christ Church, Church St.   1864   Newman and Billing.   £4,800.
Byzantine. Brick with stone facings. Parish suppressed and church closed 1936. Demolished 1937. (Dews, 1884; Basil).

— Emmanuel, Brookmill Rd.   1888.   E. C. Ayton-Lee.   £2,250.
Red brick. Chancel added 1899 for £1,300. Built as chapel-of-ease to Holy Trinity, Greenwich. Bombed 1940 and subsequently demolished. (Basil; Baker, 1961).

—* C. of E., St John, Lewisham High Rd. (Lewisham Way).   1855.   P. C. Hardwick.
Early Dec. Kentish rag. Tall spire. (Dews, 1884).

— M.H., St John's, King St. (Harton St.)   1873.
Plain. Banded brick. Sometime Rechabites and lately Celestial Church of Christ. (Dews, 1884; K; Baker, 1961.).

— C. of E., St Luke, Evelyn St.   1870–2.   T. H. Watson.
Gothic. Rag. Lancets. (Dews, 1884; Pev).

— C. of E., St Mark, Edward St., Amersham Vale.   1883.   Arthur H. Newman.   £4,500.
Early French. Brick with stone dressings. Bellcote. Built by Dove Bros. Bombed 1941. Closed 1955 and converted 1978 as youth and community centre. (Dews, 1884; Basil; Sports Council, 1978).

DEPTFORD (*continued*)   R.C., Our Lady of the Assumption, High St.   1844–6.   £2,000.
EE. Yellow brick and stone dressings. Chancel designed and built by Canon North 1859. Consecrated 19 May 1890. (Dews, 1884).

--   Bapt., Zion, Florence Place.   1846.
Amalgamated with Zion New Cross Rd. *c.* 1862. (Baker, 1961).

—   St. Bapt., Zion, New Cross Rd.   1847.
Classical. Brick with stone dressings. Enlarged 1876. Damaged 1944, reopened 1946. (Timpson, 1859; *Gospel Herald*; Dews, 1884; Whitley, 1928; Baker, 1961).

—   Bapt., Bethel.   1849.
Vanished by 1856. (Whitley, 1928).

—   Bapt., Midway Place.   1857.
Closed and demolished *c.* 1920. (Baker, 1961).

—   Bapt., China Hall Gate.   1861.
Sold 1873 to Independents. (Whitley, 1928).

—   Bapt., Brockley Rd. (Upper Brockley Rd.).   1867.   Gray Searle and Son.
Dec. Rag with stone dressings and slate roof. Geom. tracery. Bldr. Wm. Higgs. Damaged several times during WW II. (Dews, 1884; Baker, 1961).

—   Indep. Bapt., Olivet, Octavius St. (schoolroom 1867 extended to chapel).   1868.
Classical. Red and white brick. Closed December 1980 when the congregation moved to new premises in Arklow Rd. (Dews, 1884; Revd. Don Bishop, min.).

—   Bapt. M.H., Creek St.   1877.
Mission of Brockley Rd. chapel. Closed and sold 1935. (Dews, 1877; Rowberry and Hunt, 1960).

—   Bapt., Lewisham Rd.   1881.
Extinct by 1928. (Whitley, 1928).

—   Bapt. Alliance hall, High St.   1885.
Closed 1891. (Baker, 1961).

—*   Cong., High St.   1861–2.   Francis Pouget.   £5,000.
Italianate. Portland cement. Galleries. New church built 1955. (C, 1863; Dews, 1884; Baker, 1961).

—   Cong. M., Amersham Grove.   Post-1865.
Iron room superseding rented stable. Appropriated by North Kent Railway Co. (Hope-Bell, 1954).

—   Cong. M.H., Napier St.   1881.
Mission of St David's, Lewisham High Rd. Sunday school 1883. Closed and sold 1946. Baptists moved in 1948. Demolished. (Dews, 1884; Hope-Bell, 1954; Baker, 1961).

—   W.M. Free, St John's Rd.   1841.
Later Brunswick chapel (United Methodist). Closed post-1933. (Dews, 1884; K; SD; Baker, 1961).

—   W. preaching station and Sunday school, Garden Row (Friendly St.)   1846.
Wesleyan Methodist Free surviving here 1880. (K; Baker, 1961).

—   W., New Cross Rd.   1872.
Destroyed 1944. (Baker, 1961).

—   Meth. New Connexion, Victoria, Grove St.   1857.
Closed post-1884. (Dews, 1884; K; Baker, 1961).

—   City Mission, New St.   1838.   £800.
Sometime Congregational mission hall. Destroyed 1941. (Dews, 1884; Baker, 1961).

—   London City Mission, Blackhorse Bridge.   1857.
Closed ante-1890. (Dews, 1884; K).

DEPTFORD (*continued*)   Swedenborg, New Jerusalem, Warwick St. (Warwickshire Path).   1871.
    'Commodious and handsome'. Closed 1949, used sometime as British Legion then demolished
    for residential development. (Dews, 1884; Baker, 1961).

—   City Mission, Evelyn Hall, William St. (Staunton St.).   Ante-1884.
    Plain. Brick, rendered. Brethren from 1935 and latterly Bible Truth Church of God. (Dews,
    1884; Baker, 1961).

—   Moody and Sankey Mission, New Cross Rd.   1884.
    Iron. Closed within three weeks. (Baker, 1961).

—   C.C., Brockley Rd.   1858.
    Bombed WW II. (Meller, 1981).

—   R.C., St Michael and the Holy Angels cemetery chapel, Brockley Rd.   1866–8. Corbels
    by Boulton.
    Built by Sir Stuart Knill, Bart. Destroyed 1944. (CD; K; Dews, 1884: Baker, 1961).

DOVER   St Bartholomew Mission, Tower Hamlets.   1873.
    Iron. Succeeded by permanent building 1878. (*Dover Guide*, 1876).

—   C. of E., St Bartholomew, Templar St.   1878.   Joseph Clarke.
    EE. Flint and stone. Glass by Kempe 1887. Demolition scheme 1974. (K; Binney and Burman,
    1977; parish magazine, October 1972).

—   C. of E., Christ Church, Folkestone Rd.   1843–4.   Scott and Moffatt.
    EE. Rag. Lancets. Galleries. Built by John and Parker Ayres. Chancel and SW spirelet 1895
    by Stenning and Jennings of Dover for £1,050. Closed 1973 and demolished December 1977.
    (E, 1860; SD; Basil; *Kentish Gazette*, 14 October 1977).

—   C. of E., Holy Trinity, Stroud St.   1883–5.   W. M. Edmunds.   £7,973 incl. land.
    Dec. Pinnacles. Bellcote. Commissioners contributed £3,596. Built by Messrs. Youden of
    Dover. Demolished after war damage. (K; SD; Cent, 1935; Port, 1961; Green, 1978).

—   C. of E., St James the Apostle, Maison Dieu Rd.   1859–62.   Thos. Talbot Bury.   £12,000.
    Early Dec. Kentish rag with Bath stone dressings. NW tower with crockets, pinnacles and
    spire. Demolished 1952 after war damage. (SD; K. Eastlake, 1872; Pev).

—   C. of E., St Peter and St Paul, St Alphege Rd.   1893.   Jas. Brooks.
    EE. Rag. Rebuilding of older church that had proven too small. (SD; Basil; Betj).

—*   R.C., St Paul, Maison Dieu Rd.   1867–8.   E. W. Pugin.   £3,100.
    EE. Ragstone. Bellcote. Consec. 1897. (CD; SD; K. Little, 1966; Buckingham, 1968).

—   Bapt., Salem, Biggin St.   1840.   Frank Hight.
    Classical. Rendered. Pediment. Joseph Stiff, bldr. New façade and pediment 1879. Closed
    and demolished 1970. (Holyoak, 1914; Green, 1980; Mr. D. J. Cook, sec.)

—   Bapt., Maxton tabernacle, Churchill Rd.   1880.   £3,000.
    Demolished *c.* 1969. (B, 1881).

—   Indep., Zion ('Pent-side chapel'), Commercial Quay, Snargate St.   1823.   £1,205.
    Particular Baptist by 1876, sold to Pent-side Baptists 1902, closed 1909, then variously used
    as picture palace, covered market and leather merchants. (Batcheller, 1828; RC; Holyoak,
    1914; RFC; chap, 1959).

—   Indep., Russell St.   1838.   £1,780 excl. land.
    Occupied until High St. Church was built 1904. Destroyed WW II. (RC; C, 1855; Timpson,
    1859; chap, 1959; Green, 1978).

—   Cong., Ark room.   1847.
    Short lived. (RC).

—*   Gen. Bapt., Adrian St.   1820.   Thos. Read.
    Neo-classical. Yellow brick. Irregular octagon with pediments on major sides. Now Unitarian.
    (SD; Pev; Drummond, 1938).

DOVER (*continued*)   W., St John's, Middle Row (Blenheim Square).   1823.
'Extremely plain'. Closed 1827, sometime in Countess of Huntingdon's Connexion and rented from 1839 by Church of England. Later enlarged as St John's church (Free Church of England). Fell into disuse early 1900s. (Batcheller, 1828; Timpson, 1859; Holy Trinity cent.).

—   W., Snargate St.   1834.
Classical. Brick and stone dressings. Pediment. Demolished early 1970s. (RC; Goulden's *Guide*; NMR; Mr. Ivan Green).

—   W. centenary, London Rd.   1839.
Classical. Brick with rendered façade. Long closed: sometime Sea Scouts and now bingo. (Goulden's *Guide*; NMR; Dr. Christopher Stell).

—   W. M.H., Tower Hamlets.   1850.
Vernacular. Brick with slated roof and rendered façade. Porch. (SD; *Dover Express*, 28 February 1975: Godfrey Johns, min.).

—   Jubilee Prim. M., Peter St.   1860.
Closed 1901 and incorporated within engineering works. (K; Green, 1978; Revd. Godfrey Johns).

—   Prim. M., Roundhouse St.   1874.
(Green, 1978).

—   Prim. M., Belgrave St.   1882.   A. Wills.
Pointed. Brick and rendered. Built by Lewis and Co. Used post-war as timber workshop and from 1981 as auction rooms. (SD; Green, 1978).

—   Synagogue, Hawkesbury St.   1835.
Community survived until WW II. Also references to 'a fine synagogue' built in Northampton St. 1863. (RC; Goulden's *Guide*; K; Roth, 1950).

—   C.C., St Mary's cemetery, Charlton (Connaught Rd.).   Formed 1835.
EE. Ashlar with variegated tiled roof. Bellcote. (K).

—*   C.C. St James cemetery, Old Charlton Rd.   1860.
Lancets. Knapped flint and stone quoining. Two chapels a distance apart, the one demolished 1961 and the other surviving as a toolshed. (K; KAO).

—*   C.C., St Mary's cemetery, Copt Hill.   1870.
Consec. Two chapels no longer there. (K; KAO).

—   C.C. Charlton cemetery, Old Charlton Rd.   1872.
Consec. Dec. Sandstone. Plate tracery. Two chapels aside porte cochère, one now a toolshed. (K).

DOWNE   Priv., Manor land (Luxted Rd.).   Pre-1851.
Plain. Clapboard. Erected by lord of the manor, Mr. Smith. Acquired by Baptists *c.* 1851, reformed as Strict Communion 1861: chapel demolished 1961 and replaced by hall. (RFC; chap, 1969).

DUNKIRK   C. of E., Christ Church.   1840.   John Whichcord.   £2,350.
Flint with stone dressings. Buttressed tower. (K; Basil; Pev).

DUNTON GREEN   C. of E., St John Ev., London Rd.   1889--90.   M. T. Potter of Sevenoaks.
        £1,900.
EE. Red brick and Bath stone; slate roof. Lancets. Bellcote. (K; Pev).

—   Cong., London Rd.   1873.
Vernacular. Yellow brick and red brick dressings; slate roof. Acquired by Assemblies of God after Congregationalists moved to their present church in Station Rd. 1937. (C, 1875; Miss K. E. B. Lowin, sec.).

—   W.   1831.
Extant 1851.   (RC).

DYMCHURCH   Bapt., High St.   1835.
Plain. Brick. Closed ante-1887. Here is now Treasure Trove. (RC; K; Revd. C. R. Edmundson, min. of New Romney).

DYMCHURCH (*continued*)   W., High St.   1880.
Roundheaded windows. Rendered with slated roof. Porch. (K; Mr. Jack Newman).

EASTCHURCH   Bapt., Zion.   1835.
Closed early 1870s. (RC; B, 1871, 1875).

—   W., High St.   1821.   Rebuilt 1886 for £386.
Plain. Brick with slated roof. Porch. (W, 1887).

EAST FARLEIGH   Bapt.   1845.
In use 1851. (RC).

EAST LANGDON   Prim. M., The Street.   1875.
Plain. Brick with slated roof. Closed by 1920 then used as church hall; later derelict and used as village shop from 1947 to present day. (K; Occ).

EAST MALLING   W.   1844.
Superseded and vanished. (RC; McNay, 1980).

EAST PECKHAM   C. of E., Holy Trinity, Church Lane.   1842.   Whichcord and Walker.
EE. Stone. Bellcote. Restored 1892 for £800. Vestry added 1900. (K; Pev; Revd. Edmund Haviland, rector).

—   C. of E., Mission church (St Mary), Laddingford.   Ante-1895.
EE. Red and white brick with tiled roof. Attached to Church of England primary school. (OS).

—   St. Bapt., Providence, The Freehold.   1857.
Pointed windows. Brick, now rendered. Porch. (RFC).

—   W.   1823.
Succeeded 1887. (RC).

—   W., Laddingford.   1872.
Plain. Brick with white. Closed post–1964 and now village hall. (Tonbridge jub., 1964; Bailey, 1970).

—   W., Pound Rd.   1886-7.   S. W. Haughton of East Grinstead.
Pointed windows. Red brick and white brick dressings. Bldr. C. J. Jones of Tonbridge. Succeeds chapel of 1820. Extended 1923. (Tonbridge Circuit jub. programme, 1964).

—   S.A. Hall, Freehold.   1885.
Plain. Brick. Roundedheaded windows. (Lawrence, 1979; Major David Blackwell, Salvation Army).

EASTRY   Bapt., Zion, Lower St.   1824.
Plain. Brick, with slated hipped roof. Porch.

—   W., Providence, Mill Lane.   1822.
Domestic. Red brick. Hipped roof. On the market 1977 and Pentecostal since 1979; now 'New Life Chapel'. (*East Kent Mercury*, 16 November 1978).

—   Union (Eastry Hospital), Mill Lane.   1873.   £1,000.
EE. Stone beneath tiled roof. Bellcote. Lancets. (K).

EAST WICKHAM   Prim. M., Upper Wickham Lane.   1899.
Lancet style. Brick with stone dressings and red brick façade. Pinnacles. Latterly FIEC. (K).

EDENBRIDGE   Bapt., Bethel, High St.   1841.
Brick. Enlarged 1853 and 1892-3 and is now roundheaded; red brick with slated roof; pinnacles and finials; Baptist Union. (B, 1894; RFC; Bradford, 1972).

—   Presb., St John's Greybury church, Marsh Green.   1882.
EE. Red brick banded with white; stone dressings and slated roofs. Spire. Plate tracery. Adjacent Presbyterian day school surviving. (Bradford, 1972).

—   Gospel Hall, Bombers Farm.   1898.
Hut. Congregation removed 1913 to iron room at Crockham Hill. (Bradford, 1972).

EGERTON   St. Bapt., Potters Forstal Rd.   1825.
　　　Plain. Red brick with burnt headers and slated roof. Porch. Closed 1974, repaired and opened
　　　as Free Church 1975. (RFC; P. H. Oliver, min.).

ELHAM   Indep., Linpire.   1839.
　　　Congregational listing ceases 1855. (RC; C. 1855, 1856).

—*   W. centenary, High St.   1839.
　　　Classical. Flint and brick with stucco façade. Doric pilasters and high door surmounted by
　　　pediment. Galleries. Succeeds 1814 chapel now adjoining as Sunday school. (Toy, 1968;
　　　Bernard Budd, Q.C.).

—   Bible Ch., Ebenezer, The Row.   1862.   £136 14s. 9d.
　　　Plain. Flint and brick with slated roof. Follows chapel of 1832, closed 1935, used as fire
　　　station WW II and later as garage. (RC; *Bible Christian Magazine*, 1862; Elham *Circuit
　　　Messenger*, May 1912; Miss Mary Smith of Kingpost).

ELMLEY   Church.   1827.
　　　Built out of ruins of desecrated chapel and described by its curate in 1851 as 'the meanest and
　　　smallest in the United Kingdom'. Rebuilt as St James, 1853, EE, Rag. Closed 1940s. (RC;K;
　　　Woodthorpe, 1951).

ELTHAM   C. of E., All Saints mission, Foot's Cray Rd.   1884. Tin.
　　　Succeeded by permanent building in Bercta Rd. 1894. (Harris, 1885; Baker 1961).

—   C. of E., All Saints, Bercta Rd.   1894.   Richd. J. Lovell. £8,000.
　　　Lancets. Brick. Built by Peter Dollar. Perp. chancel 1930. (*Builder* 64, 1893; Clarke, 1966;
　　　All Saints vicarage).

—*   C. of E., Holy Trinity, Southend Crescent.   1869-9.   G. E. Street.   £4,500.
　　　EE. Sandstone with tile roof. Lead spirelet (now gone), kingpost roof, plate tracery. Glass by
　　　Clayton and Bell. Bombed 1944, reopened 1946. (BA, 1870; Vincent, 1890; Baker, 1961,
　　　Clarke, 1966).

—   C. of E., St John Baptist, High St.   1875.   A. W. Blomfield.   £10,000.
　　　EE. Rag. Broached spire, clerestoried nave, plate tracery. Glass by Comper. (BA, 1876; Glynne,
　　　1877; Vincent, 1890; Rivers, 1904; Baker, 1961; Clarke, 1966; *Caring for Churches*, 1975).

—   R.C., St Mary, High St.   1890.
　　　Classical. Brick. Superseded by Christ Church 1912 and surviving as Roman Catholic primary
　　　school. (Bernard Kelly, 1907).

—   Cong., High St. (Arcade).   1839.   £1,200.
　　　Cost borne by Wm. Joynson. Superseded by more commodious building in 1868. (Timpson,
　　　1859; chap, 1971).

—   Cong., High St. (corner of Well Hall Rd.).   1867-8.   Thos. Chatfield Clarke.   £4,500.
　　　Gothic. Rag and Bath stone. SW tower and spire 100 ft. Schoolrooms. Closed and sold for
　　　demolition 1935. (C, 1868; chap, 1971).

—   Cong., M., Foot's Cray Rd., New Eltham.   1875.
　　　Red and yellow brick. Schoolroom added 1882. Closed and sold 1930; Co-op built on site
　　　1931. (Mr. Tom Bunce).

—   Bible Ch., Elizabeth Terrace.   1841.
　　　Superseded by Park Place chapel 1881, then used as dwelling and office. Demolished post-
　　　1961. (Baker, 1961).

—   Bible Ch., Park Place (Passey Place).   1880-1.
　　　Gothic. Stock brick, banded with red, and with red brick façade. Brethren in 1961 and demo-
　　　lished thereafter for development. (*Bible Christian Magazine*, 13 January 1881; Baker, 1961).

ERITH   C. of E., St Augustine (St Augustine's Rd.), Belvedere.   1884.
　　　Iron. Superseded by permanent church 1916. Site now occupied by vicarage. (Harris, 1885;
　　　Mrs. Sellick, churchwarden).

—   C. of E., Christ Church, Victoria Rd.   1874.   Jas. Piers St Aubyn.   £8,000.
　　　EE. Stock brick relieved with red. On land given by Col. Wheatley. Tower and spire 1914.
　　　(K; Harris, 1855; Basil).

ERITH (*continued*)   Mission chapel, Arthur St.   1885.
   Associated with Christ Church. Closed post-1903 and demolished. (Harris, 1885; K).

— R.C., St Fidelis, West St.   1870.
   Lancets. Brick banded with red. Founded by Capuchins. Served as chapel-of-ease since opening
   of Our Lady of the Angels 1903. (Bernard Kelly, 1907).

— Bapt., Bexley Rd., Belvedere.   1863.
   Site given by Sir Culling Eardley. Formed by secession from Nuxley Rd. Strict Baptist chapel.
   Damaged by gunpowder explosion of two barges 1864. Enlarged and schoolroom added 1900.
   Bombed 1941 and rebuilt 1950. (B, 1864; Harris, 1885; Prichard, 1974).

— Bapt., Queen St.   1877.   Hesketh.   £1,350 incl. schools.
   Brick. Lancets. Survives alongside 1891 chapel.

— Bapt., Queen St.   1891.
   Dec. Brick.

— Bapt., Abbey Rd., Belvedere.   1899.   £750.
   Extant 1928. (B, 1898; K. Whitley, 1928).

— Bapt. M., Northumberland Heath (Belmont Rd.).   1901.
   Brick. Used as hall following building of new church 1939. (Whitley, 1928; Revd. F. W. J.
   Butler, min.).

—* Cong., Avenue (Rd.).   1858-9.   R. Moffat Smith of Manchester.   £2,300.
   Dec. Yellow brick and Bath stone. Richd. Holloway of Islington, bldr. Land given by Col.
   Wheatley. Closed and demolished 1973. (C, 1859; Harris, 1885; Mr. Trevor Robin, organist).

— Cong., Pickardy Hill (Picardy Rd.).   1897.   Chas. Pertwee of Chelmsford.   £2,000 incl. schools.
   Geom. Stock brick, Bath stone and tiles. Lancets. Follows iron chapel of 1865. (Mearns,
   1882; C, 1895 and 1898).

— W., Providence. Bexley Rd.   1823.
   Plain. Brick. Sometime Salvation Army from whom purchased and opened as Strict Baptist
   1897. (RC; Whitley, 1928; RFC).

— W., Pier Rd.   1876.
   Iron. Cleared *c.* 1972. (K; Mrs. J. Fraser, local preacher).

— Prim. M., Picardy Rd.   1876.   Habershon and Pite.
   Lancet style. Yellow brick banded with red; slated roof. Porch.

— Prim. M., Riverdale Rd.   1901.
   Long closed, sometime cinema and latterly Jehovah's Witnesses. (K; Mrs. J. Fraser, local
   preacher).

— Ev. Alliance, Tower Church, Lessness Heath (Belvedere).   1848.
   Built by Sir Culling Eardley with the pulpit 'open to every faithful minister' and demolished
   after his death. (RC; Timpson, 1859; K. Prichard, 1974).

— Indep., Nuxley Rd.   1853-61.   W. G. and E. Habershon.   £6,000.
   EE. Knapped flint and stone dressings. Spire. Built as proprietary chapel for Sir Culling Eardley.
   Opened as Church of England 1856 and survives as All Saints. Transepts 1864. (Timpson,
   1859; Harris, 1885; Pev).

— London City Mission, Mill Rd., Spike Island (Northumberland Heath).   1877.
   Plain. Brick with slated roof. Spirelet. Follows chapel of 1857. Gift of Alfred A. Larking.
   (*L.C.M. Magazine*, 1 October 1857 and Jan.-Feb. 1977; Vincent, 1890; Mr. R. Courts,
   missioner).

— C.C., Riverdale Rd.   1894.   Harold Hinde.
   Lancet style. Brick with tiled roofs. Bellcote. (Cemetery office, Bexley council).

ETCHINGHILL*   St Mary's Hospital.   1895.   Joseph Gardner and John Ladds.
   EE. Red brick and tiled roof. Lancets.

FARNBOROUGH   Chapel-of-ease, on vicar's premises.   *c.* 1881.
Temporary. (K).

—   Part. Bapt., Providence.   *c.* 1840.
Followed by Beulah. (RC).

—   St. Bapt., Beulah, Locks Bottom (Wellbrook Rd.).   1870.
Roundheaded. Brick, now rendered. Closed 1920, used as a garage and now by Markplan
Systems. (B, 1872; *Gospel Herald*, 1881; RFC).

—   Breth., Gospel Hall, High St.   Ante-1887.
Plain. Rendered. Surviving. (K).

FARNINGHAM   W.   1850.
Superseded by wooden chapel 1902. (RC; W, 1901).

FAVERSHAM   C. of E., St Andrew, Water Lane.   1872.
Enlarged 1874. Quayside mission. Closed *c.* WW II and used as warehouse. (K; Dane, 1954).

—   C. of E., St John the Evangelist, Brents.   1881.   Kirk and Son of Sleaford.
EE. Flint and Bath stone. Costs borne by Mrs. Hall of Syndale House, Ospringe. (Pev).

—   C. of E., St Saviour, Whitstable Rd.   1885.
Pointed. Iron. Bellcote. Mission church of St Mary. Closed 1950 and successively used as
parish hall, for printing works, tent hire and now antiques. (K; *Evening Standard*, 10 February
1950; Dane, 1954).

—   Part. Bapt., Gatefield Lane.   1818.
Superseded by larger chapel 1833. (Giraud and Donne, 1876).

—   Part. Bapt., Gatefield Lane.   1833.
Passed to Plymouth Brethren 1857, sold *c.* 1885 and adapted as Faversham Club. (RC;
Giraud and Donne, 1876).

—   Bapt., St Mary's Rd.   1872.   £1,800.
Roundheaded. Polychromatic brick. Built by Lewis Shrubsole of Faversham. Red brick
extensions are 1912. (B, 1874; Dane, 1975).

—   Cong., Newton Rd.   1878-9.   Joseph Gardner of Folkestone.
Classical. Pediment. Called 'the Nonconformist cathedral'. Demolished 1972 and replaced by
public library. (Dane, 1954; Pev; Faversham library).

—   W., Brents.   1847.
In use 1851. (RC).

—   W., Preston St.   1860-1.
Nonconformist Gothic. Brick with rag façade, limestone quoining and slate roof. Pinnacles,
buttresses and gabled sides. Enlarged and galleries 1870. Building shared with URC since 1980.
(Dane, 1954; Swaine, 1969; Dane, 1975).

—   Bible Ch., Water Lane.   1831.
Superseded 1852. (RFC).

—   Bible Ch., Abbey Place.   1852.
Classical. Stock brick dressed with red. Used by Primitives after 1898 when the Bible Christians
removed to Stone St., and subsequently as a store. (Dane, 1954; Dane, 1975).

—   Bible Ch., Stone St.   1898.   Edwin Pover.
Classical. Red brick and slate roof. Vacated 1933 upon union with the Preston St. Methodists
and now used as a store. (*Faversham Guide*, 1908; Dane, 1975).

—   Latter Day Saints, Brents.   1850.
Listings cease 1880s. (RC; K).

—   Gospel mission, Tanners St.   1888-9.
Step gabled. Stock brick dressed with red; slate roofs. (K; Dane, 1954).

FAVERSHAM (*continued*)   C.C., Love Lane.   1898.   Edwin Pover, Borough Surveyor.
EE. Red brick with stone dressings. Porch. Bellcote. (*Faversham Guide*, 1908).

—   Almshouse, South Rd.   1856-64.   Hooker and Wheeler.
Gothic. Ashlar with tiled roof. C. W. Chinnock of Southampton, bldr. Lump of plaster fell on
Canon Basil Clarke's head 1970 but repaired 1981. Still in use. (Basil; Dane, 1975).

FOLKESTONE   C. of E., Christ Church, Sandgate Rd.   1850.   Sydney Smirke.
Gothic. Rag. Built by Lord Radnor. Bombed 1942 and only the square tower survives.
(Bishop, 1973).

—   C. of E., Holy Trinity, Sandgate Rd.   1868.   Ewan Christian.
EE. Ragstone with slate roof. Plate tracery. Clerestoried nave. Cost defrayed by Earl of Radnor.
(Bishop, 1973; Pev).

—   C. of E., St John the Baptist, Foord.   1878.   A. Rowland Barker.   £4,000.
Dec. and Perp. Rag with Bath stone; red brick interior. Clerestoried nave; plate tracery.
Chancel to original design added 1894. (Pev.)

—   C. of E. St Michael and All Angels, Dover Rd.   1873.   G. F. Bodley.   Original cost £4,000,
and £9,000 for enlargements.
Flamboyant Flemish. Stone. Lofty steeple. flowing tracery. Bombed and demolished. Replaced
wooden gabled church of 1864 nicknamed 'the red barn'. (Clarke, 1938; Bishop, 1973; Binney
and Burman, 1977).

—   C. of E., St Peter, East Cliff.   1862-4.   R. C. Hussey. (N aisle 1870 by Spencer Slingsby
Stallwood of Folkestone).
Dec. Rag with slate roofs. Spirelet. 'The mariners' church'. Maintains a catholic tradition.
(BA, 1865; Bishop, 1973).

—   C. of E., St Saviour, Canterbury Rd.   1891-2.   J. T. Micklethwaite and Somers Clarke.
Neo-Perp. Ragstone. Red brick and terracotta. Whitened interior, with altar now in nave
beneath hanging rood. Built by Dunk of Folkestone. Consec. 1900. (*Builder*, 1892; Pev).

—   Emmanuel Mission, Cheriton Rd.   Ante-1882.
Plain. Brick. Ceased post-1909. (K; SD).

—   R.C., Our Lady Help of Christians and St Aloysius, Guildhall St.   1889.   Leonard Stokes.
£6,000.
Dec. Red brick banded with ashlar. Long boarded aisleless interior. Succeeded unpretending
red brick chapel in Martello Rd. Consec. 1939. (Mackie, 1883; SD; Bernard Kelly, 1907; CD;
Little, 1966).

—   Un. Bapt., Uphill.   1832.
Listed until 1876. (RC; B, 1876).

—*   Bapt., Salem., Rendezvous St.   1873-4.   Joseph Gardner of Folkestone.   £5,300.
Very classical. Corinthian façade, now rendered brick sides. Replaces 1845 chapel on adjacent
site. (B, 1875; Mackie, 1883; Bishop, 1973).

—   Cong., Tontine St.   1856-7.   Joseph Gardner.   £2,000.
Gothic. Rag with slated roof. Gallery. Tower 80 ft. Demolished *c.* 1978. (Timpson, 1859;
Mackie, 1883; Binney and Burman, 1977).

—   Cong., Holy Trinity, Radnor Pk.   1897.   Joseph Gardner of Folkestone.
Early Dec. Rag. Square tower, the pinnacles of which have been brought down to earth. Bldrs.
Hayward & Paramor. Now URC. (C, 1898).

—   W., High St.   1831.
Lancets. Brick. Unsafe by 1847 so closed, became *Appollonian Hall* public house; police
station from 1850 and sessions hall until 1891: then various uses inc. social club and Plummer
Roddis. Derelict 1982 pending redevelopment. (Mackie, 1883; Folkestone *Visitors' List &
Society Journal*, 15 July 1891; Bishop, 1973; Folkestone ref. library).

FOLKESTONE (*continued*)   W., Cow St. (Sandgate Rd.).   1852.   £190.
Long narrow building described by ministers as 'like preaching through a telescope'. Sold 1865 for £1,000 and converted to butcher's shop. Pulled down *c.* 1884. (*Folkestone Chronicle*, 25 November 1865; Revd. J. Howard Brown's note in Folkestone ref. library; Chamberlain, 1964).

—   W., Grace Hill.   1865.   Joseph Gardner of Folkestone.
EE. Rag with Bath stone dressings. Lancets. Galleries. Lofty octagonal steeple 133 ft. Demolished *c.* 1978. (BA, 1867; Mackie, 1883; Bishop, 1973).

—   W., Canterbury Rd.   1882, 1897.
Lancets. Brick. Spire and gables. Closed 1972 when Folkestone Methodism centralized. (Opening service leaflet 29 June 1882 in Folkestone ref. library; Mackie, 1883; Chamberlain, 1964; *Folkestone Herald*, 27 January 1973 and 26 May 1973).

—   Prim. M., Dover St.   1878.
Classical. White brick relieved with red and Bath stone dressings. Gordon club for boys from 1933 and Band of Hope 1953. Derelict 1973. (Mackie, 1883; *Folkestone Herald*, 21 November 1953; cent).

—   Église evangelique française, Victoria Grove.   Ante-1895.
Iron. Y-tracery. Stained glass. Sometime Church of the Good Shepherd in association with Christ Church. Age Concern since 1977. (K; Mrs. J. Woodward of Age Concern).

—   Victoria Gospel Hall, Cheriton Rd.   1900.
Plain. White brick; red brick and stone dressings and slated roof. Extant as Millfield evangelical fellowship. (K; SD).

—   C.C., Cheriton Rd.   1857.   Joseph Gardner.   £2,146.
Rag. Church and chapel connected by archway. Contract to Jas Porter. Ceased use 1929 and demolished 1950s. (*Folkestone Chronicle*, 22 December 1855, 22 March 1856; Mackie, 1883; Hawkinge cemetery office).

—   St Andrew's Convalescent Home, East Cliff.   1889.   Ewan Christian.
EE. Orange brick. Octagonal clock tower. Now East Cliff Hotel (since 1980) and used as social hall. (K; Pev).

FOOTS CRAY   C. of E., All Saints, Rectory Lane.   1863.   Henry Hakewill.
Perp. Flint. Thorough renewal of medieval building, preserving old W. spirelet. (K; Glynne, 1877; Basil; Pev; Binney and Burman, 1977).

—   Mission Room, Suffolk Rd.   1898.
Wood and iron. Associated with All Saints. Purchased and demolished 1982 and replaced by St John's Ambulance (K; Mrs. M. Levy).

—   Bapt., Sidcup Hill.   1885.   E. J. Norris.   £950.
Lancet style. Stock brick with rendered façade. Plate tracery. Joseph Taylor and Son, bldrs. Extension of 1840 building. (*Bromley Record*, 1 June 1885; B, 1887).

FORDCOMBE*   C. of E., St Peter.   1847.
EE. Sandstone with slate roof. Bellcote. Lancets. Costs borne by Viscount Hardinge. Vestry added 1883 by E. J. Tarver. (RC; K. Basil: Pev).

FORDWICH   Prim. M., off King St.   Ante-1887.
Given by Mr. Smith. Disused ante-1901. Variously used by Salvation Army and as private dwelling. (McIntosh, 1972).

FOREST HILL   C. of E., Christ Church, South Rd.   1852–4.   Ewan Christian.   £3,850.
Gothic. Rag. Clerestory. W Tower. Spire added 1885. (K; Port, 1961; Clarke, 1966).

—   C. of E., St Paul, Waldenshaw Rd.   1882–3.   H. D. Appleton and E. W. Mountford.   £6,555.
Red brick. Spire. Built by W. Smith of Vauxhall. Consec. 1887. Booth observed its capacity was greater than the population of the parish. Demolished by enemy action 7 October 1943. (Booth, 1902; Basil).

FOREST HILL (*continued*)   St Saviour, Brockley Hill (Brockley Rise).   1865-6.   W. Smith.
Dec. Stone. Completed 1928. Bomb damaged 1940, reopened 1952. (BA, 1867; Clarke, 1966).

— Bapt., Dartmouth Rd.   1857.   Tinkler and Morphew.   £3,240.
Geom. White brick and stone dressings. Gallery. Twin towers. Hall 1891. War damaged 1943 and 1944; reopened 1948; demolished 1977. (Cent, 1956; Pullen, 1979).

— St. Bapt., Zion, Malham Rd.   1878.
Lancet style. Brick. Closed 1963 and is now a Turkish delight store. (Mins; Paul, 1966).

—* Cong., Queens Rd. (Taymount Rise).   1863.   Jas. Hine of Plymouth and T. Roger Smith.
French 13th cent. Reigate stone with red Mansfield stone. Square NW tower and spire. Arcaded porch 'A friendly offshoot from Park chapel, Sydenham . . .'. Sometime spiritualist (St Luke's church of the Spiritual Evangel). Dedicated to St Paul after post-war repairs 1950 and consecrated January 1965 to succeed bombed Anglican church. (C, 1864; Clarke, 1966).

— Cong., Trinity, Stanstead Rd.   1867.   Henry Fuller.   £3,700.
Gothic. Stone. Demolished 1968 and rebuilt retaining stained glass in memory of John Williams, missionary. (C, 1867; Rev. Wm. J. Brown, min.).

— Presb., 'Iron kirk', Devonshire Rd.   1874.
Destroyed by fire 1882. (Baker, 1961; Pullen, 1979).

— Presb. M.H., Ewart Rd.   *c.* 1880.
Joined with St John's 1884. Bombed 1944 and since demolished. (K; Pullen, 1979).

—* Presb., St John, Devonshire Rd.   1883.   J. T. Barker.
Dec. Red brick and stone dressings. Spire. Closed 1978 and demolished 1983 for development. (K; W. C. Dowling, min.).

— Prim. M., Stanstead Rd.   1881.
Gothic. Red brick and stone dressings. Followed 1866 chapel which was then used as Sunday school. (Baker, 1961; Mr. Tom Collett, church treasurer).

— Bible Ch., West Kent Park.   1860.
Plain. Brick. Platform. Bought by Salvation Army 1909 after some years of occupation. Rebuilt 1910 following fire damage 1908. (*Bible Christian Magazine*, 1861; Jub, 1934; Major D. Blackwell, Salvation Army).

— Bible Ch., St James, Stanstead Rd.   1844.   £6,230.
EE. Rag faced. Spire. Hall. 1866. Spire removed by bomb. Amalgamated with former Primitive chapel 1966 then demolished. (Jub, 1934; Mr. Tom Collett).

— Methodist New Connexion, Trinity, Perry Vale.   *c.* 1865.
Congregation joined St James 1920, then chapel became Elim (Free) until *c.* 1927. (SD; Baker, 1961).

— Deutsche Evangelische Kirche, Dacres Rd.   1882.   £3,500.
EE. Brick. Square tower surmounted by spire. Destroyed 1944. Dietrich Bonhoeffer was pastor here 1933-5 and the rebuilt church of 1958 is named after him. (Herr Albert Plag, Min.)

FOUR ELMS   C. of E., St Paul.   1881.   Edwin Hall.   £4,500.
EE. Sandstone and tiled roof. Spirelet. Reredos by Lethaby. (K; Basil; Betj).

— Cong.   1831.
Classical. Rendered façade, red and grey brick sides. Pediment. Paid for by John Williams of Brooms Park; land purchased for one shilling. Remains Congregationalist.

FRITTENDEN   C. of E., St Mary.   1846-8.   R. C. Hussey.
Perp. Sandstone. Lightning struck in 1790 and the church had been a ruin since then; Hussey deemed a complete rebuilding necessary and the rector Edward Moore paid the £6,000. Tower and spire are 1881. (K; Pev; Gdbk).

GALLEY HILL, *see* Swanscombe.

GARLINGE   C. of E., St James, Canterbury Rd.   1872-3.   C. N. Beazley.   £3,600.
EE. Rag; interior Bath stone; tiled roof. Spire; plate tracery; clerestoried nave. (K; Basil; Pev).

—   W., High St.   1869.
Pointed. Brick with slated roof. Follows chapel of 1828 and has served as hall since erection of new Methodist church in Canterbury Rd. (RC; K).

GILLINGHAM, *see* New Brompton.

GOODNESTONE   C. of E., Holy Cross.   1839-41.   Rickman and Hussey.
EE. Knapped flint and Caen stone. Tower. Lancets. Rebuilding of nave and chancel. (Pev).

GOUDHURST*   R.C., Sacred Heart, Beresford Rd.   1882.
Vernacular. Brick with rendered interior and tile roof. Originally built in the grounds of Oakley House as chapel to Miss Dashwood's home for cripples. (K; CD; B. Kelly, 1907; Tiffin, 1935).

—   Bapt., Providence, Curtisden Green.   1878.   W. Theobalds.   £700.
Gothic. Red and white brick; interior rendered. Gallery. Built by Miles Tully and designated 'the model village chapel'. Founded by Joseph James Kendon, with material support from Thomas Wickham. Used since WW II as Bethany School chapel. (B, 1879; C. A. H. Lanzer, head of Bethany School).

—*   W., North Rd.   1878.   W. Ranger of London.
Roundheaded vernacular. Red brick with yellow brick dressings. Gallery. Former red brick and slate roofed chapel of 1836-7 now serves as the adjacent Sunday school. (Cent, 1978).

—*   Prim. M., Beresford Rd.   Post-1851.
Plain. Brick, with stone dressings and slated roof. Supersedes preaching house of ante-1800. Closed post-1937 and now a dwelling. (RC; K).

GRAIN, ISLE OF   Calvinistic, Bethel, (Chapel Rd.)   1827.
Built by Thos Castle, coastguard. Superseded 1895 and demolished for road widening *c.* 1970. (RC; Timpson, 1859; Mcdougall, 1980; Mr. W. Wise, sec.)

—*   Cong., Bethel, Chapel Rd.   1895.   John Gordon.   £421.
Lancet style. Brick with slated roof. Porch. (Gordon, 1898; Mr. W. Wise, sec.).

GRAVENEY   W.   1848.
In use 1851. (RC).

GRAVESEND   C. of E., St Andrew waterside mission, Royal Pier Rd.   1870-1.   G. E. Street.
EE. Rag. Bellcote. Lancets. Built by Miss Beaufort as memorial to her father, Rear-Admiral Francis Beaufort. To seat 153 persons, recalling Simon Peter's miraculous haul of fishes. Closed and declared redundant 1970, opened as arts centre 1976. (BA, 1873; Basil; Richard-Hugh Perks).

—   C. of E., St James, New Rd.   1851.   S. W. Dawkes.   £3,400.
Dec. Rag, with slate roofs. W gallery, massive tower and castellated parapet. Site given by Earl of Darnley. Demolished 1968. (E, 1860; K; Grayling, 1910; Port, 1961; Binney and Burman, 1977).

—   C. of E., St John the Evangelist, Milton Rd.   1834.   Wm. Jenkins.   £3,950.
Gothic. White brick on iron columns. Built as proprietary chapel. RC from 1851; insertions in that year by J. A. Hansom. Presbytery 1859. Steeple and saddlebacked roof 1873 by Goldie and Child. (Hiscock, 1976; Hiscock, 1977).

—   C. of E., St Luke, Wrotham Rd.   1890.   W. Basset Smith.
Mission church of St James. Used as hall after WW II and demolished *c.* 1967. (Hiscock, 1976; Bushell, 1976; Binney and Burman, 1977).

—   C. of E., St Mark, Rosherville.   1853.   H. and E. Rose.   £4,500.
EE. Rag. Cost borne by family of Geo. Rosher. Demolished 1976. (Basil; Cooke, 1942; Revd. D. Seymour, inc.).

—   R.C., St Gregory the Great, Chatham Rd.   1843.
Built by Fr. Gregory Stasiewicz to succeed humble chapel in Windmill St. opened *c.* 1840. Superseded 1851. (RC; Bernard Kelly, 1907).

GRAVESEND (*continued*)   Zion Baptist (Emmanuel), Windmill St.   1843.
  Classical. Brick, rendered. Pediment. (RC; K. Mr. Jack Shepherd, sec.).

—   St. B. and Part. B., Zoar, Peacock St.   1846.   J. C. Johnson.
  Classical. Brick. Pediment. (K; RFC; Paul, 1966).

—   Cong., Princes St.   1838.   John Gould.
  Classical. Pediment. Extended 1860 and 1879. Closed 1953 and demolished 1961. (Douglass, 1975; Hiscock, 1976).

—   Cong., Wycliffe Church, Wycliffe Row.   1874.   John Sulman.
  Dec. Brick, rendered. Cruciform. Demolished 1982. (BA, 1875).

—   Presb., St Andrew, The Grove.   1870.   A. Besborough.   £5,000.
  Twin spires. Demolished 1965. (*Presbyterian Handbook*, 1959-60; Hiscock, 1976; Binney and Burman, 1977).

—   W., Milton Rd.   1819.
  Plain. Brick. Enlarged with classical façade and pediment 1841. Extensions 1906 and 1956. (Hiscock, 1976; Mrs. R. Cresswell).

—   Prim. M., Darnley St.   *c.* 1876.
  Plain, classical proportions. Yellow brick and red dressings. Used since *c.* 1970 as clothes factory. (K; occ.).

GREAT CHART   W., The Street.   1843.
  Gothic windows. Red brick with tiled room. 'The Studio' 1981 converting to dwelling. (RC; Dr. Christopher Stell).

GREENHITHE   C. of E., St Mary, London Rd.   1855-6.   Geo. Vulliamy and J. Johnson.
  Dec. Rag with tiled roofs. Clerestory. Bellcote. Restored 1883. (E, 1856; K).

—   R.C., Our Lady of Mount Carmel, High St.   1874.
  Gothic. Stock brick. Gallery. Built as friary by Italian Capuchins. Sometime Convent of Mercy. Last mass 1973, demolition started the following day. (K; CD; Pev; Fr. Joseph Sheridan).

—   Cong., High St.   1819.
  Pointed windows, classical proportions. Brick with flint façade. Closed WW II, thence a factory; Thornton Brush Co. from 1956. (Mr. T. H. Hill of Thornton Brush).

—   Cong., Ingress Vale (Knockhall Rd).   1860.   £1,367 7s. 6d.
  Plain. Brick with thatched (now tiled) roofs. Porch. Extension 1862. (K; Cent, 1960).

GREENWICH   C. of E., St Andrew and St Michael, Dreadnought St.   1900-2.   Basil Champneys.
  Dec. Stock brick. Clerestory. Flying buttresses. Wrought iron bellcote. Follows iron mission hall 1870. Redundant 1965 and now derelict. (Pev; Baker, 1961: Clarke, 1966; CCC).

—* C. of E., Christ Church. Trafalgar Rd.   1848.   John Brown and Robert Kerr.   £7,741.
  Perp. Rag and brick quoining. Vestry 1887 by Thos. Dinwiddy of Greenwich (Pev; Clarke, 1966).

—   Holy Trinity M.H., Blackheath Hill.   1879-80.   Smith.   £1,490.
  EE. Stock brick. The gift of John and Wm. Penn and Thos. Lucas. Closed WW II, used as gymnasium and demolished ante-1961. (K; Basil; Sykes, 1937; Baker, 1961).

—   C. of E., St Mary, King William Walk.   1823-4.   George Basevi.   £19,626 16s. 11d.
  Ionic. Suffolk brick and Bath stone dressings. Tower; portico. Contractors Thos. and Geo. Martyr. Commissioners contributed £11,285. Always chapel-of-ease to St Alphege. Closed 1919 and demolished 1936. (Howarth, 1885; Port, 1961; Basil).

—   C. of E., St Paul, Devonshire Rd. (Drive).   1865-6.   S. S. Teulon.
  French Gothic. Rag and stone dressings. Bell turret. Plate tracery. Bombed 1944, restored 1950. Now Holy Trinity and St Paul. (Howarth, 1885; Baker, 1961; Clarke, 1966).

—   C. of E., St Peter, Bridge St.   1866.   S. S. Teulon.
  Cheap and plain. Brick; polychromatic interior with iron columns and wooden arches. Site given by Revd. Geo. Blisset of Wells. Galleries. Bombed 1941 and dismantled 1955 after parish had merged with St Alphege 1951. (Howarth, 1885; Basil).

GREENWICH (*continued*)   R.C., St Joseph, Pelton Rd.   1881.   J. A. Hansom.   £4,350.
Early Dec. Brick with stone dressings and slate roof. (CD, 1901; Bernard Kelly, 1907).

—   R.C., Our Ladye Star of the Sea, Croom's Hill.   1851.   Wm. Wilkinson Wardell.
Early Dec. Rag and Caenstone dressings. Graceful E spire. Founded by Canon Richard North,
traditionally in fulfilment of his mother's promise to Our Lady on the occasion of his
deliverance from the Thames. Decorations by Pugin. Restored 1901 and 1965. (Pev; Little,
1966; Stanton, 1971; Gdbk).

—   Bapt., Bridge St.   1827.
Purchased 1861 by Benj. Davies and united with Shooter's Hill Rd. to form Devonshire Rd.
Then closed. Survives as DIY shop. (Richardson, 1834; B, 1871; White, 1938; Mr. Ronald
Cooper).

—   Bapt., Bunyan Chapel, Lewisham Rd.   1838.
Became hall behind new church as from 1844. (Mr. Ronald Cooper).

—   Bapt., Bunyan Church, Lewisham Rd.   1844.
Small. Brick. Greatly improved 1872 for £4,000. Destroyed 1944 and demolished 1958. (B,
1867; White, 1938; Baker, 1961).

—   Bapt., Devonshire Rd. (Devonshire Drive).   1863.
Plain. Stock brick with red quoining. (White, 1938).

—   Bapt., South St.   1871–2.
Renaissance. Polychromatic brick with stone dressings. (White, 1938; Mr. Ronald Cooper, sec.).

—   Bapt. M., Caletock St.   1884.
Closed ante-1900. Building cleared 1960s. (B, 1887; Whitley, 1928; Mr. Ronald Cooper).

—   Bapt. M., Roan St.   1884.
Work ceased ante-1900. (Whitley, 1928).

—   Bapt. M., Azof St.   1892.
Roundheaded windows. Brick with slated roof. Closed 1897. Various uses, lately occupied by
Norfine. (B, 1892–7; Mr. Ronald Cooper).

—   Bapt., Lower Rd. (Woolwich Rd.)   1895.   Geo. Baines.   £3,790.
Castellated. Stock brick and stone dressings. Galleries. Pinnacles and battlemented parapets.
Contract to I. Barden of Maidstone. Becoming unsafe and demolished 1982. Congregation now
uses adjacent building. (B, 1896; Mr. Ronald Cooper).

—   Indep., Park Place, Maze Hill.   1823.
Brick. 'Commodious' for 1,000. Destroyed 1945. Congregation united with Rothbury Hall
1953. (C, 1855; Richardson, 1834; Timpson, 1859; Howarth, 1885; Baker, 1961).

—   Cong. M., Rothbury Hall, Azof St.   1893–4.   W. T. Hollands.   £9,000 excl. land and fittings.
Flemish. Red Suffolk brick and Portland stone. Contractors Edwards and Medway. Succeeds
1884 iron hall in Lanthorpe Rd. and survives in use. (C, 1894; Cent, 1954).

—   Presb., St Mark, Ashburnham Place, South St.   1850.
Perp. Stone. Spire. Destroyed 1944, new building 1953. (K; Howarth, 1855; *Presbyterian
Handbook*, 1959–60; Baker, 1961).

—   W., South St.   1878–80.   £9,037.
Stone. Succeeds George St. Chapel of 1816. 'Central Hall' from 1909. (W, 1882; Howarth,
1885; K).

—   W. M., Victoria Hall, Woolwich Rd. (opp. Yately St.)   1895.
Superseded on adjoining site 1933. (Booth, 1902; OS, 1928; Baker, 1961).

—   Bible Ch., King George St.   1872.
Plain. Brick. Porch. Brethren from 1878. Damaged 1940, restored 1952. Brethren use ceased
1979. Plans 1981–2 to convert as Christian youth hostel. (Baker, 1961; Mr. W. H. F. Ritchie
of Bexhill).

GREENWICH (*continued*)   London City Mission, East Greenwich.   1856.   £1,957.
   Gallery. Used by Wesleyans 1873 to 1893 then demolished for road widening. (Timpson, 1859; LCM mins.).

—   London City Mission, Randall Place.   1865.
   Plain. Brick. Stet. (LCM head office; Mr. Kelly, missioner).

—   Salvation Army Mission, Blackwall Lane (opp. Azof St.).   1898.
   Iron. Removed. (Booth, 1902; Baker, 1961).

—   C.C., Greenwich, Well Hall Rd.   Post-1856.
   EE. Sandstone and slated roofs. Lancets. Separate buildings, the episcopal chapel having broached spire. (Hart, 1882).

—   Queen Elizabeth's Almshouses, High Rd.   1819.   Jesse Gibson.
   Classical. Brick. Ionic portico, pediment and cupola. (Mr. R. C. Brown of Drapers' Hall).

—   Royal Herbert Hospital, Shooter's Hill Rd.   1860.   Capt. Galton R.E.
   Pointed. Hospital closed and disused since 1977. (Pev; Miss K. Prickett, former organist).

—   Greenwich Union (St Alfege's Hospital), Woolwich Rd.   1875.
   Demolition plans 1961. (Baker, 1961).

GROVE   W., Teedleham Hill.   1872.   £113.
   Brick. Demolished *c.* 1963. (W, 1872).

GROVE PARK, *see* Lee.

GUSTON   W.   1840.
   Extant 1891. (RC; K).

HADLOW   St. Bapt., Court Lane.   1830.
   Vernacular. Brick. Porch. Intersecting tracery. Converting 1982 to residential use. (B, 1849; RFC).

—   W.   1888.   Estim. £193.
   Iron. Sold 1899; subsequently retrieved and services resumed until 1941. (Tonbridge jub. 1964; Bailey, 1970).

—   W., Golden Green.   1899.
   Closed 1956, sold 1958, used as warehouse then demolished *c.* 1977. Here now stand modern dwellings. (Tonbridge circuit jub., 1964).

—   Unsectarian Gospel Hall, Maidstone Rd.   1890s.
   Plain. Banded brick with slated roofs. Porch. In use 1950. Latterly playschool. (K).

—   C.C. (Cemetery Lane).   1881.
   Gothic. Brick. Two adjoining chapels, one used as store for some years before both demolished 1980-1. (K; Revd. Tony Smith and Revd. Gerald Lane, vicars).

HALLING   C. of E., St Laurence Mission, Upper Halling.   1889.
   Iron. The gift of Lieut.-Col. W. H. Roberts. Closed 1971 and taken down 1974. (K; Gowers and Church, 1979).

—   Bapt., Vicarage Rd.   1900.
   Pointed windows. Corrugated iron. Porch. (Trust Deed; Mrs. N. Long, sec.).

—   W.   1901.
   Iron. Closed and latterly serving as Newtown social club. (W, 1901; Gowers and Church, 1979).

HALSTEAD   C. of E., St Margaret, Church Rd.   1880.   W. M. Teulon.
   EE. Flint. Bellcote. Enlarged 1897 by St Aubyn. (Pev).

HAM STREET, *see* Orlestone.

HARBLEDOWN   C. of E., St Michael.   1880-1.   J. P. St Aubyn.   £3,000.
   EE. Flint. Virtually a complete rebuilding of a medieval church. (K).

HARRIETSHAM   C. of E., Rectory Chapel, off East St.   1881.
      Plain. Wood. Good Shepherd, R.C. since 1970. (K; Fr. John Hine, parish priest).

HARTLIP   Bible Ch., Cardiphonia, The Street.   1820-1.
      Classical. Flint, rendered. Porch. Built by Wm. Drawbridge, J.P. Schoolroom 1907. (Shaw, 1965; chap. 1971; Mr. R. A. Baldwin, district archivist).

HASTINGLEIGH*   Bapt., Mission Room, off Elmsted Rd.   1895.
      Plain. Red brick, alternating with grey. Stet. as Elmsted Bapt. Mission. (K).

HAWKENBURY. *see* Tunbridge Wells.

HAWKHURST*   C. of E., All Saints, Highgate.   1861.   G. G. Scott.
      Sandstone. Conspicuous SE spire. Chancel glass 1861 by Clayton and Bell. Built and endowed by Henry Anthony Jeffreys (vicar 1839-97) and his sister Charlotte as chapel-of-ease to St Laurence. (Pev).

—   St. Bapt., Ebenezer, North Grove Rd.   1872-3.
      Vernacular. Red brick and stone dressings; tiled roof. Lancets. Bldrs. Warburton of Southill and Vinden of Tenterden. Closed 1939, reopened 1943 and now survives as Gospel Standard. (RFC; K; *Gospel Standard*, June 1981).

—*   Bapt., Meeting House, Cranbrook Rd.   1892-3.   Geo. F. Hawkes of Birmingham.   £1,620.
      Gothic. Red brick with stone dressings. Rose window. Gallery. Bldr. L. Edwards of Hawkhurst. (B, 1894).

—   Cong.   1842.
      Extant 1855, when listings cease. (C, 1855).

—*   W., Highgate Hill.   1898.   Messrs. Elworthy of St Leonards-on-Sea.
      Lancets. Red brick and stone dressings; slate roof. Buttressed sides. Bldr. Lewis Edwards of Hawkhurst.

HAWKINGE   C. of E., St Luke, Canterbury Rd.   1889.
      Iron. Bell. Destroyed by fire 1956. Successor dedicated 1959. (K; Revd. J. B. d'E. Chittenden, inc.).

—   United Nonconformist, The Street. | 1832, restored 1873 for £1,200.
      Dec. Red brick with stone dressings and sides now rendered. Pinnacles, the one being developed as a clock tower. Now Hawkinge Free church. (K).

HEADCORN   Gen. Bapt., Station Rd.   1819.
      Roundheaded vernacular. Red brick with slated roof. Gallery (RC).

—   W., High St.   1869.   £816.
      Classical proportions with lancets. Red and white brick and rag; slated roof. (W, 1869).

HERNE   W., Canterbury Rd.   1887.   £566.
      Lancet style. Red brick with stone dressings. Pinnacles. Follows chapel of 1827. (RC; W, 1889).

—   Eddington C.C., Canterbury Rd.   1880.
      EE. Stock brick and slated roof. Bellcote. (K).

HERNE BAY   C. of E., Christ Church, William St.   1835.   A. B. Clayton(?).
      Lancet style. Brick. Pinnacles, now removed. Built on spec., bought by Thomas Wilson for the Congregationalists, sold for Anglican use 1840, front extended 1868 by G. T. Vaughan and restored 1878 by Thos. Blashill for £2,000. (K; *Herne Bay Press*, 20 October 1972; Pev).

—   C. of E., St John the Evangelist, Brunswick Square.   1898.   R. Philip Day, diocesan architect.   £6,577.
      Chancel 1902. Dec. Rag, with brick and Bath stone interior. Clerestoried nave. Closed *c.* 1973 and demolished 1974. (K; *Builder*, 75; *Herne Bay Press*, 9 August 1974).

—   R.C., Our Lady of the Sacred Heart, Clarence Rd.   1890.   Albert Vicars.
      Dec. with perpendicular tracery. Rag. Paid for by Mr. Denis Broderick of Brighton, built by E. T. J. Adams and consecrated 10 August 1897. (CD).

HERNE BAY (*continued*) Bapt., High St. 1878-9. Caley of Tunbridge Wells.
Classical. Brick and stone. Pediment. Opened by Spurgeon. Adjoining school designed and built 1885 by Farley for £650. (Cent, 1979).

— Independent Calvinistic, Union. 1822. £500.
Schoolroom enlarged 1836. Congregation removed 1854 to ex-Wesleyan chapel. (RC; C, 1855; Timpson, 1859).

— Cong. Memorial, Mortimer St. 1864. Poulton and Woodman. £2,000.
Geom. Brick faced with rag. Buttresses; slender pinnacles. (C, 1863).

— W., Beach St. 1885. Chas. Bell. £3,000 incl. schoolrooms.
EE. Brick faced with rag. Spire; plate tracery; gallery. Founded by Jonathan Carter and built by Allen and Sons. (W, 1885).

HERNHILL C. of E., Chapel-of-ease, Lambert's Land. 1847.
Vernacular. Brick. Bellcote. Leaded lights. Demolished early 1900s and now two cottages, Hide-away and Glen-nor, on site (K; Mr. P. Judges, parish clerk).

— W., Dargate. 1840.
Vernacular with roundheaded windows. Red brick patterned with grey (vernacular style) and slated roof. Gabled side. (RC).

HEXTABLE W., Main Rd. 1896. £434.
Brick. (W, 1897; MCSR, 1980; Mrs. J. Curnow).

HIGH HALDEN W., Ashford Rd. 1884.
Lancets. Red brick. Rebuilding of earlier chapel. Closed 1970 and part conveyed to private dwelling 1975. (K; John Hogbin and Son, estate agents; Dr. C. P. Burnham of Wye; Mr. A. Wimble, county architect).

HIGHAM UPSHIRE C. of E., St John, Hermitage Rd. 1862. E. Stephens. £2,624.
Dec. Rag and Bath stone with slated roofs. Clerestory. Spire. Vestry rebuilt 1887-8. E end destroyed by flying bomb July 1944 and rebuilt. (Basil; Rootes and Craig, 1974; but BA, 1862 gives G. G. Scott).

— Cong., School Lane. 1890.
Dec. Red brick with tiled roof and stone dressings. Rebuilding of Ebenezer chapel, 1821. (RC; C, 1855; Timpson, 1859).

HILDENBOROUGH C. of E., St John the Evangelist, London Rd. 1843-4. Ewan Christian.
EE. Kentish rag and native sandstone. Broached spire. Lancets with glass by Morris 1876 and Burne-Jones 1881. Restored 1896 by F. W. Hunt. (K; Eastlake, 1872; Basil).

— R.C., Our Lady's Convent, Foxbush. 1866. Somers Clarke.
Gothic. Red brick with Bath stone. Latterly Foxbush school and used since 1981 as reception room. (Pev; Occ.).

— Bible Ch. Ante-1895.
Closed early 1900s. (K; Mr. Roger Thorne of Topsham).

HITHER GREEN, *see* Lewisham.

HOATH W., Maypole St. 1860.
Plain. Brick. Closed 1965, used as a store, then converted to a private residence, Chapel House, and rendered 1978. (K; Occ.).

HOLLINGBOURNE W., Eyhorne St. 1887. £410.
Vernacular. Stone. Built by John C. West to succeed chapel of 1823. Closed and sold 1952; now a dwelling. (RC; W. 1888; Parsons, 1981).

HONOR OAK C. of E., St Augustine, One Tree Hill (Honor Oak Rd.). 1872-3. Wm. Oakley.
EE. Rag. Messrs. Roberts, bldrs. W tower 1888. (K; Pullen, 1979).

HOO ST WERBURGH Bible Ch., Stoke Rd. 1831.
Superseded 1968 and demolished 1979. (Macdougall, 1980; Mrs. I. W. Samuels).

HORSMONDEN*   C. of E., All Saints.   1869.   R. Wheeler of Brenchley.   £1,600.
   EE. Banded brick and tiled roof. Round apse. Built as a chapel-of-ease and in R.C. use since
   1972. (K; CD; Pev; *Kent Messenger*, 29 January 1971).

—   Calvinistic Bapt., Ram's Hill.   1851.
   Plain. Brick. Plymouth Brethren from post-1882 until superseded by Furnace Lane. Demolished
   post-1962. (RC; K. Paul, 1966; Miss June Harding, former member).

—   Bapt., Bramble St.   1889.
   Vernacular with pointed windows. Red brick with white brick dressings and slate roof. Porch.
   Y tracery. Founded by Robert Burr and built by M. C. Tulley of Capel. Closed *c.* 1971, sold
   1977 and undergoing sensitive conversion to dwelling house. (Young, 1972; Mr. Tom Lynham,
   Occ.).

—   Prim. M., Goudhurst Rd.   1846.
   Plain. Brick with slated roof. Vacated 1964 and demolished 1969. (Igglesden, 1902; Mr. P.
   Gregory, former steward).

HORTON KIRBY   C. of E., Farningham Homes for Little Boys (Southdowns Church) (Gorringe
   Avenue).   1866.
   EE. Rag and stone dressings. Lancets. Closed 1961 and from 1975 serving the Retirement
   Homes Association. (Revd. Laker, vicar).

HOUGHAM WITHOUT   W., The Street.   1840.
   Rendered walls, hipped slated roof, sides of flint rubble. Shared with Anglicans 1974. Consent
   to demolish 1979. (RC; Dr. Christopher Stell).

HYTHE*   C. of E., St Michael and All Angels Mission Church, Portland Rd.   1893.
   Pointed. Iron with boarded interior. W porch; polygonal chancel. (K; SD).

—   R.C., Virgin Mother of Good Counsel, Seabrook Rd.   1893–4.   A. E. Purdie.   £4,000.
   EE. Lancets. W gallery. (K; Bernard Kelly, 1907).

—   Cong., High St.   1867–8.   Joseph Gardner.
   Gothic. Ashlar. Geom. tracery; buttresses; clerestoried nave. Bldr. W. Hazell. Schoolrooms
   1870 also by Gardner, built by W. M. Amos. Succeeded a consecrated billiard-room and a
   chapel of 1816. (Timpson, 1859).

—*   W., Rampart Rd.   1897.
   Geom. Ashlar with slated roof. Spire. Follows chapel of 1845. (RC).

ICKHAM   W. Mission Room, Bramling Hill ('The Hollies').   1875.
   Brick. Erected in memory of H. Hall. Closed ante-1970. (K; Mr. J. J. Pirt of Ash).

IDE HILL   C. of E., St. Mary Virgin.   1865–6.   C. H. Cooke.
   Dec. Rag with ashlar dressings. NE spire. Plate and Geom. tracery. (BA, 1867).

—   C. of E., Mission Chapel, Goathurst Common.   Ante-1895.
   Associated with St Mary and entirely supported by Mrs. Rycroft of Everlands. Closed *c.* 1939,
   sold post-1946 and now a dwelling. (K; Canon Peter Baker).

—   Calvinistic, Ark.   1840.
   Wood. Closed 1938 and demolished 1941. (RC; RFC).

IDEN GREEN   Cong.   1835.
   Plain. Weatherboarded, painted white without and varnished within. Ruined in WW II and
   succeeded by 1953 building opposite Post Office. (C, 1855; Timpson, 1959; Young, 1972).

IGHTHAM   W., Chapel Row.   1848.
   Classical. Sandstone with brick dressings and slated roof. Pediment. Porch.

IVYCHURCH*   W., Hamstreet Rd.   1877.
   Vernacular. Roundheaded windows. Side porch. Extended 1905. Closed 1966 and now used
   by Boy Scouts. (K; Mr. L. M. Chowns, circuit archivist).

KEMSING   C. of E., Chapel-of-ease, 'Noah's ark' ('Noah's ark mission'.)   1887.
Iron. Closed 1961 and now Kemsing coachworks. (K; Mr. Victor Bowden of Kemsing).

—   W.   1846.
Superseded 1885. (RC).

—   W., St. Edith's Rd.   1885.   £185.
Wood. Sometime Bible Christian and Free Church. Closed 1950s. (W, 1887; Mr. Victor
Bowden of Kemsing).

KENNINGTON   Cong., The Street.   1863.
Plain. Brick. Demolished and replaced 1971. (Watson, 1979; Miss M. H. Box).

KESTON   Indep., Keston Chapel, Westerham Rd.   1842.   £232 incl. land.
Roundheaded windows. Brick. Succeeds smaller building of 1828 leased to the London
Itinerant Society. Closed c. 1942, used as carpenter's shop then from 1965 as garage. (C,
1855; Timpson, 1859).

—   C. of E., St Audrey, Commonside.   1888.
Lancet style with timbered and herringbone façade. Red brick. Porch. Built as private chapel
by Lord Sackville. (K).

—   W., Prospect Place (Croydon Rd.).   1828.
Plain. Wood. Erected by Geo. Cole Esq. in his front garden. Succeeded 1927 by the
present chapel across the road. (Jub, 1976).

KIDBROOKE*   C. of E., St James, Kidbrooke Park Rd.   1866-7.   Newman and Billing.   £7,000
excluding fittings.
Dec. Kentish rag with Bath stone dressings. NE spire 160 ft. Dove Bros. Bldrs. Cost borne
chiefly by Lewis Glenton of Pagoda cottage. War damaged 1940-1 and 1945; restored with
copper roofs and diminutive spire 1954-5. (BA, 1868; *Builder*, 21 November 1868; Vincent,
1890; Clarke, 1966).

KILNDOWN*   C. of E., Christ Church.   1839-41.   Anthony Salvin, latterly with the vigilance of
Beresford-Hope.
Sandstone hewn across the road. Gothic revival rescue of a plain design, parapet concealing
low-pitched roof and the interior enhanced by Butterfield, Carpenter and Franz Eggert's
Munich glass. In its day, the Ecclesiologists' showcase. Tomb of founder Viscount Beresford
outside S wall. Severely bomb damaged 1941.

—   W.   1835.
Superseded on site 1885. (RC; Tindall, 1874; Goudhurst cent, 1978).

—   W.   1885.   £650.
Plain. Brick. Polygonal end (demolished). Sometime shop and now dwelling. (K).

KINGSDOWN, near Deal   C. of E., St John the Evangelist, Upper St.   1850.   Hay of Liverpool.
£4,500.
Florid Gothic. Stone. Bell gable. Paid for by Wm. Curling. (K; Pev; Revd. P. M. Rampton).

KINGSDOWN, near Sevenoaks   C. of E., St Mary the Virgin, Woodlands.   1850.   Talbot Bury.
Flint. Bell gable. The gift of Major Vincent. (Pev; Mr. Halbert, churchwarden).

KINGSDOWN, near Sittingbourne   C. of E., St Catherine.   1865.   E. W. Pugin.
Dec. Rag. Rebuilding on old site for Lord Kingsdown. (K; Revd. W. H. G. Hill).

KINGSNORTH   Bible Ch.   1837.
Rebuilt 1879. Vernacular. White brick with red dressings and tiled roof. Porch. Schoolroom
1907. Sold to Pentecostals in 1969. (K; Bible Christian mins, 1907; Mr. L. M. Chowns, circuit
archivist).

KNOCKHOLT   Calvinistic   Post-1858.
Wood. Superseded by Providence iron chapel 1925 and closed WW II. (K; RFC).

—   W.   1825.
Wood. Superseded 1887. Stet. 1932. (RC; Judd, 1932).

KNOCKHOLT (*continued*)   W., Townend Memorial, Old London Rd.   1887.   John Wills.   £981.
Plain. Brick. Wm. Wiltshire, bldr. Superseding wooden chapel of 1825. Now Evangelical
(W, 1887 and 1890; Judd, 1932).

LADDINGFORD, *see* East Peckham.

LAMBERHURST   St. B. and Part. B., Pound Hill.   1851.
Neo-classical. Red and grey brick. Rebuilding of 1816 chapel. (Pearce, 1904; Pastor J. Field).

—   W.   Ante-1882.
Extant 1937. (K; OS).

LAMORBEY, *see* Sidcup.

LANGLEY   C. of E., St Mary.   1853-5.   Wm. Butterfield.
EE. On plan of earlier building destroyed by fire. Rag. W broach spire. (Gdbk).

LANGTON GREEN   C. of E., All Saints.   1862-3.   Geo. Gilbert Scott.
EE. Sandstone. Bellcote. Glass by Burne Jones, Ford Madox Brown, William Morris and C. E.
Kempe. Erected as chapel-of-ease and enlarged for that purpose 1889, 1902 and 1911. (K;
SD; Pev).

—   W., Stonewall Park Rd.   1871.
Roundheaded. Polychromatic brick with slated roof. Porch. Closed *c.* WW II and converted to
dwelling 1954. (W, 1872; Pearce, 1904; SD; Mr. A. Wimble, county architect).

LARKFIELD, *see* New Hythe.

LEE   C. of E., St Augustine, Grove Park (Baring Rd).   1886.   Chas. Bell.
Early French Gothic. Rag and white brick. John Allen and Son, bldrs. Perpendicular nave and
aisles by Percy Leeds added 1912. (Grayling, 1910; Clarke, 1966; Baker, 1961).

—   C. of E., Christ Church, Lee Place.   1853-5.   G. G. Scott.   £7,863 0s. 9d.
Early Dec. Rag. W gallery and gabled aisles. Tower and steeple 1877 by E. Francis Clarke for
£1,580. Builders Piper and Sons on both occasions. Bombed September 1940 and demolished
1944. (Hart, 1882; Port, 1961; Basil; Cole, 1980).

—   C. of E., Good Shepherd, Hendon Rd.   1881. Ernest Newton.
Domestic. Brick with tiled roof. Roundheaded windows. Bell turret. Maides and Harper of
Croydon, bldrs. Given by Lord Northbrook as chapel-of-ease to St Margaret. Demolished by
bombing 1940 and succeeded on site temporarily 1941 and permanently 1957. (Hart, 1882;
Clarke, 1966; Basil).

—*   C. of E., Holy Trinity, Belgrave Villas (Glenton Rd.)   1862-3.   W. Swinden Barber of Halifax.
13th-cent. French. Rag and Bath stone. Cruciform. Oak bell-turret and shingled spire. W
gallery. Gift of Lewis Glenton. Bombed 1944 and repaired; closed 1948, dismantled 1960.
(BA, 1865; Hart, 1882; Basil; Baker, 1961).

—*   C. of E., St Margaret, Lee Terrace.   1839-41.   John Brown of Norwich.
EE. Ashlar. Lancets. W spire 136 ft. Vaulting by James Brooks 1876, when original galleries
were removed. (BA, 1841; Hart, 1882; Basil; Clarke, 1966).

—   C. of E., St Mildred, Ronver Rd.   1872.
Iron. Burnt down 1879. (Baker, 1961).

—   C. of E., St Mildred, St Mildred's Rd.   1878-9.   H. Elliott.
Dec. Rag on brick. Clerestory. G. Coles and Sons of Croydon, bldrs. Earl Northbrook,
benefactor. Polygonal apse by Sir A. Blomfield added 1910. (Hart, 1882; Grayling, 1910;
Clarke, 1966).

—   C. of E., St Peter, St Peter's Rd., Eltham.   1870-1.   Newman and Billing.   £4,000.
EE. Brick and stone. Site donated. Bldrs. G. B. and W. T. Gates. Vestry 1895 by Newman
and Newman and W porch 1909 by R. A. Briggs. Succeeds iron church in Eltham Rd.
Damaged and closed 1941. Demolished 1961. (Hart, 1882; Grayling, 1910; Basil; Baker, 1961).

LEE (*continued*)   R.C., St Winefride, Manor Way.   1892.
Perp. Red brick with stone tracery. Superseded by Our Lady of Lourdes 1939 and now serves as school hall. (CD, 1901).

—*   St. Bapt., Kingswood Place, Dacre Park.   1852.
Lancet style. Brick. Congregation formed by secession from Boone St. chapel. Closed 1908. Bought by St Margaret's as church hall. Bombed 1940 and restored 1958. (Timpson, 1859; Hart, 1882; K. Baker, 1961).

—   Bapt. School, Burnt Ash Hill (Baring Rd).   1874.   £2,000.
Roundheaded. Brick. (B, 1875; cent).

—   Bapt., Burnt Ash Hill (Baring Rd).   1896.
'South Lee tabernacle' from 1902. Permanent church followed 1911. (Cent, 1974; South Lee Christian centre).

—   Indep., Boone St.   1838.
'Neat'. Supplied by Baptists late 1850s. Closed ante-1961 and since demolished. (Timpson, 1859; Baker, 1961).

—   Cong., Burnt Ash Lane (Burnt Ash Rd.).   1874.   Osborn and Russell.   £8,000.
Gothic. Rag. Blitzed 1944 and new church built 1955. (K, Baker, 1961).

—   Cong., School, Burnt Ash Lane (Burnt Ash Rd.).   1885-6.   W. Howard Seth-Smith.
Gothic. Rag faced. Plate tracery. Messrs. Lennard, bldrs. (C, 1887).

—   W., Burnt Ash Hill.   1882-3.   £1,108.
Bombed 1940 and succeeded 1965 by a church on adjacent site, acquired for the purpose in 1935. (W, 1885; chap, 1965).

—   Bible Ch., High Rd.   1882-4.   Wm. Theobalds.   £5,000.
EE. Rag. Damaged 1944, restored 1950. New Testament Church of God since 1977. (K; Albert North's chap., 1937; Baker, 1961).

—   Free Church, Lee Chapel, High Rd.   1853-4.   £4,700.
EE. Lancets. Buttresses. Schoolroom 1857. Destroyed 1941. (Timpson, 1859; Hart, 1882; Duncan, 1908; Gregory and Nunn, 1924; Baker, 1961).

—   Boone's Chapel, High Rd.   1875.
EE. Red brick and tiled roof. Lancets. Damaged 1944, restored 1947. Sold 1963, modernised and reopened as Emmanuel Pentecostal. (Booth, 1902; Baker, 1961).

—   Free Church, People's Hall, Frant Place.   1896.
Closed 1919. Used sometime by Pentecostals who removed to Boone's chapel. Since cleared. (Baker, 1961).

—   Lee C.C. (Hither Green Cemetery), Verdant Lane.   1873.   Francis Freeman Thorne of Lee.
Dec. Rag. Two chapels with spires. (K; cemetery office).

LEEDS   Cong., Providence.   1844.
Closed *c*. 1889. (RC; K).

—   W.   1848.
Superseded 1891. (RC).

—   W., Horseshoe Lane, Langley Heath.   1891.   £1,158.
Plain. Red brick with tiled roof and terracotta dressings. The gift of Mr. Walter Kruse. Plans to convert to dwelling 1982. (K; W, 1900).

LEIGH   W.   1826.
Extant 1851. (RC).

—   Undenominational, and Schools, High St.   1871.   Geo. Devey.
Perp. tracery. Patterned brick with slated roofs. Castellated vestibule. Built by Samuel Morley, after whose death in 1886 the chapel became C. of E. Closed before WW I. Latterly British Legion. (K; Mr. L. A. Biddle, trustee).

LENHAM   C. of E., Chapel-of-ease, Platt's Heath.   Ante-1886.
Pointed. Brick. Flèche.| Believed former Primitive Methodist school. (K; Rev. R. A. Sheekey, inc.).

—   Cong., Ebenezer, Maidstone Rd.   1824.   Restored 1881 for £600.
Roundheaded. Brick. Galleries. Bombed WW II and replaced 1951. (C, 1855; Timpson, 1859; K; Eames, n.d.; Revd. Alan Duncan, min.).

—   Cong., Ebenezer, 'at the extremity of the village'.   1829.
Operating until post-1850 in addition to Ebenezer 1824. (RC).

—   Prim. M., Lenham Heath.   1870.
Extant 1938. (K).

LEWISHAM   Ascension Mission Room, Lethbridge Rd. (Lethbridge Estate).   *c.* 1875.
Plain. Brick. Later enlarged to mission hall. Bombed 1940 and finally demolished 1944. (Mr. Edward Heward).

—   C. of E., St Mark the Evangelist, Clarendon Rise.   1870.   Wm. Coppard Banks.
Dec. Rag and Bath stone. Tower and spire 160 ft. Followed iron church 1868. Demolished following union of parish with St Stephen 1964. (BA, 1870; Clarke, 1966; CCC).

—   C. of E., St Stephen, High St.   1863–5.   Geo. Gilbert Scott.   £16,500.
EE. Rag and Bath stone. Glass by Clayton and Bell. Cost borne by Revd. S. Russell Davies. Now St Stephen and St Mark. (Clarke, 1938; Clarke, 1966).

—   C. of E., St Swithun Mission, Hither Green Lane.   1884.
EE. Brick. Lancets. Adjoined by the church proper in 1892 and now serves as church hall. (K; Judge, 1973).

—   C. of E., St Swithun, Hither Green Lane.   1892–3.   Ernest Newton; details by Lethaby.
Dec. Red brick and stone. Parmenter of Braintree bldrs. Chancel and transepts 1904–5. Damaged 1940, repaired 1946. (*Builder*, 1896; Pev; Clarke, 1966).

—   C. of E., Transfiguration, Algernon Rd.   1881.   Jas. Brooks.
EE. Red brick. Plate tracery; flèche.| Built as a mission church for St Stephen's. Succeeded mission hall 1868. Renamed St Barnabas when in 1953 Royal Association in Aid of the Deaf and Dumb moved here from Evelyn St. Now Bibleway Tabernacle, West Indian Pentecostal. (K; Pev; Clarke, 1938, Basil).

—   R.C. School, High St.   1897.
Brick. Plain. Built on site of John Wesley's house. Now used by St Saviour's school. (Bernard Kelly, 1907; St Saviour's presbytery).

—   St. Bapt., College Park, Clarendon Rise.   1873–4.   Wm. Rickwood.   £1,000.
Dec. Brick with stone dressings and slate roof. Built by William Lawrance. (B, 1875; K).

—   Bapt., 78 Albacore Crescent.   1893.
Plain hall style. Brick with red dressings and slate roof. Purchased by Brethren 1954. (Baker, 1961).

—   Bapt., Brightside Rd.   1896.
Iron. Succeeded 1903 by Theodore Rd. and sold for £90. (Jub, 1956; Baker, 1961).

—   Indep., Union, High St.   1823.
Galleries 1837 and 1840. Closed 1866 when new chapel was built; then school of art and subsequently Unitarian. Destroyed WW II. (C, 1855; Timpson, 1859; Duncan, 1908; Baker, 1961).

—   Cong., Tanners Hill.   1840.   £374.
Schoolroom added 1842. (Mearns, 1882; Dews, 1884; Baker, 1961).

—   Cong. M., Cross St.   1843.
Closed ante-1878. (C, 1844; Timpson, 1859; Baker, 1961).

LEWISHAM (*continued*)   Cong., High Rd. (Lewisham Way). 'Evening chapel'.   1853-4.   St David's Church.   1859-60.   £9,000.
Dec. Rag. Broached spire. Clerestory. Named after former Lord Mayor David Wire and believed to be 'the first Independent church with a saintly title'. Galleries and alterations 1869, £1,760. (C, 1855; Timpson, 1859; BA, 1860; Mearns, 1882; Dews, 1884; K).

—   Cong., Courthill Rd.   1866.   John Tarring.
Dec. Grey rag with Bath stone dressings. Tall spire. Part of an extensive complex of buildings. Sunday school 1880. Destroyed 1940 and restored 1957. (C, 1867; Dews, 1884; Duncan, 1908; Baker, 1961).

—   Cong. School, Algernon Rd.   1881.
Pointed. Brick. Intended church never built. War damaged 1940, destroyed 1944, rebuilt 1953. (Mearns, 1882; K; Baker, 1961; Miss D. French, sec.).

—   Cong., Hither Green Mission Room, Nightingale Grove.   c. 1890.
Brick. Demolished c. WW II. (K; Mr. Monty Hillier).

—   Cong., Ladywell Mission Hall, Prospect Place.   1901.
Surviving 1930s. (K; Booth, 1902).

—   W., Avenue Rd.   1838.
Enlarged 1863. Superseded 1870. Occupied 1900s by Salvation Army. (Duncan, 1908).

—   W., Albion Rd.   1870.   £5,620.
Rag. Pointed. Paid from Sir Francis Lycett memorial fund. Bombed WW II and pulled down. (W, 1871; *Lewisham Journal*, 7 April 1905; Baker, 1961; Mr. K. L. Chanter of Chislehurst).

—   W., Wellmeadow Rd.   1900.
Brick. Tall tower. In its day 'the best attended Wesleyan church in Lewisham'. Bombed and flattened 1940. (Mudie-Smith, 1904; Baker, 1961; Judge, 1973; Mr. Monty Hillier).

—   Welsh Calvinistic Methodist, Capel Cymraeg, Undercliff Rd.   1901.
Domestic. Brick. Sold to Brethren 1924. Rebuilt and now functioning as Loampit Evangelical church. (Baker, 1961).

—   Ladywell C.C., Brockley Grove.   1858.
Dec. Rag with stone dressings and high-pitched slated roof. (K; cemetery supt.).

LEYSDOWN   C. of E., St Clement.   1874.   R. Wheeler.
EE. Rag dressed with white brick and tiled roof. Bellcote. Lancets. (Pev).

LINTON   Maidstone Union Workhouse (Linton Hospital), Coxheath (Heath Rd.)   1883.
Lancet style with Dec. E window. Rag with slated roof. Strange turret. Now Holy Trinity, Coxheath. (K; Revd. C. J. Caley, chap.).

LITTLEBOURNE   Indep., Nargate St.   1882.
Plain, to classical proportions. Red brick. (Timpson, 1859).

LOOSE

—   Bapt., Church St.   1888.   £1,000.
Gothic. Rag faced. Jas. Wood of Boughton Monchelsea, bldr. Supersedes iron building opp. Malthouse Hill. (B, 1889; Thornburgh, 1978).

LOWER HALSTOW   Bible Ch., Ebenezer.   1880.
Lancet style. Stock brick with red dressings and slated roof. Succeeded wooden chapel on the Green. Closed 1973 and amalgamated with Hartlip. Now builder's workshop. (Mr. R. A. Baldwin, district archivist; Roger Thorne of Topsham).

LOWER HARDRES*   C. of E., St Mary.   1831-2.   Rickman and Hutchinson.
EE. Flint. Lancets. Octagonal steeple surmounting square tower. (K; Pev).

LUTON, *see* Chatham.

LYDD   R.C., St Martin of Tours, High St.   1890.
Wood and iron. Superseded by present church 1931. (Bernard Kelly, 1907; OS, 1907).

LYDD (*continued*)   Bapt., Ness Rd.   1893.
> Iron. Mission of New Romney. Closed 1960. (B, 1893 and 1960; Revd. C. R. Edmundson, min.).

—   W., New St.   1866.   £1,450.
> Pointed. Polychromatic brick, rendered sides and slated roof. (K).

LYDDEN   W.   1866?
> Flint and brick. Follows chapel of 1811. Known locally as 'the cathedral'. Cost borne by Ald. Philip Stiff. Superseded 1915. (RC; Buckingham, 1967).

LYMINGE   W., Church Rd.   1894-5.   £2,273 1s. 9d.
> Rag and blue Pluckley brick. Built by Alfred J. Camburn. Cost borne largely by Mr. T. Rigden of Etchinghill. Demolished by one of the last flying bombs of WW II. Superseded 1835 chapel which was sold 1894. (K; builder's receipts in Folkestone ref. library; Bernard Budd, Q.C.).

MAIDSTONE   C. of E., St Faith's Mission, Station Rd.   1862.
> Iron. 'For the spiritual destitution of the waterside population'. Removed 1871 for foundation of present building. (Cent, 1971).

—* C. of E., St Faith, Station Rd.   1872.   E. W. Stephens.
> EE. Rag. SW tower 1880-1 bereft of pinnacles 1938. Bldrs. Vaughan Bros. (Russell, 1881; K; Basil).

—* C. of E., Holy Trinity, Church St.   1826-8.   John Whichcord sen.   £11,900.
> Classical. Stone. Tower and spire. Commissioners gave £7,373 towards cost. Closed 1965, sold 1981 and converting 1982 to a multipurpose hall. (Russell, 1881; Basil; Port, 1961; Amery, 1975; Mr. Neville Hargreaves).

—   C. of E., St John the Evangelist, Willington St.   1861.   H. Blandford of Maidstone.
> EE. Bath stone with tiled roof. Bell turret. Redundant 1968, demolition order 1971, occupied by Pentecostals from 1975 and subsequently used for handicapped children. (BA, 1862; K; Russell, 1881; *London Gazette*, 12 February 1971; CCC).

—   C. of E., St Luke Mission, Wheeler St.   1886.   £1,200.
> Conducted by clergy of St Paul. Survived opening of permanent church 1897. (K).

—   C. of E., St Luke, St Luke's Rd.   1896-7.   Wm. Howard Seth-Smith.   £4,000.
> Art nouveau. Rag and ashlar with Monks Park stone dressings and tiled roofs. Bell turret. (K; Pev; Betj; Basil).

—   C. of E., St Michael.   1841.   £2,978 16s. 2d.
> (RC).

—   C. of E., St Michael and All Angels, Tonbridge Rd.   1876.   Arthur Blomfield.
> Dec. Rag. Castellated tower 74 ft. Clerestory. (K; Russell, 1881).

—   C. of E., St Michael's Mission, Milton St.   1885.
> Closed 1930s. (K; SD).

—   C. of E., St Michael's Mission Room, Scrubbs Lane.   Ante-1887.
> Extant 1949, subsequently Apostolic. (K).

—   C. of E., St Paul, Perryfield.   1859.   Peck and Stephens of Maidstone.   £5,000.
> Dec. Rag. Gabled. Spire. Gutted by fire 1963; redundant and demolished 1971. Here now stands Elizabeth House. (BA, 1862; Basil; CCC; Baldock and Hales, 1980).

—   C. of E., St Philip, Waterloo St.   1856-8.   Whichcord and Whichcord.   £2,500.
> EE. Rag. Spire. Extensions 1869 and 1878 by E. W. Stephens. (BA, 1859; K; Russell, 1881; Pev).

—   C. of E., St Stephen, Church Rd., Tovil.   1839-41.   John Whichcord sen.
> EE. Rag. Recessed spire. (K; Russell, 1881; Basil).

—* R.C., St Francis, Week St.   1880.   C. G. Wray.   Est. cost £2,044; actual £3,098.
> Dec. Red brick with stone dressings. Built by James G. Naylor of Rochester. Spire now dismantled. (CD; K; Basil; Cent, 1980).

MAIDSTONE (*continued*)   Part. Bapt., Providence, Mote Rd.   1820.
Roundheaded vernacular. Brick. Hipped roof. Porch. Built by seceders from old Rose Yard meeting. Closed 1960 and now Christian Science. (RC; Russell, 1881; RFC; B, 1960 and 1961; SD; Paul, 1966).

—   Part. Bapt., King St.   1822.
Formed by defection from old Rose Yard meeting. Condemned and demolished 1860-1. (RC; Paul, 1966).

—   Part. Bapt., Zion, Brewer St.   1831.   £1,000.
Pointed. Brick. Jas. Steer, bldr. In Countess of Huntingdon's Connexion from 1838. Freemason's hall post-1881; then varied secular uses from drill hall to toffee factory until acquired by Assemblies of God 1945. New façade 1959. (RC; C, 1855; Russell, 1881; Paul, 1965; Parfitt, 1977).

—   Bethel Bapt., Union St.   1834.
Plain. Brick. Built by Samuel Cornford. Renovated. Classical façade and pediment 1877 and 1888. Salvation Army since 1905 when Baptists removed to Knightrider St. (Russell, 1881; B, 1878 and 1889; K; Paul, 1966; Mr. R. Jeal, sec.).

—   St. Bapt., Priory, Priory Rd.   1886.
Lancet style. Rag. Porch. Formed by secession of Pudding Lane Baptists and now Gospel Standard. Bombed 1940 and repaired. (RFC; Paul, 1966; Mr. Joseph Pollington, trustee).

—*   Cong., Week St.   1865.   Habershon and Pite.   £2,149 and school £500.
Classical. White brick and stone dressings. (BA, 1866; C, 1865).

—   Cong., Bower Chapel, Tonbridge Rd.   1875.   C. Pertwee.
Lancets. Rag and Bath stone. Demolished late 1970s having long stood empty. (C, 1874; Russell, 1881; Pratt Boorman, 1965; Baldock and Hales, 1980).

—   W., Union St.   1823.
Brick with stucco façade. On site of 1805 chapel. Survived arson 1977. (RC; Russell, 1881; *Methodist Recorder*, 14 July 1977).

—   W., Tonbridge Rd.   1882.   Ruckson and Smith.   £4,137.
Lancet style. Rag with tiled roof. Spirelet. Richd. Avard, bldr. (W, 1882 and 1885).

—   Prim. M., Brewer St.   Ante-1881.
Roundheaded. Stock brick with yellow dressings and slated roof. In use until late 1930s, sometime Rechabite and now school of dancing. (Russell, 1881; K; SD; Mr. Peter Preedy).

—   Undenominational, King St.   1860-2.   Peck and Stephens.
Superseding Baptist chapel of 1822. Latterly Congregational. Demolished mid-1970s. (Russell, 1881; K; Paul, 1966; Binney and Burman, 1977).

—   Jezreelite Hall, Tonbridge Rd.   1886.
Iron. Brought here from Napier Rd, New Brompton. (Gillingham reference library, 6).

—   C.C., Sutton Rd.   1858.   Peck and Stephens.
Dec. Rag faced. Spires. Nonconformist chapel, some distance from the other, demolished 1959. (Pev; Mr. R. H. Leigh, supt.).

—   West Kent Infirmary (West Kent general hospital), Queen Anne Rd.   1833.
Brick. Closed 1983. ('L', 1834; Revd. John Cossins, chaplain).

—   Prison, County Rd.   1818.   D. A. Alexander.
Rag. In accordance with contemporary practice in prisons, seating was arranged so that worshippers could see the chaplain but not each other. Superseded by present chapel 1910-14. (S.C.L., 1834; Pev; Revd. F. H. Sisley, chaplain).

MANSTON   C. of E., St Catherine, Preston Rd.   1873-4.   W. E. Smith of London.   £1,000.
EE. Brick, Staffordshire blues and Bath stone; slated roof. Built by Smith and Son of Ramsgate as chapel-of-ease to St Lawrence. 'Rather ugly looking', comments Canon Basil Clarke in his notes, 'as though it had strayed from the Midlands.' (K; Basil; Jub. 1923).

MANSTON (*continued*)   W., High St.   1856.
   Lancet style. Knapped flint dressed with brick. Porch.

MARDEN   St. Bapt., Providence, High St.   1894.
   Vernacular. Red brick with tiled roof. Now closed and idle. (Miss E. D. Thunder of Cousley
   Wood).

—   W., High St.   1844.
   Altered 1888. Known locally as 'the little chapel'. Sometime Old Gipsy Williams' preaching
   house. Part demolished and reconstructed 1966 to form hall for parish church. (RC; W, 1888;
   Mr. A. Wimble, county architect).

—   Prim. M., Plain Rd.   1865.
   Plain. Brick with slated roof, hipped. Porch.

MARGATE   C. of E., All Saints' Mission, Westbrook Cottages.   1874.
   Pointed. Brick. Store-room from 1927 and Greek Orthodox since 1964. (Mr. John
   Christodoulou).

—   C. of E., All Saints, Hartsdown Rd., Westbrook.   1894.   Thos. Andrews of Margate.   £4,500.
   Transitional. Rag. Lancets. Tower 1909 by Caröe. (SD; Pev).

—   C. of E., St. Augustine, College Rd.   1901.
   Lancet style. Red brick. Bell gable. Built as chapel-of-ease to St John. High church. Demolished
   1966. (SD; CCC).

—*   C. of E., Holy Trinity, Trinity Square.   1825–8.   Wm. Edmunds of Margate.   £24,983.
   Perp. Brick, faced with Bath stone. Pinnacles. Tower 135 ft. Built by White, Jenkins and
   Mercer. Parliament contributed £10,000. Bombed and demolished. (Port, 1961).

—   C. of E., St Mary, Northdown (Park Rd.)   1893.   Thos. Andrews.
   EE. Knapped flint dressed with red brick; tiled roof. Lancets. Major extension 1959 and now
   called Holy Trinity. (K).

—*   C. of E., St Paul, Northdown Rd., Cliftonville.   1872–3.   R. K. Blessley of Eastbourne.   £8,000.
   EE. Rag. SW tower; clerestory, nave. Completed by R. Wheeler. (SD).

—   St. Bapt., Bethel, Hanover Place.   1828.
   Converted to Bethel Cottages, 1857. Now demolished. (K; RFC).

—   St. Bapt., Mount Ephraim, Thanet Rd.   1875.
   Sold 1917 upon opening of Rehoboth. (RFC).

—   Bapt., Cecil Square.   H. T. A. Chidgey of London.
   Perp. windows. Rag and stone dressings. Flèche. Built by Paramor and Sons of Margate.

—*   Cong., Union Crescent.   1860.   Poulton and Woodman of Reading.   £2,900.
   Dec. Rag and stone dressings. Spire; buttresses. Schools added 1872, galleries later. (C, 1859;
   K; Cent, 1945).

—   Countess of Huntingdon's Connexion, Emmanuel, Victoria Rd.   1881–2.
   EE. Red brick. SE tower and 100 ft. spire. Now occupied by manufacturing company. (K).

—*   W., Northdown Rd., Cliftonville.   1876–8.   Alfred Drewe and Wm. Geo. Bower.   £6,000.
   Early French Gothic. Rag. Now St Stephen's Methodist. (*Kent Conservation Bulletin*, 1982).

—   W., Hawley Square.   1896.   R. Dalby Reeve.   £5,000.
   French Gothic. Stucco and brick. Contractor E. Padgett. Major extension of 1811 chapel. (K;
   SD; Cent, 1911; Messrs. Stewart Gore, estate agents).

—   Prim. M., Dane Hill.   1871.
   Pointed. Polychromatic brick with slated roof. Gabled. Closed and now used as carpentry
   workshop.

—   Ply. Breth., Dane Rd.   Ante-1887.
   Plain. Brick with slated roof. Closed 1970 and builders' suppliers from 1979. (K; Mr. J. Wilson
   of Cliftonville; Occ.).

MARGATE (*continued*) Disciples of Christ, Margate Tabernacle, Union Crescent. Ante-1899.
Listings cease 1913. (K).

— C.C., St John's, Manston Rd. 1856. Birch of Margate.
EE. Rag with tiled roofs. Two chapels, the one gabled with bellcote. G. Hadlow, bldr. (K;
Miss H. Westgarth, cemetery registrar).

— Royal Sea Bathing Hospital, Canterbury Rd. 1833. Jas. Knowles.
Dec. tracery. Red brick and stone dressings; slate roof. (Pev).

MARK BEECH C. of E., Holy Trinity. 1852. David Brandon.
EE. Sandstone. Spire. Lancets. Gift of the Hon. John Chetwynd Talbot. Chancel 1892 by
Bodley, roof destroyed 1958. (K; Pev).

MARLPIT HILL Bapt., Hilders Lane. 1888. £227.
Plain. Stock brick with slated roof. (Bradford, 1972).

MATFIELD C. of E., St Luke. 1874-6. Basil Champneys. £2,000.
Dec. tracery. Sandstone with tiled roof. Spirelet. (K; Pev).

MEOPHAM C. of E., School Church, Culverstone Green. 1873.
Brick. Purchased by council 1937 and demolished early 1960s. (K; Revd. D. M. P. Giles,
vicar).

— St. Bapt., Mount Zion, Leading St. 1828. £660.
Classical. Brick. Porch. Formed by dismission from Eynsford. Gallery 1835. (Chap; RFC).

MERSHAM W. 1828.
Extant 1851. (RC).

— W., Frithgate. 1846.
Roundheaded. Rendered with slated roof. Closed 1970, sold for conversion to dwellings 1975.
(RC; Dr. Christopher Stell; Dr. C. P. Burnham of Wye).

MILTON next Gravesend C. of E., Christ Church, Parrock St. 1856. R. C. Carpenter (later
Wm. Slater). £2,670.
Dec. Stone. Central tower. Followed mission church of 1851, enlarged 1870, closed 1932,
dismantled 1934 and rebuilt in Old Rd. East. (K; Goodhart-Rendel, 1953; Port, 1961;
Hiscock, 1976; Binney and Burman, 1977).

— C. of E., Holy Trinity, Milton Place. 1844. J. Wilson. £4,539.
Dec. Kentish rag beneath a slated roof. Cruciform. Pinnacled tower, spire never built.
Demolished after fire 1963. (K; Basil; Port, 1961; Hiscock, 1976; Binney and Burman, 1977).

—* Cong., Clarence Place. 1873-4. John Sulman. Initial contract £4,128.
EE. Blue rag and Bath stone under a green and blue slated roof. Formed by secession from
Princes St. Closed 1955, then used as warehouse and from 1968 as Sikh temple. (C, 1874; B,
1874; Douglass, 1975; Hiscock, 1976).

MILTON REGIS or Milton next Sittingbourne C. of E., St Mary, Park Rd. 1901. R. Philip Day.
EE. Brick. (K; Revd. Francis Turner, rural dean).

— C. of E., St Paul, St Paul's St. 1863.
Brick. Chapel-of-ease. Demolished late 1940s. (Bethune, 1973; Revd. W. Drury).

— Bapt. M., Flushing St. 1890.
Closed 1914. (Revd. G. Breed; chap.).

— Indep., Paradise, Crown Rd. 1860. Poulton and Woodman of Reading. £1,247 10s. 1½d.
Dec. Stock brick with dressings of white brick and Bath stone. Spire (now dismantled) and
schoolrooms 1865. Now Boy Scouts. (C, 1861; J. B. Jones, 1910).

— Indep., Bethel Mission. *c.* 1895.
Iron. Lancets. Porch. Bellcote. Erected by seceders from Paradise chapel who reunited 1909.
(J. B. Jones, 1910).

MINSTER, Isle of Sheppey   Cong., Bethel, Chapel St.   1869.
  Classical. Rendered. Survives in affiliation to the Congregational Federation. (Timpson, 1859;
  C, 1870).

—   W., Hermon Hill.   1830.
  Extant 1851. (RC).

MINSTER-IN-THANET   R.C., St Mildred, St Mildred's Rd.   1878.
  EE. Stock brick banded with red and slated roof. Lancets. Porch. Consec. 1901. (Bernard
  Kelly, 1907).

—   W., High St.   1850.
  EE. Red brick. Porch. Survives in Methodist use. (SD).

—   Prim. M., High St.   c. 1870.
  Lancet style. Brick (now rendered) with slated roofs. Pinnacles. Closed after Methodist union,
  used since as Co-op and for various purposes. (Tindall, 1874; K; Mrs. Nicholls of Westgate-
  on-Sea).

MOLASH or Moldash   W.   Ante-1873.
  Plain. Brick. Now a dwelling. (Tindall, 1874; K; OS).

MONKTON   Calvinistic.   c. 1821.
  Extant 1851. (RC).

—   W., High St.   1877.
  Classical. Brick with rendered façade. Porch. (MCSR, 1980).

MOTTINGHAM   C. of E., St Andrew, Court Rd.   1879.   E. F. C. Clarke.
  EE. Red brick and stone dressings; tiled roof. War damaged 1944 and repaired. (Vincent,
  1890; K; Clarke, 1966).

—   W., Mottingham Rd.   1883.   £1,383.
  EE. Brick faced with rags and slated roof. War damaged 1941 and restored 1942. (W, 1884;
  Baker, 1961).

—   Royal Navy College, Grove Park Rd.   1853.
  Iron. Stood in quadrangle and was dismantled when new chapel (now Eltham College) was
  built 1904. (K; Elthamian, December 1904; Mr. D. L. Jones, librarian of Eltham College).

MURSTON   C. of E.   All Saints, Church Rd.   1873-4.   William Burges.   £3,000.
  13th cent. French. Knapped flint and stone dressings. Incorporates medieval N arcade.
  W tower heightened 1959. (K; Basil).

NEW BEXLEY, see Bexley Heath.

NEW BROMPTON   C. of E., St Barnabas, Nelson Rd.   1889-90.   J. E. K. and J. P. Cutts.   £2,550.
  EE. Red brick and stone dressings. Lancets. Flèche. Succeeds mission of 1886. Chancel 1899.
  Chapel 1914. (K; Basil).

—   C. of E., St Mark, Canterbury St.   1864-6.   J. P. St Aubyn.   £5,800.
  EE. Stock brick and Bath stone dressings. Lancets. Clerestoried nave. Follows wood building
  1862. (BA, 1867; Eastlake, 1872; Basil; Gillingham public library, 6).

—   C. of E., St Mark Mission.   1891.
  Blew down forthwith. (Gillingham reference library, 6).

—   C. of E., St Mark Mission, Virginia Rd.   1891.
  Pointed. Brick. Became hall after building of permanent church 1907-8. (K; Revd. B. Lamb).

—   R.C., Our Lady of Gillingham, Gillingham Avenue.   1896.
  Plain. Yellow brick banded with red. Enlarged 1902. (CD; K; Bernard Kelly, 1907; Basil;
  Fr. Arthur Porter).

—   Bapt., Green St.   1881.
  Plain. Flint. Demolished 1888 and replaced by the Tabernacle. (Tomlinson, 1979).

NEW BROMPTON (*continued*)* Bapt. Tabernacle, Green St. 1889. John Wills of Derby.
£3,800 incl. schoolrooms.
Early Gothic. Rag faced brick with dressings of Monk's Park stone. Buttresses and pinnacles.
J. Naylor of Rochester, bldr. Extended 1901. (B, 1889; K; Tomlinson, 1979).

—* Cong., Railway St. (High St.) 1869. Habershon and Brock. £1,700.
Geom. Yellow brick banded, Bath stone dressings. Gallery. Closed 1945 and now a shoe shop.
(C, 1869; Revd. Chas. Teal, min.).

— W., Christmas St. 1828.
Plain. Rebuilding of 1797 chapel. Extant as St Andrew's. (Wright's *Topography*, 1838; RC;
Gillingham reference library).

— W., Arden St. 1850.
Converted to girls' school 1878. (Tomlinson, 1979; Gillingham public library, 6).

— W., Canterbury St. 1882. £2,373.
Pointed. Brick. Slated roof. Porch. Closed 1962 and demolished *c.* 1965. (W, 1883; Tomlinson,
1979; Gillingham reference library).

— Prim. M., Gillingham Rd. 1869.
Closed *c.* 1926. Succeeded by Nelson Rd. (Gillingham reference library).

— Bible Ch., Bethesda, Marlborough Rd. 1821.
Closed *c.* 1886 and transferred to Trafalgar St. Now veterans' club. (RC; Gillingham reference
library).

— Bible Ch., Jubilee, Trafalgar St. 1887.
Pointed. Brick under slated roof. Merged with former Wesleyan chapel 1960s, modernised and
extant as St Peter's church and community centre. (Gillingham public library, 6; Mr. Roger
Thorne of Topsham).

— Meth., Zion, Gad's Hill. 1852.
Listings cease 1970. (SD; Gillingham reference library).

— United Meth. Free, Arden St. 1887.
Closed 1920s, transferred to St Paul's, Third Avenue. Demolished 1970s? (Gillingham
reference library).

— Church of Scotland, St Margaret, Paget St. 1866.
Pointed. Rendered beneath a slated roof. Extant.

— Ply. Breth., Skinner St. 1884.
Plain. Roundheaded windows. Brick rendered. Hall 1935. (Mins; Mr. A. A. Cotterrill of
Gillingham).

—* Christian Israelite Temple, Chatham Hill. 1892. Messrs. Margetts of Chatham.
Castellated. Yellow brick. Founded by 'Jas. Jershom Jezreel' (pseud.) and built by Naylor of
Rochester and Honey and Nye. Not completed; claimed by the builders when sponsors failed
to pay. In periodic experimental uses but eventually demolished 1960-1. (K; Montgomery,
1962; Rogers, 1963).

— Salvation Army Barracks, Gardiner St. 1900.
Plain. Brick. Roundheaded windows. C. E. Gooding, bldr. New building in Green St. 1931.
(Tomlinson, 1979; Major David Blackwell, ARIBA).

— Peculiar People, Beresford St. 1901-2.
Roundheaded. Yellow brick with red dressings. Survives in religious use. (*Peculiar People*,
September 1901; Mr. Mark Sorrell of Thundersley).

NEWENDEN C. of E., St Peter. 1859. G. M. Hills.
Perp. Sandstone. Tower and shingled spire built on to 14th cent. nave, the tower and chancel
having been 'ruines' since late 17th cent. New chancel added 1930-1. (Pev).

NEW HYTHE   C. of E., Holy Trinity, Larkfield.   1854.   R. P. Pope.
EE. Rag. Chapel-of-ease to St James, East Malling. (K; Pev).

NEWINGTON   W., Church Lane.   1880.
Renaissance. Polychromatic brick with slated roof.

NEWNHAM   Indep.   1823.
Followed cottage meetings from 1816. Associated with Faversham Congregationalists from 1840. Surviving 1903. (RC; Timpson, 1859; C, 1863: K).

NEW ROMNEY   Bapt., North St.   1886.
Simple roundheaded. Rendered, with slate roof. Enlargement of building of 1832. (Pastor C. R. Edmonton).

—   W., Lydd Rd.   1836.
Brick. Superseded on site by present building 1929, old schoolroom surviving until 1970s. (RC; Mr. Peter Brown).

NORTHBOURNE   W., The Street, Finglesham.   1869.   £180.
Plain. Closed 1979 and now used as builder's store. (W, 1869; Revd. R. L. H. Peacock, min.).

NORTH CRAY   C. of E., St James, North Cray Rd.   1850-2 nave;   1857 tower;   1871 chancel.
Edwin Nash.
Perp. Rag. Shingled spire. Rebuilding. (Pev).

NORTHFLEET   C. of E., All Saints, Perry St.   1868-70.   Jas. Brooks.
EE. Rag with ashlar dressings. Bell gable. Clerestoried nave. John Edmeads and the Rosher family, benefactors. (K; Cooke, 1942; Pev).

—   RC, Our Immaculate Mother and St. Joseph, Rose St.   1867.   J. Multon.
Superseded by Giles Gilbert Scott's church in 1914. Survives in commercial use. (CD, 1870; BA, 1873; Fr. David O'Regan, parish priest).

—   Cong., Dover Rd.   1850.   Plot £169 7s. 0d.; building £798 9s. 9d.
Red brick and stone dressings. Pediment. (C, 1855; Timpson, 1859; Cooke, 1942).

—   W., Portland Rd.   1885.   £737,
Closed post-1938 and demolished. (W, 1885; K).

—   Prim. M., Wood St.   1875.
Roundheaded windows. Brick. Survives in Methodist use.

—   C.C., Springhead Rd.   1893.   £5,000 incl. land.
Dec. Sandstone with slated roofs. Two chapels. Porte cochere surmounted by bell turret and spire. (K).

—   Huggens College, High St.   1847.   W. Chadwick.
Lancet style. Stock brick and stone dressings. Spire. Founded by John Huggens of Sitting-bourne for 'ladies of reduced circumstances'. Demolished 1968. (K; Basil; Hiscock, 1976).

OARE   W., The Street.   1877.
Brick. Derelict and demolished after WW II.

OFFHAM   Prim. M.   1848.
Superseded 1892. (RC).

—   Prim. M., Teston Rd.   1892.
Plain. Brick. Surviving in use. (MCSR, 1980).

OLD BROMPTON   C. of E., Holy Trinity.   1848.   L. W. Dawkes.   £10,150.
EE. Tower and spire. Demolished c. 1955. (CCC).

—   W., Middle St. 1835.
Secession as United Methodist from c. 1851. (RC; Gillingham reference library).

—*   W. Garrison, Prospect Row.   1891-3.   A. W. Smith.   £5,200.
Perp. Rag. Pinnacled tower. Galleries. Sold 1953 and demolished. (W, 1891; K; Tomlinson, 1979; Major Hancock, Royal Engineers library).

ORLESTONE*   W., Ham St. (New Romney Rd.).   1872.
> Vernacular. Brick and stone under tiled roof. Extended 1887. Altered 1976 and since then 'The Shared Church' with C. of E. (Mr. L. M. Chowns, circuit archivist: Dr. C. P. Burnham of Wye).

ORPINGTON   C. of E., St Andrew, Building Field (Lower Rd.), South Cray.   1892-3.   John E. Newberry.   £3,800.
> EE. Brick with stone dressings. Central bell turret. (K; Basil).

—   C. of E., St Paul, Crofton Rd.   1887.
> Lancet style with Tudor façade. Red brick. W bell turret, now dismantled. Reflects St Audrey, Keston. Built as chapel-of-ease and used as church hall since the appearance of a new building adjoining in 1958. (K).

—   Bapt., High St.   1883.   £1,500.
> Closed 1967, sold and demolished for development. (B, 1884; Mr. A. A. Mercer sec.).

—   Bapt., Green Street Green.   1899.
> Iron. Permanent church built alongside 1906; moved to rear when Sunday school built 1922 and survives in young people's use. (Mr. Brian Marley, sec.).

OSPRINGE   C. of E., St Peter and St Paul, Water Lane.   1858.
> (Rebuilding of medieval church) and 1866 (NW saddlebacked tower). Knapped flint.

—   Cong. M., Ospringe Rd.   1887.   £500.
> Brick. Superseding cottage converted in 1839. Closed post WW I and latterly used as car spray workshop. (RC; C, 1855; *Kentish Express*, 22 April 1911 and 6 May 1911; Mr. D. G. Green of Faversham).

OTFORD   C. of E., Mission chapel, Twitton.   1900.
> Iron. Enlarged 1950 and survived as Church of the Good Shepherd until 1982, when closed. (K; Revd. Christopher Bunch, vicar).

PADDOCK WOOD*   C. of E., St Andrew, Queen St.   1860.
> EE. Rag. Bombed 1940 and replaced 1953. (K; Grayling, 1913; *Kent and Sussex Courier*, 20 February 1953).

—   W., Commercial Rd.   1888.   £640.
> Plain, pointed windows. Red brick. Porch. Now jointly used by Anglicans and Methodists. (W, 1891).

PEMBURY*   C. of E., St Peter, Hastings Rd.   1846-7.   E. W. Stephens.   £2,500.
> Perp. Sandstone. Spire. Cost borne by Marquess Camden. (K; Pev).

—   Bapt., Bopeep.   1834.
> Extant 1851. (RC).

—   Indep., Bethel, Lower Green.   1835.   £458 8s. 3d.
> Lancet style. Rendered. Porch. Cost borne largely by Stephen and Daniel Dickenson. Condemned and demolished 1885. (RC; Timpson, 1859; Pearce, 1904; Standen, 1947).

—*   Bapt. and Cong., Union, Lower Green (Romford Rd.).   1887.   J. Wallis Chapman.   £1,241.
> Queen Anne style. Red brick with green slate roof. Elliptical windows. Built by G. and F. Penn of Pembury. Known since 1920s as Pembury Free Church. (B, 1888).

—   W.   1835.
> Superseded 1884. (RC).

—*   W., Hastings Rd.   1884.   S. W. Haughton.   £800.
> Gothic. Banded brick with slated roof. Porch. G. and F. Penn, bldrs. Now private dwelling. (Pearce, 1912).

PENSHURST   Cong., Smarts Hill.   1866.   £250.
> Lancet style. Brick, rendered. Succeeds rented skittle alley. Closed 1970s. (Pearce, 1904; Strange, 1930; Bailey, 1970).

PENSHURST (*continued*)   W., Pound's Bridge.   1852.
 Unsafe 1903, pulled down and replaced. (K; Pearce, 1904).

—   C.C., Pound's Bridge.   1889.   Mervyn Ed. Macartney.
 EE. Sandstone and tiled roof. Bellcote. Lancets. Rebuilding of 1854 chapel. (Architect's drawings in KAO).

PERRY STREET, *see* Gravesend.

PETHAM*   Prim. M.   1863.
 Plain. Brick. Superseding room from 1850. Now FIEC. (RC; OS, 1908; Dr. C. P. Burnham of Wye).

PLAISTOW, *see also* Bromley   C.C., Burnt Ash Lane.   1892.   W. R. Mallett.   Estim. £1,000.
 EE. Rag faced beneath a tiled roof. Flèche. (SD; *Bromley Record*, 1 January 1892 and 1 March 1892).

PLATT   C. of E., St Mary, Longmill Lane.   1841-2.   Whichcord and Walker.   £3,363.
 EE. Stone. Cruciform. (RC; Basil).

PLAXTOLE   Cong., Long Mill Lane.   1899.
 Pointed. Rag, brick and slated roof. Porch. Now Dunks Green Evangelical Free Church. (K).

—   W., School Lane.   1893.
 Pointed. Red brick beneath tiled roof. Porch. Closed and converting 1982 to residential use. (MCSR, 1980).

PLUCKLEY   C. of E., St Mary, Bethersden Rd.   1882.
 EE. Red brick with stone dressings and tiled roof. Site given by Sir Edward Cholmeley Dering, Bart. (K).

—   W.   Ante-1873.
 Iron. Superseded by present building 1904. A case of Wesleyans being banned from sites in the village. (WA; K; Mr. Nichols of Smarden; Mr. Gordon Crust of Ashford).

PLUMSTEAD   C. of E., All Saints, Shooter's Hill (Ripon Rd.).   1873-5.   W. G. Habershon.
 Rag and Bath stone. Hammer beam roof. Chancel 1879, tower 1881. Began 1867 as tent mission of St Margaret, Eglinton Rd., then iron church from 1868. Destroyed in air raid 30 August 1944. (Basil; Clarke, 1966).

—   C. of E., St John the Baptist, Robert St.   1883-4.   C. H. Cooke.   £4,000.
 EE. Red brick. Spirelet. One of the Bishop of London's Ten Churches. Built by John Walker to succeed mission conducted from 1866 in Inverness Place. Destroyed 1941. Parish united with St James 1953. Demolished 1959. (Vincent, 1890; Basil; Baker, 1961).

—   C. of E., St Margaret, Vicarage Rd.   1858-9.   Wm. Rickwood of Plumstead.
 Perp. Rag and tiled roof. Pinnacled Tower. Dec. chancel 1899 by R. J. Lovell. Redundant and riddled with dry rot 1974, then demolished. (Vincent, 1890; Clarke, 1966; CCC).

—   C. of E., St Mark, Old Mill Lane.   1901.   C. H. M. Mileham.
 Romanesque. Rendered. Twin towers. Demolished following Order in Council 1972. (Basil; Clarke, 1966; CCC).

—   C. of E., St Paul, Hector St.   1901.   W. Bassett Smith.   £4,150.
 Dec. Red brick and Bath stone with slated roofs. Spirelet. Reprieved from demolition order 1968 to become St Patrick (R.C.). (Clarke, 1966; CCC).

—   R.C., St Patrick, Griffin Rd.   1893.   F. A. Walters.
 Romanesque. Red brick with tiled roof. Succeeds temporary iron building in Coupland Terrace. 1891. Converted to school hall, 1970. (Bernard Kelly, 1907; Baker, 1961; Fr. Rodell, parish priest).

—   Part. Bapt., Plumstead Tabernacle, Maxey Rd.   1861.
 Gospel Standard 1890. Closed *c*. 1930. Since demolished. (Vincent, 1890; Baker, 1961).

—   Bapt., Conduit Rd.   1865.   £1,200.
 EE. Stock brick with stone dressings and high-pitched slated roof. Lancets. Closed 1969 upon merger with Tabernacle and sold to council for demolition. (Vincent, 1890; Mr. B. Orford, sec.).

PLUMSTEAD (*continued*)   Bapt., Union Church, Park Rd. (Waverley Crescent).   1885.
 Lancet. Polychromatic brick and slated roof. Offshoot of Conduit Rd. Baptists, reunited 1907; then used by Peculiar People; Strict and Particular Baptists 1934–54; subsequently used as a store and now as Scout headquarters. (Vincent, 1890; Baker, 1961).

— Bapt., Station Rd. (Southport Rd.), East Plumstead.   1887.
 Iron. Succeeded by Elm St. mission hall, 1890. (Whitley, 1928; Baker, 1961).

— Indep., Ebenezer, Plumstead Common Rd.   1842.
 Sold to Wesleyans 1846, enlarged 1849. Surviving here 1933. (Vincent, 1890; K; Baker, 1961).

— Indep., St James, St James's Place (Burrage Rd.).   1855.   £3,000.
 Italianate. Stock brick. Bell turret. Consecrated for the use of the established church 1878. Closed 1966 and now Greenwich Young People's Theatre. (Timpson, 1859; Vincent, 1890; Baker, 1961; Clarke, 1966; CCC).

— Unitarian, Dallin Rd.   1894.
 Plain. Wood. Closed 1939, then acquired as All Saints church hall. Now derelict. (*Unitarian Yearbook*, 1940; Baker, 1961).

— W., Burrage Rd.   1863.
 Damaged 1940 and demolished 1949. (Baker, 1961).

— Prim. M., Deadman's Lane (Vicarage Rd.).   1850.
 Enlarged 1857. Succeeded by Robert St. 1863. (Baker, 1961).

— Prim. M., Robert St.   1863.
 Burnt down 1908, rebuilt 1909, damaged 1940, restored 1956, now disappeared. (Vincent, 1890; Baker, 1961).

— Prim. M., Eglinton Rd.   1883.   £1,000.
 Closed after Methodist union, used for youth work 1935 until destroyed 1944. (Vincent, 1890; Baker, 1961).

— Bible Ch., Herbert Rd.   1886.   J. K. Cole.   £4,000.
 EE. Red brick and stone dressings. E. G. Covil, bldr. 'An architectural ornament which has no superior in church or chapel at Plumstead'. R.C. since 1972. (Vincent, 1890; St Joseph's presbytery).

— Indep. W., Crescent Rd.   1861.
 Congregational from 1863. United Methodist from 1880. Mission hall for St. James parish church from 1911. (Vincent, 1891; K; Baker, 1961).

— Cage Lane Mission, Cage Lane (Lakedale Rd.).   1879.
 Closed 1905, subsequently in commercial use. (Vincent, 1890; K; Baker, 1961).

— Peculiar People, Brewery Rd.   1882.
 Simple pointed. Rendered with slate roof. FIEC from 1957 and Air Scouts from 1970. (Baker, 1961; Sorrell, 1979).

— Breth., Richmond Hall, Vicarage Rd.   1898.
 Plain. Brick. Built by Brothers Geo. and Harry Sandford. Succeeded stable in Richmond Place, whence the work took its name. Demolished 1970. (Mr. D. Jenner).

— C.C., Bostall Heath (Cemetery Rd.).   1890.   £6,000 incl. lodges.
 French Gothic. Sandstone. Spire. (K; Meller, 1981).

PRESTON, near Wingham   Cong., The Street.   1825.
 Pointed. Stock brick with tiled roof. Porch. Enlarged 1836. (Timpson, 1859; K).

QUEENBOROUGH   Cong., Bethel, North Rd.   1897.   W. T. Rule.
 Classical. Brick and stone dressings. Portico. Closed 1982. (Gordon, 1898; Mr. G. Whitaker, sec.).

— W., High St.   1888.   £637.
 Lancet style. Banded brick. Turret. Now vandalised and derelict. (W, 1889).

RAINHAM   C. of E., Preaching Room.   1862,   £75,
     Built on to front of house. Founded by Thos. Stanley Wakeley and surrendered by him in
     1865 when he left the established church. (Wakeley, 1902).

—   St. Bapt., Providence.   1884.
     Brick. Roundheaded. Porch. Founded by Thos. Stanley Wakeley, after whose death in 1899
     the cause dwindled and expired. (RFC; Wakeley, 1902).

—   Indep., Chapel Lane (Mares Court Rd.)   1848.   £260 excl. land.
     Superseded 1891 and recently demolished. (RC; C, 1855; Timpson, 1859; Revd. Chas. Teal,
     min.).

—   Cong., High St.   1891.
     Pointed. Brick with red dressings and slated roof.

—   W., Lower Rainham (opp. Bloors Wharf Rd.).   1852.
     Plain. Brick. Closed post-1938 and now derelict. (OS; Revd. Ray Norgate).

—   Bible Ch.   c. 1825.
     Superseded 1899. (RC).

—   Bible Ch., Station Rd.   1899.
     Polychromatic brick and slated roof. Survives in Methodist use. (Mr. Roger Thorne of Topsham;
     Revd. Ray Norgate, min.).

—   United Methodist Free, Ivy St.   1874?
     Closed 1953. Subsequently Masonic. (Mr. Brian Davies of Sittingbourne; Gillingham reference
     library).

RAMSGATE   C. of E., Christ Church, Vale Square.   1846-7.   Geo. Gilbert Scott.
     EE. Rag. Slate roof. NE spire. (Pev; Muthesius, 1972).

—*   C. of E., St George the Martyr, Broad St.   1827.   Henry Hemsley, then H. E. Kendall.
     £23,034.
     Perp. White brick and stone. Hexagonal lantern tower. Church Commissioners gave £9,000
     and lent £13,000. Contractors D. M. Jarman and Thos. Grundy. (Port, 1961; Betj; Pev).

—   C. of E., St Luke, Hollicondane Rd.   1875-6.   W. E. Smith.   £8,300.
     Gothic. Dec. tracery. Brick construction faced with rag laid crazy-paving style. (K; Pev).

—   C. of E., St Paul, King St.   1873-4.   Robert Wheeler of Tunbridge Wells.   £1,400.
     EE. Spirelet. Lancets. Porch. Demolished 1957. (BA, 1875; Richardson, 1885; Haslewood,
     1976; CCC).

—   C. of E., Trinity, Arklow Square, East Cliff.   1844-5.   Stephens and Alexander of London.
     £3,000.
     Gothic. Black knapped flint and Caen stone dressings. Clerestoried nave; EE bellcote.
     Largely the gift of Lady Truro. (Pev).

—   R.C., St Augustine, West Cliff.   1847-51.   A. Welby Pugin.   £20,000.
     Loyal Dec. Knapped black flint, Whitby stone dressings and dim religious light. Cost borne
     mainly by Pugin and built under his close supervision by Myers. Since 1856 an abbatial church
     of the Benedictines. Consec. 1884. Digby Chantry is post-1857 by Edward Pugin. Illustrated
     on endpapers. (Gdbk; Ferriday, 1964; Stanton, 1971).

—   St Augustine's Monastery, Grange Rd.   1860.   E. W. Pugin.
     Perp. Knapped flint banded with red brick. (Pev; Bro. Damian).

—   Part. Bapt., Bethesda, Bethesda St.   1829.
     Vacated 1843 upon removal to Mount Zion and subsequently occupied by Primitive Metho-
     dists. In use as ironmongers' early 1950s and since demolished. (RC; RFC).

—   Particular and Calvinistic, Cavendish Chapel, Cavendish St.   1840.   Jas. Wilson of Bath.   £4,000.
     Neo-Norman. White brick (no longer!) Turretts and Prince of Wales' feathers, solidly done, for a
     finial. Galleries. Open communion from 1860. Schools 1899 by John Wills of Derby, red brick;
     contract to W. W. Martin of Ramsgate. (BA, 1841; B, 1866 and 1900; Hitchcock, 1954; RFC).

RAMSGATE (*continued*)   Part. Bapt., Mount Zion, Clover Hill. (Camden Rd.).   1843.
Gothic. Brick and stone dressings. Intersecting tracery. Demolished post-1954. (RC; RFC; Haslewood, 1976).

— Bapt., Ellington, Crescent Rd.   1891.   £870.
Demolished early 1970s and now an unofficial tip. (B, 1892; Haslewood, 1976).

— Cong., Meeting St.   1838.   Jas. Wilson of Bath.
Neo-Norman. Formerly white brick. Lancets. Closed October 1979. (Timpson, 1859; *Kentish Express*, 5 April 1949; Pev.)

— Prim. M., Foads Lane, Cliff's End.   1871.
Lancet style. Brick with slated roof. Rented by C. of E. from WW II and opened as St Mary the Virgin, 1954. (Mrs. Joan Franklin, churchwarden).

— Prim. M., Queen St.   1874.   £2,000.
Gothic. Polychromatic brick and stone dressings. Marble columns. Rebuilding of chapel of 1868, £1,425, burnt down 1873. Closed WW II, used by RAF then as toy factory; now furniture showroom. (Richardson, 1885; Occ.).

— Prim. M., Denmark Rd.   *c.* 1890.
Demolished by enemy action WW II. (PO; K; Haslewood, 1976).

— 'No name but that of Christian' Church, Broad St.   1837.
(RC).

— Sailors' Room, Queen St.   1837.
Extant 1851. (RC).

— Sailors' Bethel, Leopold St.
Listed 1874 to 1891.   (K).

— Sailors' Home and Mission, Military Rd., Royal Harbour.   1878.
Lancets. Brick. Dormitories upstairs. Opened by Marquess Conyngham. Restored 1981. (K; Matkin, 1982).

— Holiness Mission, Naivesink Villa, Mays Rd.   1882.
(Villa built 1878). Neo-classical. Rendered. Porch. Mays Hall (Brethren) since ante-WW II. Rear extension 1948. (Haslewood, 1976; Mrs. Butcher and deeds).

— Salvation Army Citadel, High St.   1885.   Prob. E. J. Sherwood.
Classical. Red brick. Pediment. Young people's hall at rear (Belmont Rd.) added 1890. Coxhead and Morgan, bldrs. (Major David Blackwell, Salvation Army architect; *Kent Advertiser*, 1 December 1936).

— The Grange, St. Augustine's Rd.   1844.   A. W. N. Pugin.
Yellow brick. The private chapel in Pugin's home, now used as a retreat house. (Pev; Bro. Damian).

— Jewish Synagogue, Honeysuckle Rd.   1833.   David Mocatta.   Estim. £1,900.
Regency. Stucco. Given by Sir Moses Montefiore. (Cardozo and Goodman, 1933).

— C.C., Cecilia Rd.   1871.   Geo. Gilbert Scott.   Estim. £6,000.
EE. Flint with stone dressings and tiled roofs. Castellated tower with Kentish turret. (K; anon. MS in Ramsgate reference library; Miss H. Westgarth, cemetery registrar).

READING STREET*   C. of E., St Mary the Virgin.   1858.   S. S. Teulon.   £270.
EE and Perp. Sandstone with tiled roof. Bellcote (replacing spire). Originally built on the Isle of Ebony (one mile south) and moved here when it proved inaccessible for want of footpaths; the whole operation was conducted within three months by Bourne and Chambers of Woodchurch. (Mace, 1902).

RECULVER   C. of E., St Mary the Virgin, Hillborough.   1876.   Joseph Clarke.
EE. Knapped flint with stone dressings; tiled roof. Bellcote. Sympathetic extension 1962. (Pev).

RHODES MINNIS   United Methodist, off White Horse Lane.   1888.   £250.
    Vernacular. Brick with slated roof. Barge-boards. Porch. Geo Boughton, bldr. Survives in
Methodist use. (Elham *Circuit Messenger*, May 1912; Mr. Derek Boughton of Elham).

RIPPLE   C. of E., St Mary the Virgin.   1861.   Ashpitel.
    Norman. Flint. W spire. Rebuilding of 13th cent. church. Copy of Barfrestone. (K; Basil).

—   C. of E., Mission Room, on parish boundary with Ringwould.   Ante-1887.
    Stone. Services conducted by Lieut.-Col. Joseph Sladen of Ripple Court. Vacated by 1921
and believed exported to Australia. (K; Mrs. D. H. Moat of Ripple Court).

—   Various sects, Mission.   1874.
    Plain. Rendered with slated roof. Porch. Closed post-1938 and now inhabited as Chapel
Cottage. (K; OS).

RIVER   C. of E., St Peter, Minnis Lane.   1832.   B. J. Reeve.
    EE. Knapped flint. Tower. Apsidal chancel 1876. (Pev).

—   W., Common Lane.   1876.   Mr. Tucker of Dover.   £162.
    Plain. Brick with slated roof. Porch. Built by Joseph Stiff. Has served as Methodist hall since
building of current chapel in 1956. (*Dover Express*, 27 February 1976; Welby, 1978).

RIVERHEAD   C. of E., St Mary.   1831.   Decimus Burton.
    EE. Rag. Recessed spire; lancets; rib vaulting. Chancel 1882 by A. W. Blomfield. (Eastlake,
1872; Pev).

ROCHESTER   C. of E., St Andrews Mission, Cossack St.   1889.
    Lancet style. Stock brick. Now Gurudawara Sabaha.

—   C. of E., St Peter, King St.   1858–60.   Ewan Christian.   £6,000.
    Early Dec. Rag and polychromatic brick. Cross gables. Saddlebacked roof. Demolished 1973.
(K; Eastlake, 1872; Pev).

—   Part. Bapt., Adullam, Hangman's Lane.   1848
    In use 1851. (RC).

—   Bapt. School, Crow Lane (sometime Maidstone Rd.)   1890.   £713.
    Lancets. Red brick and stone. Adjoining Baptist church 1907 by C. E. Bond. (K).

—*   Cong., Vines, Crow Lane.   1853–4.   John Tarring.   £3,000.
    Dec. Rag with slate roof. Built by Ford and Son of Rochester. (C, 1856; Timpson, 1859).

—   Cong., Star Hill.   1856.
    Lancet style. Brick with rag façade. Formed by a faction of Vines Congregational church
under Revd. Dr. Jenkyn. United Methodist Free church 1882–1928 and now Elim Pentecostal.
(K; SD).

—   Free, Bartholomew, Delce Rd.   1878.
    Galleries. Purchased by Quakers 1910 for £680. Sold to corporation and demolished 1966.
(K; Chatham *Almanac*, 1878; Showler, 1970).

—*   Jewish Synagogue, High St.   1865.   H. H. Collins.
    Romanesque. Rag with stone dressings. Supplied by Simon Magnus to the memory of his only
son. Bldr. J. G. Naylor. Occupies site of earlier synagogue *c.* 1750. (K; Roth, 1950).

—   C.C., St Nicholas, Maidstone Rd.   1856.
    Separate buildings, the Episcopal chapel having bell tower. Demolished WW II. (*Rochester
Gazette*, 27 May 1856; K; Rochester reference library).

—   C.C., St Margaret's, Maidstone Rd.   1865.   M. Bulmer.
    Dec. Ashlar and flint with tiled roofs. Free standing octagonal steeple joined by arches to
chapels on either side. (Pev).

RODMERSHAM   Bible Ch., Providence, The Green.   1848.
    Brick. Cause failed 1950s and demolished. (RC; Mr. Roger Thorne of Topsham).

ROLVENDEN   C. of E., Mission Room, Rolvenden Layne.   1890s.
Brick. Bell. Associated with parish church. Demolished 1960s. (K; Mrs. Jenner of Rolvenden).

—   Bible Ch., Rolvenden Layne.   1849.
Brick with slated roof. Closed 1970 and demolished 1972. (*Bible Christian Magazine*, 1848; RC; Dr. C. P. Burnham; Mrs. Jenner, former Sunday school leader).

ROSHERVILLE, *see* Gravesend.

RUCKINGE*   W., Oak Ridge.   1839.
Vernacular. Rendered with slate roof. Survives as Methodist.

RUSTHALL*   C. of E., St Paul, Rusthall Common.   1849–50.   H. J. Stevens of Derby with N. E. Stevens (local).
EE with Dec. Native sandstone. N aisle added 1864. (SD; Savidge, 1975).

—   C. of E., St Paul's Mission, High St.   1887.   Henry Taylor.   £1,000.
Brick and tiled roof. Lancets. Bell gable. Given by Mr. J. Stone-Wigg. Enlarged 1908. (Cent, 1950).

—   Cong. School, High St.   1861.
Plain. Brick. Wilson and Finch, bldrs. Extended 1907. Demolished for petrol station 1967. (SD; Pearce, 1904; Strange, 1930; Bailey, 1970).

—   W. Mission Room, High St.   *c.* 1894.
'Homely'. Succeeded 1902 by the present building which after various unsuccessful unions was bought out by the Congregationalists in 1967. (Pearce, 1904; Bailey, 1970).

RYARSH   Bapt., Jireh, Chapel St.   1863–4.
Plain. Brick, rendered. Now Strict Baptist. (B, 1865; RFC).

ST LAWRENCE*   W., Chapel Rd.   1897.   J. Wills.   £1,480.
Lancet style. Brick with stone dressings. Contractor W. W. Martin of Ramsgate. (W, 1897).

ST MARY CRAY   R.C., St Joseph, High St.   1895.
Dec. Bombed 1941 and superseded. (Bernard Kelly, 1907; Blake, 1980).

—   Bapt.   1869.
Extinct ante-1928. (Whitley, 1928).

—   Bapt., Zion.   1887.
Renovated 1894. Extinct ante-1928. (B, 1894; Whitley, 1928).

—   Cong., The Temple, High St.   1851.   £12,000.
Italianate. Cost defrayed by Wm. Joynson. Windowless, being lit by enormous glass dome. Bombed 1941 and demolished 1953. Survived by Bonella and Paull's 1893 schoolrooms, £1,967. (C, 1851 and 1893; Timpson, 1859; Mrs. M. Palmer).

—   C.C., Star Lane.   1881.   Edward Clarke.
EE. Red brick with tiled roof. Bellcote.

ST NICHOLAS-AT-WADE   W., Down Barton Rd.   1822.
Vernacular. Brick with slated roof. Closed post-1974 and now youth club. (RC; K; Dr. Christopher Stell).

ST PETER'S*   W., Ranelagh Grove.   1871.
Neo-classical. Brick. Occupied since 1973 as Elim Pentecostal, having previously served as social club. (Revd. C. R. Gidney, min.).

—   Prim. M., Northwood.   1846.
Purchased by Wesleyans 1892 for £66. (RC; W, 1892).

—   Orphanage, Lanthorne House Rd.   1869.   J. P. Seddon.
Dec. Flint with red brick diapers. Polygonal apse. Occupied W wing of upper two storeys. Bombed WW II and demolished 1953. (*Visitors' Guide*, 1879; Lapthorne, 1971).

SANDGATE   C. of E., St Paul, High St.   1849.   S. S. Teulon.
Spireless Gothic. Polychromatic; brick with stone dressings. Cross gables. Galleries until Temple Moore, who disliked the church, removed them in 1920. Elevated from chapel-of-ease to parish status 1888. (Gdbk).

—   Cong.   1882.
Iron. Superseded by High St. chapel converted to theatre 1965. (K; Mr. A. Wimble, county architect).

—   W., Chapel St.   1819.   £325 4s. 8d.
Enlarged 1862. Sold 1900 to pay for new chapel and used latterly as a store. (RC; Stace's *Sandgate Almanac*, 1873; Pitts, 1969).

—   W., Gough Rd.   1900.   Gordon Lowther and Gunton.   £2,000.
Gothic. Rag and tiled roof. Pinnacled. Lantern tower. Demolished 1970s. (W, 1897; Pitts, 1969).

SANDWICH   W., New St.   1874.   £2,096.
Closed 1965 and sold 1966. (W, 1874; K, Methodist circuit archives).

—   Prim. M., Moat Sole.   1862.
Plain. Brick. Roundheaded windows. Closed 1932 and sold for £300. Now Moat Sole clinic. (Methodist circuit archives; Occ.).

SARRE   Prim. M., off Old Rd.   Ante-1887.
Plain, roundheaded windows. Brick with slated roof. Closed *c.* 1966 and converted to dwelling 1975-7. (K; Mr. A. Wimble, county architect).

SEAL, near Sevenoaks   C. of E., St Lawrence, Stone St., Seal Chart.   1867-8.   C. H. Howell.
Rectilinear. Sandstone with tiled roof. Lancets. W. Constable, bldr. Tower 1888 by F. W. Hunt. (K; Basil).

—   Bible Ch., Church St.   1881.
Renaissance. Yellow brick and red dressings. Now Seal Baptist mission. (K; Mr. V. Bowden of Kemsing; Revd. J. Tattersall, min.).

SELLINDGE   W., Hythe Rd.   1883.   Albert Wm. Smith.
Plain. Rag. Porch. A. J. Camburn of Folkestone, bldr. Thos. Rigden, benefactor. (W, 1883).

SEVENOAKS   C. of E., St John, St John's Hill.   1858-9.   Morphew and Green.
(N aisle 1878). Early Dec. Rag faced. Chancel and vestries, unsympathetic red brick and stone dressings, added 1901, on too large a scale. (BA, 1860; K).

—   C. of E., St Mary, Kippington.   1878-80.   J. M. Hooker of Kippington.   £12,500 excl. land.
EE. Rag and Westwood stone dressings. Lancets. Glass by Clayton and Bell. Founded by William James Thompson and his sister Esther and built by W. B. Wilson of Canterbury. (K; Standen, 1958).

—   C. of E., Kippington Church, Granville Rd.   1878.
Iron, tarred and lined with matchboarding. Became parish room when St Mary Kippington was completed in 1880. (SD; Standen, 1958).

—   R.C., St Thomas of Canterbury, Granville Rd.   1896.   F. A. Walters.
Romanesque. Rendered with stone dressings. Spirelet. Incorporates earlier chapel of The Most Holy Trinity, 1884. (CD; K; Little, 1966).

—   Bapt., The Vine.   1886.   John Wills of Derby.   £3,120.
Gothic. Rag and Monks Park stone. Lancets and traceried windows. Gallery. Pinnacles surmounting buttresses with carved finials. Built by W. Wiltshire. Adjoining schools 1888. (B, 1887, 1888).

—   Cong., St John's Hill.   1865-6.   J. Tarring.   £2,460.
Dec. Rag and Bath stone. Cross gables and buttresses. Spire 127 ft. dismantled 1880 and the tower latterly balded of its pinnacles. (C, 1866).

SEVENOAKS (*continued*)   General Bapt., Bethel, Harts Lands (— Lane).   1842.
  (RC).

— W., Market Square.   1852.   W. W. Pocock.
  EE. Rag. Lancets. N porch. Succeeded hired premises. Congregation removed to The Drive 1904. Now converted to shops with a restaurant in the upper storey. (*Methodist Recorder*, 7 April 1904; Judd, 1932; Horton, 1979).

— Bible Ch., St John's Hill.   1882.
  Lancet style. Red brick and terracotta. Closed 1961 and sold to freemasons. (Horton, 1979; Mr. Roger Thorne of Topsham).

SEVENOAKS WEALD   C. of E., St George, Church Rd.   1820.
  EE. Stone. Castellated W tower. Chancel 1872 by T. G. Jackson. (K; Pev).

— W., The Green.   1843.
  Renaissance façade. Brick. (Judd, 1932).

— Breth., Gospel Hall, Glebe Rd.   1875.
  Plain. Red brick and hung tiles. Residence attached. (Mr. J. Jackson, Occ.).

SHADOXHURST   W., The Green.   *c.* 1832.
  Wood. Demolished *c.* 1868. (Chowns, 1977).

— W., Church Lane.   1868.
  Lancet style. Rag dressed with brick, slated roof. Schoolroom 1931. (Chowns, 1977).

SHEERNESS   C. of E., Holy Trinity, Edward St.   1835-6.   G. L. Taylor.   £4,128.
  Yellow brick and stone. S tower. Built by Wm. Ranger. Commissioners gave £2,595. Enlarged 1851. (Daly, 1904; Basil; Port, 1961).

— St Paul (Garrison Church), Station Rd.   1872.   Robert Wheeler of Tunbridge Wells.
  Byzantine. Brick. Disused and demolished (proposal 1962). (BA, 1873; Daly, 1904; Woodthorpe, 1951; Basil; Revd. A. B. Sharpe).

—* R.C., St Henry and St Elizabeth, Broadway.   1865-6.   E. W. Pugin.   £3,710.
  EE and Dec. Stock brick banded with black. Bell turret. (BA, 1865; Bernard Kelly, 1907; Basil).

— Bapt. M., Winstanley Rd.   1869.   £270.
  Plain. Brick. Survives next to Strode Crescent. (B, 1871).

— Bapt., Strode Crescent.   1878.   Thos. Seward.   £1,406 16s.
  Renaissance. Red brick with dressings and columns of Portland cement and arches of Bath stone. Built by J. G. Naylor of Rochester. (B, 1879, 1880).

— Cong., Bethel School., Hope St., Mile Town.   1832.   £300.
  Classical. Brick with slated roof. Roundheaded windows. Extended 1863 and 1872. Became Christian institute 1883. (Timpson, 1859; Gordon, 1898).

— Cong., Alma Rd.   1862.
  Dec. Red brick. Porches. Destroyed by fire 1942. (Gordon, 1898; A. T. Sears, sec.).

— Cong., School Chapel, Hope St.   1882-3.
  Classical. Brick with red dressings. Succeeding 1832 school. Survives as URC. (Gordon, 1898).

— Cong. School, Meyrick Rd.   1891.   T. W. Parrish.   £1,250.
  Gothic. Brick and red dressings. W. Taylor, bldr. Used WW II as British restaurant and currently as Sheppey Little Theatre. (Gordon, 1898; Mrs. L. Hogben).

— W., Hope St.   1841.
  Wood. Demolished post-1925, used as builders' yard and subsequently developed. (RC; K; Mrs. L. Hogben).

— Prim. M., Providence, Mile Town.   1828.
  Extant 1851. (RC).

SHEERNESS   Bible Ch., Ebenezer, Alexandra Rd.   1821.
Lancets. (Rendered) with slated roof. Porch. Opened by Wm. O'Bryan. Internal alterations 1863. Closed c. 1972. (*Bible Christian Magazine*, 1863; Shaw, 1965; Mr. Roger Thorne of Topsham).

—   Catholic Apostolic, Chapel St., Mile Town.   1845.
Surviving in Russell St. 1891. (RC; K).

—   C.C., Halfway.   1857.   £1,300 incl. land.
Pointed brick. Pulled down post WW II and replaced by toilets. (K; Mrs. L. Hogben).

SHELDWICH   C. of E., Church Mission Room, Perry Wood.   Ante-1887.
Closed post-1909. (K).

SHIPBOURNE   C. of E., St Giles.   1881.   Mann and Saunders.
EE. Rag and Bath stone dressings. Norman capped central tower. The gift of Edward Cazalet of Fairlawn, replacing church of 1722. (K; SD; Basil; Pev).

SHOREHAM   Bapt., Crown Rd.   1896.
Plain. Weather-boarded. Fleche. Enlarged 1903. Closed 1982. (K; B, 1904; Revd. E. W. R. David, vicar).

—   W.   1836.
Plain. Brick. Hipped roof. Closed ante-1932 and used as public reading room. (RC; K. Judd, 1932).

—   W., Romney St.   1846.
Plain. Flints, hand picked from the fields by local farmer Mr. Booker. (RC; Judd, 1932).

SHORNCLIFFE   St Mark (Garrison), Military Rd.   1855.
Plain. Wood and iron. W gallery added c. 1870. Part blown down by a 1936 gale and formally demolished 1937. Succeeded 1939. (Gdbk).

—   R.C., Most Holy Name, Hospital Hill, Shorncliffe Camp.   1894.
Iron and weatherboarding. Demolished 1967 and succeeded by new garrison chapel. (K; CD; Bernard Kelly, 1907; chaplain).

SHORNE   W., Zion, Ridgeway.   1838.
Brick with slated roof. Closed 1976 and subsequently used as studio. (RC; Dr. Christopher Stell; Revd. Roger Cresswell, min.).

—   Prim. M., The Street.   1893.
Plain. Brick. Survives in use. (MCSR, 1980; Revd. Roger Cresswell, min.).

SHOTTENDEN   Prim. M.   1875.
Lancets. Red brick with slated roof. Now private dwelling.

SIBERTSWOLD (Shepherdswell)   C. of E., St Andrew, Mill Lane.   1863.   Benj. Ferrey.
EE. Flint with Bath stone dressings. Bellcote. Plate tracery. (K; Basil; Pev).

—   W., Church Hill.   1870.
Pointed. Rag faced and rendered with slated roof.

SIDCUP   C. of E., Christ Church.   1872.   Mr. Kent.
Iron. Temporary. Superseded 1900. (*The Cray*, 2 September 1872; K).

—   C. of E., Christ Church, Main Rd.   1900–1.   A. R. Barker and Son.
EE. Rag and ashlar with slated roofs. Plate tracery. Succeeds iron church of 1887. (K; Pev).

—   C. of E., Holy Trinity, Lamorbey (Station Rd.).   1879.   Ewan Christian.
Dec. Rag with tiled roof. Destroyed by enemy action October 1944, restored 1949. (K; Pev).

—   C. of E., St John the Evangelist, Church Rd.   1844.   Wollaston.
Byzantine. Brick and flint. W towers. Succeeded by present building. Canon Basil Clarke commented, 'Its removal is no loss'. (Basil).

—   C. of E., St John the Evangelist, Church Rd.   1882–99.   Fellowes-Prynne.
EE. Stock brick. Clerestory. Spacious interior lined with red brick. (Pev).

SIDCUP (*continued*)   Bapt., Hatherleigh Rd.   1890.
'A picture of grace and neatness'. Alterations incl. raising of roof 1899. Succeeded by Main Rd. chapel 1922 and demolished. (B, 1899; K).

—   Cong., Station Rd.   1887–8.   Geo. Baines.   £3,804.
Gothic. Rag and Bath stone. Spirelet and plate tracery. Built by Geo. Dobson. Now united with Methodists. (C, 1889).

—   W. School.   1884.   Dunk and Geden.   £1,872.
Plain. Stock brick. Perp. windows. John Otway of Chislehurst, bldr. (W, 1883 and 1885).

—   Breth., Gospel Hall, Birkbeck Rd.   1879.
Plain. Brick. Named Nathaniel Hall after 1895. Enlarged, modernised and renamed Birkbeck chapel 1965. (Mr. Frank Smale).

—   Breth., Manor Room, Manor Rd.   *c.* 1890.
Plain. Brick. Survives windowless, rendered and in Exclusive Brethren use. (K).

SISSINGHURST*   C. of E., Trinity.   1838.   J. Jennings of Hawkhurst.   £1,525 1s. 7d.
After the design of Casterton, nr. Stamford. Native sandstone. Lancets, buttresses, castellated tower. James Reed of Hawkhurst, bldr., left bankrupt. The gifr of Captain A. King, R.N., land and stone given by Lord Cornwallis. Restored and enlarged 1893. (Pile, 1980).

—*   W., High St.   1869.
Pointed. Red and white brick. Y tracery. Kent peg-tile roof. Disused; conversion to dwelling-house pending 1981. (Director of Planning, Cranbrook).

SITTINGBOURNE   C. of E., Holy Trinity, Dover St.   1867.   R. C. Hussey.
Dec. Rag. Chancel and tower 1873 by Joseph Clarke. (Pev).

—   R.C., Sacred Heart, West St.   1892.   W. L. Grant.
Lancets and square tower. Brick and stone dressings. Cons. 1902. (Pev; CD).

—   Bapt., West St.   1867.   £1,700.
Classical. Round arched. Brick and stone dressings. Enlarged 1887 by Wm. Leon. Grant of Sittingbourne. (K; Revd. G. R. Breed, min.).

—   Bapt. M., Bayford Rd.   1889.
Closed 1934. (Revd. G. R. Breed, min.).

—   Cong., Latimer, High St.   1841.
Gothic. Rag faced brick. Spire. (C, 1855; Timpson, 1859).

—   W., High St.   1863.
White brick. Followed wooden chapel on site. Bombed and destroyed 1944. (K; Mr. Brian Davies).

—   Prim. M., Shakespeare Rd.   1881.
Brick. Closed and now in secular use. (K; Mrs. Eric Maynard).

—   Bible Ch., East St. (High St.).   1887–8.   W. L. Grant.
Gothic. Red brick and Bath stone dressings. Gallery. Replaced George St. chapel which continued as mission. Closed and sold 1980 upon amalgamation with former Wesleyan church. Now sports centre. (*Bible Christian Magazine*, 1888; K; Mr. Roger Thorne of Topsham; Mr. Brian Davies of Sittingbourne).

—   Cemetery, Bell Rd.   1860.   Wimble and Molyneux.
A Gothic pair linked by garbled arch. Rag. Tiled roof. (Pev).

SMARDEN   Bapt., Zion, High St.   1841.
Classical. Pediment. Stuccoed. (Pev).

—   St. Bapt., Tilden, off Bethersden Rd.   1892.
Vernacular chapel style. Brick. School detached. Succeeds the earlier chapel of 1726, given by Jas. Tilden. Yeoman of High Halden (K; RFC).

SMARDEN (*continued*)   Old Baptist Union, Bethel, Bethersden Rd.   1901.
 Vernacular. Corrugated iron. Prefabricated by F. Smith and Co. of Stratford. Affiliated to Assemblies of God 1926. Walls rendered 1970. (Mrs. G. M. Brooker, pastor).

SNODLAND   C. of E., Christ Church, Malling Rd.   1893.
 EE. Rag under tiled roof. Lancets. Built as chapel-of-ease to All Saints, Birling. (K).

— C. of E., Mission Church, Holborough.   1880s.
 Iron. Given by Col. W. H. Roberts in memory of Wm. Lee. Disposed *c.* WW II. (Woolmer, 1894; Mr. Gerald Edgeler).

— Bapt., Church Field.   1898.
 Iron. Porch. Acquired by Lead Wool Co. 1939 and used as works canteen until demolished 1982. (Mr. C. W. Pestell of Lead Wool).

— Cong., Providence, Holborough Rd.   1855.   £500.
 'Neat!' Sold 1887 to the Misses Hook for school purposes. (Timpson, 1859; Woolmer, 1894; Wall, 1928).

— Cong., High St.   1888.
 EE. Stock brick and Bath stone. J. Welford, bldr. Now united with Methodist. (Woolmer, 1894; Wall, 1928; MCSR, 1980).

— Prim. M., Malling Rd.   1899–1900.
 Renaissance. Brick and red dressings. J. Wilford, bldr. Closed and used by C. Bishop, household furniture, since 1976. (Occ.).

— Church of the New Jerusalem (Swedenborg), St John the Evangelist, High St.   1881–2.
  £5,000.
 EE. Rag and stone dressings with tiled roof. Tower. Lancets. Cost borne by the Misses Hook and Col. Holland. (*Intellectual Repository*, May 1881; Woolmer, 1894; Funnell, 1980).

— C.C., Constitution Hill.   1895.   £2,000 incl. land.
 Tudor. Sandstone. Adjoins lodge. (K; Mr. Gerald Edgeler).

SOUTHBOROUGH, Tunbridge Wells   C. of E., Christ Church, Brightridge Lane (Prospect Rd).
  1870–1.   T. K. Green.   £2,400.
 Completed 1889. EE. Banded sandstone with tiled roof. Flèche. Built as chapel-of-ease to St Peter. (BA, 1872; SD).

— C. of E., St Matthew, High Brooms Rd.   1886.
 Brick and stone. Mission church succeeded by permanent building 1902. (*Kent and Sussex Courier*, 12 August 1949; Jub, 1952).

— C. of E., St Peter, Church Rd.   1830–1.   Decimus Burton.
 EE. Yellow brick and sandstone, slate roof. Capacity extended 1866; W tower and spire 1883 by Ewan Christian. (Pev).

— C. of E., St Thomas, Pennington Rd.   1860.   H. Pownall.   £2,400.
 Dec. Rag and Bath stone dressings. Bellcote. Given by Mrs. Sarah Pugh and built by Jackson and Shaw of Westminster. S transept 1888 by R. H. Garling. (*Sussex Weekly Advertiser*, 11 December 1860; Pev).

— St. Bapt., Bethel, Western Rd.   1882.
 Classical. Stucco. (RFC).

— W., London Rd.   1870–1.   Cattermole and Eade of Norwich.
 Gothic. Polychromatic brick and Bath stone. Aaron Brown of Southborough, bldr. Succeeds chapel of 1845 on adjacent site. Replaced by new chapel 1936. (Pearce, 1904; Bailey, 1970).

— W., High Brooms Rd.   1898.   Herbert Murkin Caley of Tunbridge Wells.
 Lightly Gothic. Red brick with stone dressings and tiled roof. Bldr. J. Jarvis. Now Bethel Evangelical Free Church. (*Builder*, 1898).

SOUTHEND   C. of E., St John, Bromley Rd.   1824.
 Lightly classical. Brick with slated roof. Proprietary chapel endowed by John Foster, succeeded by new building 1928 and has since served as church hall. (Baker, 1961; Clarke, 1966).

SOUTHFLEET   Cong., Warren Rd.   1896.
  Plain. Brick. (Douglass, 1975).

SPELDHURST   C. of E., St Mary the Virgin.   1870.   G. G. Scott, jnr.   £7,000.
  EE. Ashlar. Rebuilding of earlier church incorporating old tower. (BA, 1872; SD; Betj).

—   C. of E., Mission Church, Broomhill Rd.   1878.
  Perp. Sandstone. Spire. Porch. Used WW II as store and for last 25 years as Wellden hall, carpet
  cleaning. (OS, 1907; Pev; Mr. W. Crundwell, sen.).

STALISFIELD   C. of E., Vicarage Chapel, Stalisfield Green.   1878.
  Pointed. Brick. Porch. Adjoining vicarage. Sold 1971 and now privately occupied. (K; Mrs.
  Jean West, Occ.).

STANFORD   C. of E., All Saints, Church Field.   1841 and 1878.
  EE. Stone. Bellcote. (K).

—   W., Stone St.   1845, rebuilt 1868.
  Plain. Brick. Closed ante-1930s, truncated and occupied until the present day as 'St David's
  bungalow'. (K; Mr. Eli Simpson, Occ.).

STAPLE   C. of E., Sunday School, Shatterling.   c. 1880.
  Lancets. Brick with slated roof. Attached to parish church. Used since 1950s as farm store.
  (Mr. Eric Pay, Occ.).

STAPLEHURST   Indep. Chapel, High St.   1825.
  Plain. Brick. Schoolrooms added 1830. Enlarged to present condition (1889 EE. Red brick.
  Plate tracery) as memorial to Wm. Jull, minister 1825–77. Survives as URC. (Timpson, 1859).

STELLING*   W.   1855.
  Neo-classical. Brick and flint. Bldr., Edwd. Boughton. Having no address it is distinguished
  locally as 'the top chapel' or 'the chapel near the mill'. (Mr. Derek Boughton).

—   Prim. M., Ebenezer, Church Lane, Stelling Minnis.   1862.
  Vernacular. Knapped flint and brick dressings. Chas. Boughton, bldr. Sometime called 'the
  ranters' chapel'. Closed 1982 with a view to sale. (Mr. Derek Boughton of Elham; Dr. Doreen
  Rosman, University of Kent).

STOCKBURY   W., South Green.   1888.   £268.
  Plain. Brick. (W, 1889; MCSR, 1980; Mrs. Eric Maynard).

—   Bible Ch.   1822.
  Closed ante-1907. (RC; K; Mr. Roger Thorne of Topsham).

STOKE   R.C., St George, The Street.   Ante-1882.
  Pointed. Brick with slated roof. Closed post-WW II and demolished c. 1960. (K; Mr. Philip
  Beck, churchwarden of Stoke).

—   Part. Bapt., Zion.   1842.
  In use 1851. (RC).

—   Bible Ch., Providence.   1843.
  Superseded 1889 and subsequently demolished. (RC; Macdougall, 1980).

—   Bible Ch., Allhallows Rd.   1889.
  EE. Stock brick and red dressings and slated roofs. Lancets. Survives in Methodist use. (K).

STONE, near Dartford.   C. of E., Mission Church, Mile Stone Rd.   1878.
  Plain. Flint and stone dressings, now rendered. Commandeered WW II, used previously and
  subsequently as Sunday school. Deemed c. 1968 to be council property and sold to Jehovah's
  witnesses with whom it remains. (Mrs. I. Lineham).

—   C. of E., St Michael's Mission, Invicta Rd.   1883.   £500.
  Plain. Iron. Bell turret. Closed c. 1933 and sold to Stone House hospital; now industrial
  therapy unit. (K. Mrs. I. Lineham).

STONE (*continued*)   Prim. M., Hill House Rd.   *c.* 1890.
Survived in use until Methodist union. (K).

—   C.C., St James's Lane.   1899.   £5,500.
Lancet style. Banded brick with slated roof. Two chapels joined by arch bearing bell-turret. (K).

—   Lunatic Asylum (Stone House Hospital).   1898.   Andrew Murray.
Dec. Knapped flint. Spirelet. (Pev).

STOURMOUTH   Indep.   1840.
Enlarged 1851. Associated with Wingham Congregationalists. Extant 1863. (RC; Timpson, 1859; C, 1863).

STOWTING   W., Stowting Common.   1838.
Sold to Bible Christians 1860. Ruined by fire 1876 and demolished 1940s. (RC; Elham *Circuit Messenger*, 1912; Mr. John Hammon of Stowting).

—   Bible Ch., Fiddling Chapel, Mill Lane.   1844.
Converted to dwelling 1860 and since demolished. (Mr. John Hammon of Stowting).

STROOD*   C. of E., St Mary, Vicarage Rd.   1868–9.   Arthur Blomfield.   £6,083.
EE. Rag and yellow brick. Slender spire. Clerestory. Built by Messrs. Foord. Cost borne by Mrs. Griffiths. (BA, 1871; Smetham, 1899; Pev).

—   Cong., St Mary's Rd.   1880.
Pointed. Iron. Porch. Now Boy Scouts. (Smetham, 1899; K).

—   W., North St.   1859.   Keeling.
Succeeded chapel 1813. Schoolroom added 1861 for £240. Bought by Salvation Army 1889 and sold to the town for clearance 1970. (Smetham, 1899; Major David Blackwell, Salvation Army).

—   W.M., Jubilee, Frindsbury Rd.   1887.   J. W. Nash.   £5,700.
EE. Red brick and Bath stone. Flèche. Demolished. (Smetham, 1899).

—   W. Hall, Stonehorse Lane (Cliffe Rd.).   1898–9.   J. W. Nash and Son.   £1,650.
Gothic. Red brick. Built by H. Wyles. Used 1914–18 as auxiliary hospital and survives as Strood Methodist church. (Smetham, 1899).

—   Gospel Mission, Brompton Lane.   1895.   J. W. Nash of Rochester.
Plain. Stock brick. Survives with name unchanged. (Smetham, 1899).

—   C.C., Cuxton Rd.   1883.   £4,750 incl. land.
EE. Red brick with tiled roofs. Lancets. Two chapels joined by double arch. (K).

STURRY   R.C., St Anne's Convent (Notre Dame des Missions), Westbere Lane.   1889.
EE. Red brick (now rendered). Here in the sanctuary rests the foundress, Adela Euphrasia Barbier, who built this initially as a hall, being unable to obtain permission for a chapel. (Fr. Leonard Whatmore; Sr. Veronica Kavanagh, RNDM).

—   W.   1827.
Plain. Follows certified dwelling house. Closed WW I; modernised 1943 and 1973 to serve as social centre. (RC; McIntosh, 1979).

SUNDRIDGE   Cong.   1840.
Extant 1855. (C, 1855).

SUTTON-AT-HONE   Part. Bapt., Bethesda, Main Rd.   1834.
Plain. Brick with slate roof. Formed by dismission from Eynsford, closed *c.* 1930, revived 1934 and surviving. (RC; RFC).

—   W., Ship Lane.   1880.
Lancets. Rendered with slated roof. Porch. (MCSR, 1980).

SUTTON VALENCE   C. of E., St Mary.   1828.   W. Ashenden and Sons.
Dec. Kentish rag and Bath stone. Tower. Restoration 1874 by G. M. Hills. (K; Basil; Pev).

SUTTON VALENCE (*continued*) Cong., Broad St.   1873.   Sulman and Rhodes.   Contract £1.275.
Gothic. Rag and Bath stone, brick interior and tiled roof. Spire. Gallery. Closed 1975,
purchased for Sutton Valence school and opened 1981 as 'the Gulland Hall' arts centre. (C,
1873; school bursar).

SWALECLIFFE*   C. of E., St John the Baptist.   1875-6.   R. Wheeler.
EE. Ragstone with yellow brick dressings and tiled roof. Flèche. (BA, 1877; Pev).

SWANLEY   C. of E., St Mary the Virgin, Swanley Junction.   1900-1.   Dudley Newman.   £6,000.
Gothic. Brick. Site presented by Rt. Hon. Sir Wm. Dyke, Bart. (K; Betj; Revd. R. L. Gwyther,
inc.).

—   C. of E., St Paul, Swanley Village.   1860-1.   Ewan Christian.
Dec. Rag and yellow brick. Tower 1862-5.   (BA, 1863; Pev).

—   C. of E., Iron Mission, Swanley Junction.   1895.
Superseded by St Mary. (K; Revd. R. L. Gwyther, inc.).

SWANSCOMBE   C. of E., All Saints Mission, Galley Hill.   1882.
Iron. Used as social club following building of permanent church. (K).

—   C. of E., All Saints, Galley Hill Rd.   1893.   R. Norman Shaw.
EE. Knapped flint and white stone dressings. Provided by Bazley White cement works for its
employees. Declared redundant 1971. (K; Blomfield, 1940; Basil; *London Gazette*, 8 June
1971).

—   Cong.   1836.
Extant 1855. (RC; C, 1855).

—   W., Galley Hill.   1884.   £604.
Extant 1903. (W, 1884; K).

—   Prim. M., Milton Rd.   1888.
Classical proportions with pointed windows. Stock brick with red dressings. Survives in
Methodist use.

SWINGFIELD   Bible Ch.   1845.   £186.
Plain. Knapped flint with red brick dressings and slate roof. Porch. Survives in Methodist
use. (Elham *Circuit Messenger*, May 1912).

SYDENHAM   All Saints, Trewsbury Rd.   1901-3.   G. H. Fellowes-Prynne.
Gothic. Red brick and stone dressings. Aisled. Barrel roof. White stone traceried rood. Bldr.,
Goddard. W front and cupola wanting. (Clarke, 1966).

—*   C. of E., St Bartholomew, West Hill (Westwood Hill).   1827-32.   Lewis Vulliamy.   £9,357.
Perp. Suffolk brick with stone dressings. Built by Wm. Woods and, later, Thos. Smith, with
Commissioners' money. Apsidal chancel 1857-8 by Edwin Nash. Body of church rebuilt
1874-5. Tower now bereft of pinnacles. (K; Clarke, 1966; Port, 1961).

—   C. of E., Holy Trinity, Sydenham Park.   1865-6.   John Emmett.   £15,000.
EE. Ashlar. Glass by Morris. Closed 1976 and demolished 1981. (BA, 1868; Revd. G. Hayter,
inc.).

—   C. of E., St Matthew, Panmure Rd.   1879-82.   J. E. K. Cutts.   £8,000.
Early French Gothic. Brick. Chapel-of-ease to St Bartholomew, succeeding iron church bought
in 1871 for £268 from St Luke, West Norwood, where it had never been used. Building closed
1938 and demolished 1939. (K; Basil; Baker, 1961).

—   C. of E., St Michael and All Angels, Bell Green (Champion Crescent).   1863-4.   J. T.
Knowles.   £4,500.
Perp. Stone. Octagonal bell turret, crocketed spire, seven-sided apse. Cost borne by W.
Woodgate of Hyde Park. Chapel-of-ease to St Bartholomew until 1879. Destroyed in air raid
10 September 1940. (K; Basil; Clarke, 1966).

SYDENHAM (*continued*)   C. of E., St Philip the Apostle, Taylors Lane.   1864–7. Edwin Nash
       and J. Round.   £6,350.
EE. Reigate stone, interior rendered. S chapel 1896 by C. H. M. Mileham. Closed 1982 for
demolition and new building. (BA, 1867; Clarke, 1966).

—   R.C., Our Lady and St Philip Neri, Sydenham Rd.   1882.   F. A. Walters.
Followed iron church of 1872. Destroyed 1940 and rebuilt 1959. (Bernard Kelly, 1907;
Baker, 1961).

—   Bapt. M.H., Bell Green.   1883.
Lightly classical. Brick with slated roof. Salvation Army 1931; now Church of God of
Prophecy. (Whitley, 1928; Baker, 1961).

—   Bapt. Lecture Hall, Perry Rise.   1900.   W. H. Woodroffe.
Perp. tracery. Red brick and stone. Bldrs. Messrs. Holliday and Greenwood. Church added
1914. (Baker, 1961).

—   Cong., Lower Sydenham.   1819.
Later used as British school and reopened 1851. (Timpson, 1859; Baker, 1961).

—   Cong., Park Chapel, Albert Rd. (Sydenham Park).   1850.   Matthew Trimen.
EE. Flint with Calne stone dressings. Closed 1852, reopened 1853 (?), renamed Park Hall and
continued as Sunday School until WW II; thence a store. (C, 1850; Timpson, 1859; Baker,
1961).

—   Cong. M., Wells Rd. (Wells Park Rd.).   1849.
Rented by Baptists 1854–7. Purchased by St Bartholomew's as church hall 1881. Closed 1938.
Wrecked during VE celebrations 1945. (C, 1855; Baker, 1961).

—   Cong., Church-in-the-Grove, Jews' Walk.   1867.   £6,100.
Succeeded Park chapel and followed on site 1974 by the Grove Centre (Baptist–URC). (Mearns,
1882; Baker, 1961).

—   C. of E., Christ Church, Sydenham Rd.   Post-1866.
Rebuilding(?) of 18th-cent. Nonconformist chapel.. Lancet style. Brick, rendered. Chapel-of-
ease to St Michael, later becoming hall to All Saints, Trewsbury Rd. (Clarke, 1966).

—   Breth., Mayow Hall, Mayow Rd.   1889.
Plain. Grey brick. High-pitched slated roof. (Mr. F. W. Mountford).

—   London City Mission, Emmanuel Hall, Maddin Rd. (Porthcawl Rd.).   1894.
Plain. Brick with red dressings. Porch. Extended 1924. (Jub, 1944; Mr. Stephen Frost,
missioner).

TENTERDEN*   C. of E., St Michael and All Angels, Boar's Isle.   1863.   Gordon Hills.
Ragstone. Lancets. SE tower and conspicuous spire added 1865. Built by Bourne of Woodchurch. Founded by Seaman Beale, the first vicar, who established the adjacent school the
previous year. (Mace, 1902).

—*   Part. Bapt., Zion, High St.   1835.
(Rebuilt 1887). Classical. Red brick and stone dressings. Now Baptist Union. (B, 1889; Bicent,
1967).

—*   St. and Part. Bapt., Jireh, Boar's Isle.   1869.
Vernacular. Weatherboarded. Porch. Renovated 1961 and extended 1967. (Jub, 1919).

—*   W., West Cross.   1884.   Jas. Weir.
Perp. Red brick and stone dressings; tile roof. Panel tracery. Flèche. M. J. Bingham of
Headcorn, bldr. (Mace, 1902).

—   Bible Ch., Ebenezer, Bird's Isle.   1838.
Plain. Wood and brick. Sold 1954 and demolished c. 1970. (RC; Mr. L. M. Chowns, circuit
archivist).

TEYNHAM   C. of E., St Andrew Mission, Green St.   Ante-1887.
Brick. Bombed 1940, restored but demolished. (K; Dane, *War Years*).

— W., London Rd.   1841.
Roundheaded windows. Brick and slated roof; now rendered. Closed 1929; since used as billiards hall and auction rooms. (RC; Mr. Stanley of Lynsted; Mr. Brian Davies of Sittingbourne).

— W. School, Lynsted Lane.   1868.
Plain. Brick with red dressings. Stet.

— Bible Ch., Green St.   1831.
Extant 1851. (RC).

— Bible Ch., Ebenezer.   1833.
Extant 1851. (RC).

— Bible Ch., Green St.   1842.
Extant 1851. (RC).

THROWLEY   Bible Ch., Bethel.   1829?
Plain. Brick. Closed post-1878. Derelict ante-1969. (K).

THURNHAM   W., Providence, Chapel Lane.   1818.   £250.
Vernacular. Brick. Declared unsafe 1875 and subsequently demolished; succeeded by the chapel at Ware St., Bearsted. (Bourner *et al.*, n.d.).

TILMANSTONE   W., Chapel Hill.   1876.   £384.
Lancet style. Brick. Porch. Has served 15 years as parish hall. (W, 1876; Revd. J. C. Brooks of Northbourne).

TONBRIDGE   St Eanswythe's Mission, Priory Rd.   1890.
Pointed. Iron. Established by Miss Mary Caroline Gorham. (Mr. W. Horton, missioner; Chap.).

— C. of E., St Saviour, Dry Hill Pk.   1876.   Ewan Christian.
EE. Red brick. Flèche. Rounded apse. Built by John Deacon as Chapel-of-ease to Tonbridge parish church. Sustains a sacramental tradition. (K).

— C. of E., St Saviour's Mission Room, Seven Acre Square (Elm Lane).   1886.
Domestic. Banded red brick. Gabled. Closed and British Red Cross since 1963. (Neve, 1933; SD).

— C. of E., St Stephen, Quarry Hill Rd.   1851–4.   Ewan Christian.
EE. Rag. Spire. Lancets. Glass by Morris and Co. (E, 1853; Eastlake, 1872).

— C. of E., St Stephen's Mission Room, Priory Rd.   1880.
Plain. Brick. Gabled. Closed *c.* 1958, used for television repairs and since 1975 by gas engineers. (Neve, 1933; K; Occ.).

— C. of E., St Stephen's Mission Church, Lower Hayesden.   *c.* 1887
Pointed. Iron. Closed *c.* 1956 and now derelict. (SD).

— R.C., Corpus Christi, Waterloo Rd.   1894.
Corrugated iron. Succeeded by Corpus Christi, Lyons Crescent in 1904. (CD, 1901; Neve 1933).

— St. Bapt., Zion, Pembury Rd.   1867.
Classical. Brick. Pedimented porch. Gift of the Misses Nye; built by Punnetts. (K; RFC).

— Bapt. Cong., High St.   1871.   C. G. Searle of Bloomsbury.   £1,425.
Gothic. Brick and stone dressings. Built by Powell and Everest. Renamed 'Baptist church' 1878. New façade and Dec. window 1903. Severely flooded 1968, vacated 1972, sold to International Stores and demolished. (K; B, 1873, 1879; Bailey, 1970; Binney and Burman, 1977).

— Cong., High St.   1875–6.   £4,500.
Early Geom. Rag. Porch. The munificent Samuel Morley, benefactor. Gallery. Sands, bldr. Succeeds chapel in Back Lane. Replaced on site 1978. (*Tonbridge Free Press*, 14 October 1876; Neve, 1933; bicent, 1951).

TONBRIDGE (*continued*)   Indep., Ebenezer, Bradford St.   1898.
   Pointed. Red brick. Superseded Ebenezer Calvinistic ('Piper's Chapel') of 1857. Closed 1971
   and now a store. (K; Neve, 1933; Bailey, 1970).

—*   Cong., Cage Green Mission Room, Shipbourne Rd.   1874.
   Brick and tile roof. Vernacular. Gabled. Demolished 1970. Congregation removed to Bishop's
   Oak Ride. (C, 1970: Neve, 1933).

—   W., East St.   1872.   Cattermole and Eade of Ipswich.   £2,293.
   Dec. Red brick and stone dressings. Galleries. Built by C. Punnett and Sons of Tonbridge.
   Succeeds more modest chapel of 1829 built on the same site (then Swan Lane) 'in the
   "packing case" style of architecture'. (K; Neve, 1933).

—   W. School, Barden Rd.   1869.
   Dec. Banded brick. Plate tracery. Used as mission from 1890–1909. School built 1901. Now
   adult education centre. (Bailey, 1970).

—   United Methodist Free, Priory St.   1868.
   Renaissance. Polychromatic brick. Succeeds chapel across the road. Closed 1919 and since
   used for storage. (SD; Neve, 1933).

—   Free C. of E., Christ Church, Lansdowne Rd.   1874.
   Iron, nicknamed 'the Tin Tabernacle'. Erected for the Revd. William Scorer Seymour, whose
   duties at the parish church were terminated. School-room added 1875. Has served as Truscott's
   bindery, the Working Men's Club and for over fifty years as workshops for Tonbridge school.
   (Neve, 1933).

—*   Salvation Army Citadel, Lyons Crescent.   1898.   Probably Alexander Gordon.
   Dutch gable. Red brick with stone dressings. Purchased 1928 from Tonbridge Citadel Co. Ltd.
   (Major David Blackwell).

—   C.C., Shipbourne Rd.   1856-7.   Thos. Talbot Bury.   £2,300.
   Dec. Rag and stone dressings. Built by Geo. Punnett on land bought for £1,250. Two chapels,
   joined by an arch. The Noncomformist chapel now serves as a workshop. (Neve, 1933).

—*   Tonbridge School Chapel, Shipbourne Rd.   1859.   Wadmore and Baker.   £2,500.
   Dec. Sandstone. Built by George Punnett. Never consecrated. Became school museum 1892,
   since used as the school library and for general purposes. (Neve, 1933; Pev).

—   Tonbridge School Chapel, London Rd.   1900-2.   Campbell-Jones.
   Perp. Red brick and sandstone. Succeeds temporary iron chapel of 1892 on site of Ferox
   Place. *Builder* (1892) gives Jas Brooks, late 15th-cent, fan vaulting. (Neve, 1933).

TOVIL, *see* Maidstone

TUNBRIDGE WELLS   C. of E., St Barnabas, Stanley Rd.   1889-90.   J. E. K. and J. P. Cutts.
   £15,000.
   Lancet style. Red brick with stone dressings. Clerestoried nave. Flèche. Consec. 1893. (Betj;
   Pev).

—*   C. of E., Christ Church, High St.   1835-41.   R. Palmer Browne of Greenwich.   £8,500.
   Neo-Norman. White brick and stone. Castellated square tower. Galleries. Glass by Morris and
   Burne-Jones. Money given in trust to the town by Revd. Thos. Ward Franklyn. Bldrs., Cole,
   Thorpe and Scuntlebury. (SD; Pev).

—   C. of E., Good Shepherd, Vernon Rd.   1886.
   Kent. Iron. Became a school when St Barnabas was built 1890 and remained in use until the
   building of St Barnabas' schools. (Copus, 1970).

—*   C. of E., Holy Trinity, Church Rd.   1827-9.   Decimus Burton.   £10,591.
   Perp. Local sandstone. Commissioners' church built by Henry and Aaron Barrett of Tunbridge
   Wells, improved 1880, destined for demolition by verdict of the Church Commissioners, but
   reprieved and converted 1981 to an arts centre. (SD; Port, 1961).

TUNBRIDGE WELLS (*continued*)   C. of E., St James, Sandrock Rd., Calverley Plain.   1860–2.
        Ewan Christian.   £6,000.
    Dec. Jackwood sandstone and Wadhurst stone. Spire. N aisle added 1880. Fabric donated by
    the Wards of Calverley estate. (SD; Eastlake, 1872).

—*   C. of E., St John, London Rd. (St John's Rd.).   1858.   A. D. Gough.   £3,044 4s. 6d.
    Dec. Rag. Additions by Cronk and glass by Kempe. Originally built with S tower and spire,
    rebuilt in present position 1896. (SD; Cent, 1958).

—   C. of E., St John's Mission, Shatters Rd. (Silverdale Rd.)   1895.
    Demolished for St Luke 1910. (St John's cent.).

—*   C. of E., St Mark, Broadwater Down.   1864–6.   R. L. Roumieu.
    Late Italian Gothic. Bath stone and local sandstone. NW spire 140 ft. Glass by Clayton and
    Bell. Bldr., G. Mansfield. The gift of the Revd. Wm, 4th Earl of Abergavenny. (SD).

—   C. of E., St Peter, Windmill Fields (Bayhall Rd.)   1874–5.   Henry Hickman Cronk.
    Dec. Sandstone. Spire. N aisle 1889 by Cronk and Cronk. Bldrs., Willicombe and Oakley.
    (Cent. 1974).

—   C. of E., St Stephen, Camden Rd.   1870.   Arthur W. Blomfield.
    EE. Tiled. Erected as mission church for St James at sole cost of Revd. H. W. Hitchcock.
    Became a centre of ritualist controversy and was demolished 1889 for the building of St
    Barnabas on same site. (K; SD; Copus, 1970).

—   R.C., St Augustine, Grosvenor Rd.   1837–8.   Joseph Ireland.   (Campanile 1889 by Brett
        A. Elphicke).
    Classical. Local sandstone. Closed 1967 and pulled down 1968 for supermarket. (K; SD; CD;
    Hitchcock, 1954; *Kent and Sussex Courier*, 24 May 1968).

—*   St. and Part. Bapt., Hanover, Hanover Rd.   1834.   Henry Kewell.   £1,265 incl. land.
    Gable ended. Red brick. Porch. (SD; Pearce. 1904; Strange, 1930).

—   St. Bapt., Rehoboth, Chapel Pl.   1851.
    Classical. Brick with stucco façade. (SD; Pearce, 1904 RFC).

—   Bapt., Tabernacle, Calverley Rd.   1883.   Lander and Bedells of London.   £5,759.
    Early Dec. Red brick and Bath stone. Galleries. With school, to which more rooms were added
    1892. Succeeded 1938 by the new Tabernacle in Upper Grosvenor Rd. (B, 1833).

—*   Bapt., St John's Free, Mount Ephraim.   1899.   Herbert Murkin Caley of Tunbridge Wells.
        £7,560.
    Gothic. Red brick with stone dressings and slate roof. Church and porch surmounting lecture
    rooms. Fleche. Open framed roof. Built by J. Marshall, incl. adjoining Manse. Later St
    Andrew's Presbyterian church and now URC. (B, 1902).

—   Cong., Bethel, Tutty's village (Hawkenbury).   1839.   £200.
    Continued in use until 1894 when lease expired. (Timpson, 1859; Pearce, 1904; anon.
    typescript in Tunbridge Wells reference library).

—*   Cong., Mount Pleasant.   1845–8.   Possibly Jabez Scholes.   £3,700.
    Tuscan portico façade (added 1866 for £1,400). Sandstone. Succeeded chapel of 1720.
    Alterations 1871 by Chas. Pertwee of Chelmsford and 1885 R. S. Lander. Concluded religious
    life as Pentecostal 1977–80 after congregation had united with Presbyterians. Converted
    1981–3 to Habitat store. (SD; Strange, 1930; *Kent and Sussex Courier: Focus*, 28 June 1980).

—   Cong., Albion Rd.   1873.   J. Sulman.   £2,600.
    Dec. Rag and Bath stone with slated roof. Adjoining Sunday and day schools built 1876 at cost
    of J. Remington Mills. Closed *c.* 1929; used 1930s for anti-aircraft activities and since 1945 as
    a garage. (BA, 1875; C, 1875; SD; Bailey, 1970).

—*   Cong., Forest Rd. (Hawkenbury).   1889.   Potts, Sulman and Hennings.
    Plain. Red brick and tiled roof. Turret. Gift of Mr. Le Lacheur. Schoolroom added 1907, and
    church hall 1926. (C, 1889; SD; Strange, 1930).

TUNBRIDGE WELLS (*continued*) *   Countess of Huntingdon's Connexion, Emmanuel, Mount
        Ephraim.   1867.   Wimble and Taylor.   £5,000.
    Dec. Rag. with Bath stone. Side galleries; needle spire 140 ft. Succeeds humbler edifice opened
    on adjacent site by George Whitfield in 1769. Demolished 1974 and now hospital forecourt.
    SD; Pev; Binney and Burman, 1977).

—*   W., Vale Rd.   1872–3.   Chas. Bell of London.   £5,000.
    Early French Gothic. Kentish rag and Bath stone dressings; slate roof. Perp. tracery; pinnacles.
    Succeeds earlier building of 1812. Built by Willicombe and Oakley. (SD; *Sussex Weekly
    Advertiser*, 10 June 1873).

—   Bible Mission Hall, John St.   1873.
    Domestic. Rendered with slated roof. Double porch. Known 1930s as the Old Hall. Passed
    subsequently to St John's parish church and bought 1980 for use as a studio. (Pearce, 1904;
    Occ.).

—   W. Mission, Hill St.   1875.
    'Tin tabernacle' (secondhand). Replaced 1904 by the brick chapel which was taken by
    Plymouth Brethren 1934 as Salem. (Pearce, 1904; Bailey, 1970).

—   Prim. M., Down Lane (Culverden Down).   1874.
    Pointed. Brick. Sold to Congregationalists 1884, for whom it functioned as Down Lane hall,
    a branch of Mount Pleasant. Then successively occupied by Pickfords as a furniture store,
    by Pentecostals (Assemblies of God) as Glad Tidings Hall and, since 1979, as Down Lane
    Hall Antiques. (SD; Strange, 1949; deeds).

—   Prim. M., Camden Rd.   1877–8.   Weeks and Hughes.   £4,000.
    Renaissance. Brick with Bath stone dressings. Gallery on iron columns. Price exceeding
    estimates by £1,000 and hampering activities until 1900. In use as antiques saleroom since
    1982. (K; RIBA).

—   Indep., Salem, St John's Rd.   1866.
    Erected for Thos. Edwards, min. of Rehoboth, when he repudiated believers' baptism.
    Brethren 1903–34 then sold to Bus company and replaced by garage. (Pearce, 1904; RFC;
    Bailey, 1970).

—   Disciples of Christ, Commercial Rd.   1877.   £600.
    Gable ended. White brick and stone dressings. Now Church of Christ. (Pearce, 1904).

—*   Salvation Army Citadel, Varney St.   1886.   E. J. Sherwood.
    Romanesque. Red brick. Scrolls, pilasters and classical ornaments. Succeeded by Bayhall Rd.
    1970 and demolished. (Bailey, 1970; cent, 1979).

—   Breth., Meeting Room, York Rd.   *c.* 1891.
    Classical Stucco. (SD).

—   Bible Mission, St John's Rd.   1894.
    Eclectic. Ashlar. Lancets. Porch. Financed by Mrs. Bingham for Pastor John McAuliffe.
    Wesleyan from 1907. Disappeared early 1930s. (K; Pearce, 1904; SD; Bailey, 1970).

—*   Society of Friends, Grosvenor Park.   1894.   £2,100.
    Domestic. Red brick with stone dressings. Meetings were previously held in the successive
    homes of Mary Walker in Calverley Park and, from 1889, the Mechanics Institute in Dudley
    Rd. (Lewes and Chichester Monthly Meeting, viii. 1894; Pearce, 1904; Showler, 1970).

—   Breth., Gospel Hall, Quarry Rd.   1898.
    Gift of Miss Woodfell. Became builders' workshop early 1930s. (Pearce, 1904; SD; Bailey,
    1970).

—   C.C., Trinity, Woodbury Park.   1849.
    Lancets. Sandstone. (Pelton's *Guide*, 1881).

—*   C.C., Frant Forest (Benhall Mill Rd.).   1873.   E. W. Stephens of Maidstone.
    Dec. Rag. Two chapels aside an arch surmounted by a spire. Constable of Penshurst, bldr.
    (*Sussex Weekly Advertiser*, 12 August 1873; *Tunbridge Wells Gazette*, 24 October 1873).

TYLER HILL* Bapt. 1885. £210.
   Vernacular. Red and white brick with slate roof. Pointed windows. Branch of Baptist church
   at St George's Place, Canterbury. (B, 1886).

UNDERRIVER   C. of E., St Margaret.   1867.   G. G. Scott.   £2,500.
   EE. Rag. Cost borne by Rt.-Hon. J. R. Davison. (BA, 1868; Preb. D. Lynch).

UPNOR   C. of E., St Philip and St James, Upnor Rd.   1878.   Ewan Christian (though *Builder*
   says Scott).
   EE. Red brick with tiled roof. Spirelet. Lancets. Rounded apse. Paid for by Capt. and Mrs.
   Savage. (*Builder* xxxvi; Pev).

—   Cong., High St.   1898.   £700.
   Plain. Brick with stone facings. Closed ante-1967 and sold for dwelling, pulpit-rail being
   transferred to Cuxton. (C, 1899; K; Revd. S. G. Sexton of Vines, Rochester).

—   W., Lower Upnor.   1843.
   Extant 1851. (RC).

UPPER HARDRES   W.   1883.   £211.
   Extant 1939. (W, 1883; OS, 1939).

UPSTREET   Cong., Island Rd.   1848.
   Vernac. Brick. Converted 1958 to two private dwellings, 29–31 Island Rd. (C, 1848; Timpson,
   1859; McIntosh, 1979; Upstreet Post Office).

WALMER   C. of E., St Mary (New Church), St Clare's Rd.   1887-8.   Arthur Blomfield.
   EE and Tans. Rag, lined with brick. Clerestoried nave. Lancets. W tower 1893. (K; Basil;
   Clarke, 1966).

—   C. of E., St Saviour, The Strand.   1848-9.   John Johnson.
   Dec. Rag. Open wood bell turret (now removed). N aisle added 1895. Built as chapel-of-ease
   to serve the needs of boatmen. (E, 1853; Basil).

—   R.C., Sacred Heart of Jesus, Dover Rd.   1881.   Pugin and Pugin.
   Gothic. Yellow brick with stone dressings and slated roofs. Tower added 1897. Convent choir
   chapel demolished 1982; the remainder survives in use. (K; Fr. Cyril Williams, parish priest).

—   C. of E., Garrison (Royal Marines), Canada Rd.   1858.
   EE. Brick with slated roof. Bellcote and lancets. Served weekdays as school. Now a concert
   hall, following building of new chapel within barracks 1904. (K; Mr. Reed, verger).

WALTHAM*   W., Petham Rd.   1887.
   Lancet style. Flint and brick with slate roof. Façade part rendered (weatherboarded since
   1978). Adjoining meeting-room now demolished as it was sinking. Closed *c.* 1970 and appre-
   ciatively occupied as a private dwelling since 1975. (Occ.).

WAREHORNE*   Bible Ch., Providence, Leacon.   1866.
   Vernacular. Sandstone and rendered. Porch. Follows earlier chapel of 1842 and survives in
   Methodist use. (RC).

WEALD, *see* Sevenoaks Weald.

WELLING   Iron church, Hook Lane.   1869.
   Chapel-of-ease to Christ Church, given by Alfred Dean Esq. Superseded 1926 by St John,
   Danson Lane. Site sold to post office. (Bexley *Guide*, n.d.; Mr. F. W. Price, churchwarden).

—   Indep., Providence, New Rd.   1831.   £450.
   Followed tent of 1830. Closed 1846, reopened 1847, recognized as Union church 1889.
   Superseded 1960s and now in Pentecostal use. (Mearns, 1882; *Trans. Cong. Hist. Soc.* 7; Mrs.
   A. D. Dyer, sec.).

WESTERHAM   Cong., Fullers Hill.   1839.
   Classical. Rendered. Pediment. Has remained apart from URC. (C, 1855; Timpson, 1859; Miss
   K. E. Lowin of Dunton Green).

WESTGATE-ON-SEA   C. of E., St Saviour, Westgate Rd. (Westgate Bay Avenue).   1873–4.   C. N.
      Beazley.   £6,000.
    Dec. Rag; tiled roof. NW tower linked to nave. Glass 1887 by Kempe. Built by Naylor of
    Rochester. (Pev).

—*   Cong., Christ Church, Westgate Rd.   1883.   John Sulman.   £1,592.
    Gothic. Red brick. Buttressed. Campanile. (C, 1882; Mr. Tim Catherall).

WEST LANGDON   C. of E., St Mary.   1869.
    EE. Knapped flint with stone dressings. Lancet and bellcote. Rebuilding. (K).

—   Cong.   1863.
    Lancet style. Rendered brick, slated roof. (K; Revd. David Williams, min.).

WEST MALLING   Bapt., Swan St.   1836.
    Classical proportions with pointed windows. Brick; façade now rendered. Renovated 1894 for
    £399. (B, 1895; K).

WESTMARSH   C. of E., Holy Trinity, Ware.   1841.   G. Russell French.
    Lancet. Yellow brick with tiled. Porch. Bellcote. Closed c. 1970 and now a store. (K; Pev;
    Mrs. L. Foat).

—   W., next Fairview Farm.   1897.   £120.
    Iron. Cause failed and closed 1966 and sold 1970. (Worship certificate and correspondence in
    Folkestone reference library).

WESTWELL   Indep. 1821.
    Extant 1851. (RC).

—   W., 1846.
    In use 1851. (RC).

WEST WICKHAM   C. of E., St Augustine Mission, High St.   1869.
    Wood. Given by Lewis Loyd Esq. as chapel-of-ease to St John the Baptist. Known locally as
    'the village church' and early 20th cent. as St Christopher. Superseded 1933 by St Francis of
    Assisi and now occupied by Jehovah's Witnesses. (Watson, 1959; Revd. J. D. B. Poole).

—   Cong., North Rd.   1887.   Potts, Sulman and Hennings.   £315.
    Simple. Red brick and tiled with timber framing. Lancets. W. Grubb of Bromley, bldr. Closed
    1929 and succeeded by Emmanuel. (C, 1888; Sheen, 1980; Hewitt, 1964).

WHITFIELD   Cong., Forge Lane.   1867.   £150 3s. 10d.
    Lancets. Stock brick and slated roof. (Dover chap, 1959).

WHITSTABLE   C. of E., St Alphege, High St.   1844–5.   Hezekiah Marshall of Canterbury.
    Dec. tracery. Rag façade, brick sides and buttresses; slate roofs. Castellated tower. (K; Pev).

—   C. of E., St Peter Mission, Harbour Place.   Ante-1878.
    Brick. Superseded 1903 in Sydenham St. Subsequently independent. (PO; Green, 1955).

—   R.C., Church St. (— Rd.), Tankerton (Castle Rd.).   c. 1899.
    Long since removed. (K; Sister of Mercy).

—   Bapt., Middle Wall.   1875.   £500.
    Plain. Brick. Galleries. Extended 1911. (B, 1877).

—   Indep., Zion Chapel, High St.   1833.   £1,000.
    Brick. Destroyed by fire 5 October 1854. (C, 1856; Timpson, 1859).

—*   Cong., Zion, High St.   1855.
    Classical. Brick with stucco façade. Galleries. Succeeded earlier chapel destroyed by fire.
    Sunday schools 1891. Sold 1980, converted for £75,000 and opened April 1982 as Whitstable
    Playhouse. (C, 1855, 1856; Timpson, 1859; *Kent Gazette*, 16 April 1982).

—   W., Argyle Rd.   1866–8.   Thos. Grant Cozens.
    Classical. Brick with stone dressings. Named St John's Methodist church 1932; renovated
    1968. (Revd. Bernard Moss, min.).

WHITSTABLE (*continued*)   Prim. M., Albert St.   1864.
Plain. Brick with rendered façade. Closed and derelict.

— Salvation Army Barracks, High St.   1887.
Plain. Brick with rendered façade. Built and leased by Amos and Foad. (*Kent Gazette*, 6 December 1887).

— Mission Hall, Island Wall.   Ante-1895.
Iron. Winter months only. Closed *c.* 1960.

— Ply. Breth., Harbour St.   Ante-1899.
Classical façade. Brick. In Brethren use 1938, latterly Evangelical. (K).

— C.C., Millstrood Rd.   1854(first burial).
Lancet style. Rag and slated roofs. Porches. Two chapels, separate buildings, the W chapel now a store. (Cemetery supt.).

— R.C., St Vincent's Orphanage, Church St.   1901.
Ground floor served as R.C. mission until 1906, thence in educational use. (Bernard Kelly, 1907; Sisters of Mercy).

WICKHAMBREAUX   W., Wickham Rd.   1890.   £689.
Lancet style. Red brick and white dressings with slated roof. Sold 1975 and converted to private dwelling. (W, 1891; Mr. A. Wimble, county architect).

WILLESBOROUGH   C. of E., Christ Church, Hythe Rd. and Albemarle Rd.   1874.   Joseph Foster.
EE. Rag-faced. Bell turret. Proprietary chapel in the parish of St Mary Virgin. (K).

WILMINGTON   C. of E., St Michael. 1839.   (N aisle E. Cresy) and 1884 (chancel Ewan Christian).
Victorian rebuilding on to W end. (Pev).

WINGHAM   Indep., North Court Rd.   1835.   £1,000.
Classical. Stock brick. Cost defrayed by Samuel Toomer, father of the pastor, to replace old General Baptist chapel. School built 1855, restored 1885. Closed and latterly Toomer House Antiques. (Timpson, 1859; Occ.).

— W., High St.   1848.
Patterned brick and slated roof. Closed ante-1895, and used by Buffs as drill hall and latterly by printers as workshop (RC; K; Occ.).

WITTERSHAM   W., The Street.
Lancet style. Red brick with slated roof; sides of hung tiles. Closed 1980 when faithful remnant started worship to parish church. Succeeded wood and iron chapel. (Mr. C. K. Packham).

WOMENSWOULD, *see* Wymynswold.

WOODCHURCH   Bible Ch., Bethel, The Green.   1821.
Built on to back of Mr. Hukins' house. Wesleyan from 1851. Followed by present church 1902. (RC; Woodchurch Parish Magazine, January 1983).

—* Bible Ch., Zion, Front Rd.   1851.
Pointed. Brick with slated roof. Closed 1934. Converted to dwelling 1981. (RC; Mr. L. M. Chowns, circuit archivist; Woodchurch Parish Magazine, January 1983).

— Mission Room, Chapel Hill.   1899.
Red brick with tiled roof. Porch.

WOOLWICH   C. of E., Christ Church, Shooter's Hill.   1855-6.   Tress and Chambers.
EE. Rag with slate roof. Bellcote; lancets. (Vincent, 1890; Baker, 1961; Clarke, 1966).

—* Garrison Church of St George, Grand Depot Rd.   1863.   T. H. and Digby Wyatt.   £18,000.
Adapted Lombardic. Stock, red and blue brick. Iron columns. Gallery. Clerestory. War Dept. gave money. Destroyed by flying bomb 13 July 1944; consecrated grounds and ruins are preserved as memorial garden (BA, 1864; Vincent, 1890).

WOOLWICH (*continued*)   C. of E., Trinity Episcopal Chapel, Rope Walk (Beresford St.)   1833.
        J. D. Hopkins.
    Georgian. Stucco. Galleries on iron columns. W tower. Built as proprietary chapel; became
    chapel-of-ease 1850. Interior alterations 1883. Closed 1960 and demolished 1962. (Vincent,
    1890; Basil; Port, 1961; Binney and Burman, 1977).

—   C. of E., St John the Evangelist, Wellington St.   1845-6.   Francis E. H. Fowler.   £5,478.
    EE. Stock brick. Tower only to roof level. Built by Charles Kirk. Commissioners gave £2,012.
    Additions 1886 by Ewan Christian built by Dove Bros. for £1,016. Restored from decay 1912
    but war damaged and demolished 1948. (Vincent, 1890; Basil; Port, 1961; Baker, 1961).

—   C. of E., St Michael and All Angels, Borgard Rd.   1875 (chancel).
    EE. Brick. Vaulted. Clerestoried nave 1888 by Butterfield. Succeeds iron church 1868.
    Damaged both in WW I and in 1944, when services continued in the roofless church. Restored
    1955. (Vincent, 1896; Clarke, 1966).

—*   R.C., St Peter, New Rd.   1842-3.   A. W. N. Pugin.
    Dec. Brick with stone dressings. (Ferrey, 1861; Vincent, 1890; Stanton, 1971).

—   C. of E., Royal Dockyard Chapel.   1857.   George Gilbert Scott.   £8,000.
    EE. Redbrick with black bands. Galleries. Admiralty granted the money. Consec. 1863.
    Disused *c.* 1920. Removed to Rochester Way 1932 as St Barnabas. Bombed, restored 1956.
    (Basil; Baker, 1961; Clarke, 1966).

—   St. Bapt., Carmel, Anglesea Rd.   1857.
    Classical. Brick and stone dressings. Succeeding chapel in New Rd. from 1850. Closed 1884,
    reopened 1885, closed 1908, army contractors WW I, then Oddfellows and lately St Peter's
    youth club. (*Earthen Vessel*, February 1850; Vincent, 1890; K. Whitley, 1928; Baker, 1961).

—*   Bapt., Parsons Hill.   1857.
    Lancet style. Towers. Used by Woolwich tabernacle from 1879 and enlarged 1881 for £1,600.
    Sold to Co-op. 1901. (B, 1882; Vincent, 1890; Pev; Baker, 1961).

—   Bapt., Elm Grove St.   1872.
    Church divided 1873 and remnant extended work through tent missions and ceased 1876.
    (Whitley, 1928).

—   Bapt., Cave Adullam, Ordnance Rd.   1877.
    Until 1879. (Whitley, 1928).

—   Bapt. M., Purrett St.   1891.
    Until 1926. (Whitley, 1928).

—*   Bapt. Tabernacle, Beresford St.   1896.   W. H. Woodroffe.   £10,000 estim., excl. site.
    Georgian. Red brick and Monks Park stone dressings. Surmounting schoolroom-cum-lecture
    hall. Contractor Jas. Smith and Sons of South Norwood. Closed 1969 and demolished. (B,
    1896; Mr. and Mrs. E. Johns).

—   Cong., Rectory Place.   1858.   Lander and Bedells.   £3,000.
    Dec. Spire. McLennan and Bird, bldrs. Succeeds Ebenezer, an auction room in William St.
    adapted for worship in 1852. (C, 1859; Timpson, 1859; Vincent, 1890).

—   Cong., Viewland Rd.   1900.
    Pointed. Corrugated iron. Stet. as Plumstead URC. (C, 1901).

—   Scots Presb., New Rd.   1842.   £4,000 upwards.
    Brick with stone dressings. Renovated *c.* 1878. United with St Andrew 1924. (K; Cairns, 1913;
    Presbyterian Handbook, 1959-60).

—   Presb., Anglesea Hill (— Rd.).   1868.
    Iron. Removed from Salem. Replaced 1871-2. (Vincent 1890).

—   Presb., St Andrew, Anglesea Hill (— Rd.).   1872.   £7,000.
    Galleries later. United with New Rd. 1924, then used as synagogue. (Vincent, 1890; *Presby-
    terian Handbook*, 1959-60; Baker, 1961).

WOOLWICH (*continued*)   W., William St. (Calderwood St.).   1818.
Classical Brick. For many years the Methodist garrison chapel. Now Sikh temple. (Baker, 1961).

—   W., Beresford St.   1840.
Plain. Brick with slated roof. Branch of William St. United Methodist by 1890. Purchased by Salvation Army 1899 and converted to citadel. (Vincent, 1890; K; Major D. Blackwell, ARIBA).

—   W., Sand St.   1844.
Baptist from 1882. Extant 1928. (Vincent, 1890; K; Booth, 1902; Whitley, 1928).

—   W., Shooters Hill Chapel, Red Lion Lane.   1873.
Iron. Erected on plot of land behind Royal Military Academy. Dismantled soon after congregation jointed Plumstead common 1902. (Baker, 1961).

—   W., Sutcliffe Rd.   1885.
Iron. Succeeded by hall in Timbercroft Rd. (Baker, 1961).

—   Bible Ch., Zion, Upper Market St. 1828.
Built by Mr. Bossey. Converted to a school upon erection of Herbert Rd. chapel. 1887. (Vincent, 1890).

—   Woolwich C.C., King's Highway.   Post-1856.
EE. Red brick with stone dressings and slated roof. Octagonal spire. (Vincent, 1890; Meller, 1981).

WOULDHAM   Prim. M., High St.   1867.
Brick. Follows chapel of 1848. Demolished post-1936. (RC; K; OS).

WYE*   W., Bridge St.   1869.
Pointed. Polychromatic brick. Succeeds 1824 chapel in Luckley's field where is now Taylor's garage. (Hooper, 1921; Dr. C. P. Burnham).

WYMYNSWOLD   Bapt., Woolage Green.   1887.   £190.
Plain. Stock brick with slated roof. Porch. (B, 1889; K).

YALDING   Bapt., Spurgeon Memorial, Vicarage Rd.   1892.   John Wills of Derby.   £760.
Lancet style. Red brick with Bath stone dressings; slated roof. Mancktelow Bros., bldrs. Schoolroom 1894. (B, 1893 and 1895).

—   Breth., Benover.   Ante-1887.
Iron. Following meetings in old farmhouse. Closed pre WW II, used as Scout hut, dismantled 1942 by doodlebug. (RC; K; Mr. Titterall of Benover).

INDEX OF ARCHITECTS

This list includes architectural works in Kent from 1818 to 1901. New buildings are listed first within each entry and are followed by restorations, rebuildings, extensions, completions and so on in parentheses. Dates given are those of the commencement of works.

Alexander, Daniel A.
    1818   Maidstone prison chapel
Andrews, Thomas, of Margate
    1893   St Mary, Northdown, Margate
    1894   All Saints, Westbrook, Margate
Appleton, Herbert David and Mountford,
        Edward W.
    1882   St Paul, Forest Hill
    1884   Elm Road Baptist, Beckenham
Arnold, Thomas
    1887   Vanbrugh Park Presbyterian,
        Blackheath
Ashenden, W. and Sons
    1828   St Mary Sutton Valence
Ashpitel, Arthur
    1852   St John the Evangelist, Blackheath
    (St Mary Ripple 1861)
Austin, H. J.
    1867   Christ church, South Ashford
    1868   Beulah chapel, South Ashford
Ayton-Lee, E. C.
    1888   Emmanuel, Deptford

Baines, George
    1887   Sidcup Congregational
    1890   Congregational school chapel, Bexley
    1895   East Greenwich, Baptist
Banks, William Coppard
    1870   St Mark, Lewisham
    1878   St George, Catford
Barber, W. Swinden, of Halifax
    1862   Holy Trinity, Lee
Barker, A. Rowland
    1878   St John the Baptist, Folkestone
    1900   Christ church, Sidcup (and Son)
Barker, J. T.
    1883   St John, Presbyterian, Forest Hill
Barnes, David
    1829   Trinity, Broadstairs
Barnes, F.
    1863   St George, Bickley
Bartleet, W. Gibbs
    1885   St George, Beckenham
Basevi, George
    1823   St Mary, Greenwich

Beaumont, J. W. and R. F.
    1887   Cresent Rd. Congregational,
        Beckenham
Beazley, C. N.
    1872   St James, Garlinge
    1873   St Saviour, Westgate-on-Sea
    1876   St Mildred, Acol
    (All Saints, Birchington, 1864)
Bell, Charles
    1872   Tunbridge Wells Wesleyan
    1885   Herne Bay Wesleyan
    1886   St Augustine, Grove Park
    1891   Rushey Green Wesleyan, Catford
Bentley, John Francis
    1897   St Luke, Chiddingstone
Besborough, A.
    1870   St Andrew Presbyterian, Gravesend
Bignell, Jabez
    (SS Peter and Paul, Swanscombe, 1872)
Birch, of Margate
    1856   Margate cemetery
Blandford, H., of Maidstone
    1861   St John the Evangelist, Maidstone
Blashill, Thomas
    (Christ church, Herne Bay, 1878; St Mary
    Virgin, Orlestone, 1883)
Blashill, Thomas and Hayward, Charles Forster
    1876   Christ church, Beckenham
Blessley, R. K., of Eastbourne
    1872   St Paul, Margate
Blomfield, Arthur W.
    1868   St Mary, Strood
    1870   St Stephen, Tunbridge Wells
    1875   St John the Baptist, Eltham
    1876   St Michael and All Angels,
        Maidstone
    1887   St Mary, Walmer
    1890   St Cyprian, Brockley
    (Holy Trinity Dartford, 1862; St Mary
    Virgin, New Brompton 1868; All Saints,
    Snodland, 1870; SS Peter and Paul, Ley-
    bourne, 1873; St Mary Virgin, Upchurch,
    1875; St Mary, Riverhead, 1882; St Mary,
    Chatham, 1884; St Mary, Lewisham; St
    Peter, Brockley)

Bodley, George Frederick
    1873   St Michael, Folkestone
    (St James, Bicknor, 1859; Holy Trinity,
    Mark Beech, 1892)
Bond, George E., of Rochester
    1892   Ebenezer Congregational, Chatham
    1893   Primitive Methodist, Chatham
Bonella and Paull
    1893   Congregational school chapel, St
            Mary's Cray
Bonner, Horace Thomas, of Eastbourne
    1883   St Lawrence mission, Catford
Brandon, David
    1852   Holy Trinity, Mark Beech
    1870   Private chapel, Bayham Abbey
Brooks, James
    1868   All Saints, Northfleet
    1868   Annunciation, Chislehurst
    1881   Transfiguration, Lewisham
    1893   SS Peter and Paul, Dover
    (SS Peter and Paul, Worth, 1888)
Brown, John, of Norwich
    1839   St Margaret, Lee
    1848   Christ church, Greenwich
            (with Robert Kerr)
Browne, R. Palmer, of Greenwich
    1835   Christ church, Tunbridge Wells
Bulmer, Martin
    1865   St Margaret's cemetery, Rochester
Burges, William
    1873   All Saints, Murston
Burton, Decimus
    1827   Holy Trinity, Tunbridge Wells
    1830   St Peter, Southborough
    1831   St Mary, Riverhead
Bury, Thomas Talbot
    1850   St Mary Virgin, Kingsdown
    1856   Tonbridge cemetery chapels
    1859   St James, Dover
    (SS Peter and Paul Temple Ewell, 1874)
Butterfield, William
    1845   St Augustine's college, Canterbury
    1853   St Mary, Langley
    (St Nicholas, Thanington, 1846; St Nicholas,
    Ash, 1847; St Martin, Great Mongeham,
    1851; St Lawrence, Godmersham, 1865;
    St Mary, Milstead, 1872; St Andrew, Buck-
    land, 1876; St Michael, Woolwich, 1888)

Caley, Herbert Murkin, sometime mayor of
            Tunbridge Wells
    1878   Herne Bay Baptist
    1898   Southborough Wesleyan
    1899   St John's Free church, Tunbridge
            Wells
Campbell-Jones, W.
    1900   Tonbridge School new chapel

Carey
    1870   Bredgar Wesleyan
Carpenter, Richard Cromwell
    1856   Christ church, Milton
    (St Mary, Stowting, 1843; St Laurence,
    Hawkhurst, 1853)
Cattermole and Eade
    1870   Southborough Wesleyan
    1872   Tonbridge Wesleyan
Cawston, Arthur
    1886   St Luke, Bromley Common
Chadwick, W.
    1847   Huggens college, Northfleet
Champneys, Basil
    1874   St Luke, Matfield
    1900   SS Andrew and Michael, Greenwich
Chapman, J. Wallis
    1887   Union chapel, Pembury
Chidgey, H. T. A., of London
    1899   Cecil Square Baptist, Margate
Christian, Ewan
    1843   St John the Evangelist, Hildenborough
    1851   St Stephen, Tonbridge
    1852   Christ church, Forest Hill
    1858   St Peter, Rochester
    1860   St Paul, Swanley
    1860   St James, Tunbridge Wells
    1868   Holy Trinity, Folkestone
    1876   St Saviour, Tonbridge
    1878   SS Philip and James, Upnor
    1879   Holy Trinity, Lamorbey
    1889   St Andrew convalescent home,
            Folkestone
    1894   All Souls, Cheriton
    (St John the Baptist, Sutton-at-Hone 1862;
    St Mary, Horton Kirby, 1862; St Peter,
    Bredhurst, 1866; SS Peter and Paul, Sutton,
    1860s; St Margaret's-at-Cliffe, 1869; St Mary
    of Charity, Faversham, 1873; St Mary,
    Stone-in-Oxney, 1874; St John the Baptist,
    Margate, 1875; All Saints, Boxley, 1875;
    St Lawrence, Bidborough, 1876; St
    Nicholas, Sevenoaks, 1878; SS Mary and
    Sexburga, Minster-in-Sheppey, 1879; St
    Peter, Southborough, 1883; St Michael,
    Wilmington, 1884; St Mary Virgin, Woodnes-
    borough, 1884; All Saints, Allhallows, 1886;
    All Saints, Waldeshare, 1886; St John the
    Evangelist, Woolwich, 1886; St Peter
    Cudham, 1891; St Thomas, Charlton, 1892;
    St Peter, Whitfield, 1894; St Dunstan,
    Cranbrook)
Clarke, A. H.
    1899   Baptist school chapel, Broadstairs
Clarke, E. F. C.
    1879   St Mary, Mottingham
    1881   St Mary Cray cemetery

Clarke, G. Somers
1866   Our Lady convent chapel,
          Hildenborough
Clarke, Joseph
1876   St Mary Virgin, Hillborough,
          Reculver
1878   St Bartholomew, Dover
(All Saints, Brenchley, 1849; St Peter,
Broadstairs, 1852, 1859; St James, Egerton,
1854; SS Peter and Paul, Headcorn, 1854,
1868; St John the Baptist, Wateringbury,
1856; St Paulinus, Crayford, 1862; St
Clement, Sandwich, 1865; St Catherine,
Preston-next-Faversham, 1866; Holy Cross,
Hoath, 1867; St Peter Oare, 1868; St
Margaret Rainham, 1869; St Michael,
Smarden, 1869; Holy Trinity, Sittingbourne,
1873; St George, Ham, 1879; St Giles,
Wormshill, 1879; St Margaret, Wichling,
1882; SS Peter and Paul, Bilsington, 1883;
St Giles the Abbot, Farnborough, 1886)
Clarke, Thomas Chatfield
1867   Eltham Congregational
Clayton, Alfred Bowyer
1835   Christ church, Herne Bay
Clutton, Henry
1862   St Michael, Chatham (nave)
(1874   St Mary, Chislehurst, mortuary
          chapel for Louis Napoleon)
Cole, J. K.
1884   Luton Bible Christian
1886   Plumstead Bible Christian
Collins, H. H.
1865   Rochester synagogue
Cooke, C. H.
1865   St Mary Virgin, Ide Hill
1883   St John, Plumstead
Cozens, Thomas Grant
1866   Whitstable Wesleyan
Cresy, Edward
(St Michael, Wilmington, 1839; Holy
Trinity, Dartford, 1846)
Cronk, Henry Hickman
1874   St Peter, Tunbridge Wells
Cronk and Cronk
(St Peter, Tunbridge Wells, 1889)
Crowther, C. L.
1901   Wesley hall, Deal
Crutchloe, E.
1886   St John the Baptist, Chislehurst
Cutts, J. E. K.
1879   St Matthew, Sydenham
Cutts, J. E. K. and J. P.
1889   St Barnabas,
          New Brompton
1889   St Barnabas,
          Tunbridge Wells

Dawkes, Samuel Whitfield
1848   Holy Trinity, Old Brompton
1851   St James, Gravesend
Day, R. Philip, diocesan architect
1898   St John the Evangelist, Herne Bay
1901   St Mary, Milton Regis
Devey, George
1871   Leigh undenominational
Dinwiddy, Thomas, of Greenwich
(Christ church, Greenwich, 1887)
Drewe, Alfred and Bower, William George
1876   Cliftonville Wesleyan
Dunk, William and Geden, J. M.
1884   Wesleyan school chapel, Sidcup
(Blackheath Wesleyan 1884)

Edmunds, William, of Margate
1825   Holy Trinity, Margate
Edmunds, W. M.
1883   Holy Trinity, Dover
Elliott, H.
1878   St Mildred, Lee
Elphicke, Brett A.
(St Augustine, Tunbridge Wells 1889)
Elworthy, Messrs., of St Leonard's-on-Sea
1898   Hawkhurst Wesleyan
Emmett, John
1865   Holy Trinity, Sydenham

Farley
1885   Baptist school chapel, Herne Bay
Fawcett, W. M.
1895   St Barnabas, Boughton
Fellowes-Prynne, George Halford
1882   St John the Evangelist, Sidcup
1901   All Saints, Sydenham
Ferrey, Benjamin
1857   All Saints, Blackheath
1863   St Andrew, Sibertswold
(St Nicholas, Chislehurst, 1849; All Saints,
Woodchurch, 1858; St Mary V. Wingham,
1874)
Finlay, G., of Clapham Junction
1881   Brockley Rd. mission church,
          Brockley
Fletcher, Banister
1876   Brockley Wesleyan
Foster, Joseph
1874   Christ church, Willesborough
Fowler, Francis E. H.
1845   St John the Evangelist,
          Woolwich
French, G. Russell
1841   Holy Trinity, Westmarsh
Fuller, Henry
1867   Trinity Congregational,
          Forest Hill

Galton, Capt.
    1860   Herbert hospital chapel, Greenwich
Gardner, Joseph, of Folkestone
    1856   Congregational, Folkestone
    1857   Folkestone cemetery
    1865   Folkestone Wesleyan, Grace Hill
    1867   Hythe Congregational (and school-
           rooms, 1870)
    1873   Salem Baptist, Folkestone
    1878   Faversham Congregational
    1882   Deal Congregational
    1895   Etchinghill hospital chapel
           (with John Ladds)
    1897   Radnor Park Congregational,
           Folkestone
Garling, R. H.
    (St Thomas, Southborough, 1888)
Gibson, Jesse
    1819   Queen Elizabeth almshouses,
           Greenwich
Gordon, Alexander
    1898   Tonbridge Salvation Army
Gordon, John, of Sheerness
    1895   Bethel, Isle of Grain
Gough, Alexander Dick
    1853   St Paul, Chatham
    1858   St John, Tunbridge Wells
Gough, Hugh Roumieu
    1886   St Lawrence, Catford
Gough and Gough
    1875   Hospital chapel, Chartham
Gould, John
    1838   Princes Street Congregational,
           Gravesend
Grant, William Leonard, of Sittingbourne
    1887   Sittingbourne, Bible Christian
    1892   Sacred Heart, Sittingbourne
    (Sittingbourne Baptist, 1887; Holy Trinity,
    Milton Regis, 1889)
Gray, Searle and Son
    1867   Brockley Rd. Baptist, Deptford
Green, T. K.
    1870   Christ church, Southborough
Gwilt, Joseph
    1849   St Thomas, Charlton

Habershon, W. G.
    1853   Erith Independent (with brother
           Edward)
    1873   All Saints, Plumstead
    (St Peter, Boughton Monchelsea, 1874)
Habershon and Brock
    1869   New Brompton Congregational
Habershon and Pite
    1865   Maidstone Congregational
    1867   Crayford Baptist
    1868   Trinity Baptist, Bexleyheath

Habershon and Pite (*continued*)
    1871   Christ church, Chislehurst
    1876   Erith Primitive Methodist
    (St John the Baptist, Erith, 1877)
Hakewill, Henry
    1863   All Saints, Foot's Cray
    (St Margaret, Barming, 1850)
Hall, Edwin T.
    1881   St Paul, Four Elms
Hall, John Green, Canterbury city architect
    1874   St Thomas, Canterbury
    1876   Congregational, Canterbury
    1877   Canterbury cemetery
    1880   St Andrew Presbyterian, Canterbury
Hansom, Joseph Aloysius
    1881   St Joseph, Greenwich
    (St John the Evangelist, Gravesend, 1851)
Harbour, of London
    1892   St Joseph iron, Bromley
Hardwick, Philip Charles
    1847   St Margaret, Collier Street
    1855   St John, Deptford
    1857   Clergy orphan school, Canterbury
Harston, C. and A.
    1878   Imbecile asylum chapel, Darenth
Haughton, S. W., of East Grinstead
    1884   Pembury Wesleyan
    1886   East Peckham Wesleyan
Hawkes, George F., of Birmingham
    1892   Hawkhurst Baptist
Hay of Liverpool
    1850   St John the Evangelist, Kingsdown
Hellicar, Evelyn
    1887   St Mark, Bromley
Hemsley, Henry
    1827   St George, Ramsgate
Hesketh
    1877   Queen Street Baptist, Erith
Hight, Frank
    1840   Salem Baptist, Dover
Hills, Gordon M.
    1863   St Michael, Tenterden
    (St Peter, Newenden, 1859; St John,
    Chatham, 1863; St Mildred, Tenterden,
    1864: St Mary, Sutton Valence, 1874;
    St Margaret, Broomfield, 1879)
Hinde, Harold
    1894   Erith cemetery
Hinds and Son
    (Broadstairs Congregational, 1890)
Hine, George T.
    1899   Bexley hospital
Hine, James and Smith, T. Roger
    1863   Queens Rd. Congregational,
           Forest Hill
Hollands, W. T.
    1893   Rothbury hall, Greenwich

Mileham, C. H. M.
  1901   St Mark, Plumstead
  (St Philip, Sydenham, 1896)
Mocatta, David
  1833   Ramsgate synagogue
Moore, R. H.
  1864   Widmore Baptist, Bromley
Morphew and Green
  1858   St John, Sevenoaks
Multon, J.
  1867   Our Immaculate Mother, Northfleet
Murray, Andrew
  1898   Stone hospital chapel
Murray, John C. T.
  1895   Trinity Presbyterian, Bromley

Nash, Edwin
  1850   St James, North Cray
  1851   All Souls, Crockenhill
  1864   St Philip, Sydenham (with J. Round)
  (St Martin of Tours, Chelsfield, 1857; St
  Bartholomew, Sydenham, 1857; St Mary, St
  Mary Cray, 1861)
Nash, J. W.
  1887   Strood Jubilee Wesleyan
  1895   Strood Gospel mission
  1898   Wesley hall, Strood
Newberry, John E.
  1892   St Andrew, South Cray
Newman, Arthur H.
  1883   St Mark, Deptford
Newman, Dudley
  1900   St Mary Virgin, Swanley
Newman and Billing
  1864   Christ church, Deptford
  1866   St James, Kidbrooke
  1870   St Peter, Eltham
  (St George, Wrotham, 1861)
Newman and Newman
  1890   St George, Blackheath
  (St Peter, Eltham, 1895)
Newton, Ernest of Bickley
  1881   Good Shepherd, Lee
  1892   St Swithun, Hither Green
Norris, E. J.
  1885   Foot's Cray Baptist

Oakley, William
  1872   St Augustine, Honor Oak

Parrish, T. W.
  1891   Congregational school chapel,
          Sheerness
Peck and Stephens, of Maidstone
  1858   Maidstone cemetery
  1859   St Paul, Maidstone
  1860   King Street chapel, Maidstone

Pertwee, Charles, of Chelmsford
  1875   Bower chapel, Maidstone
  1897   Belvedere Congregational
  (Tunbridge Wells Congregational 1871)
Pocock, William Willmer, himself a Wesleyan
  1844   Dartford Wesleyan
  1852   Sevenoaks Wesleyan
  1875   Bromley Wesleyan
Pocock, Corfe and Parker
  (Dartford Wesleyan, 1869)
Pope, R. P.
  1854   Holy Trinity, Larkfield
  (SS Peter and Paul, Luddesdown, 1866)
Potter, M. T.
  1889   St John the Evangelist, Dunton Green
Potts, Sulman and Hennings
  1887   West Wickham Congregational
  1889   Hawkenbury Congregational
Pouget, Francis
  1861   Deptford Congregational
Poulton, W. F.
  1863   Union chapel, Canterbury
  1866   Ashford Congregational
Poulton and Woodman, of Reading
  1860   Union Crescent Congregational,
          Margate
  1860   Milton Regis Congregational
  1864   Herne Bay Congregational
Pover, Edwin
  1898   Faversham Bible Christian
  1898   Faversham cemetery
Pownall, H.
  1860   St Thomas, Southborough
Poynter, Ambrose
  1848   St Andrew, Deal
Pugin, Augustus Welby Northmore
  1842   St Peter, Woolwich
  1844   The Grange, Ramsgate
  1847   St Augustine, Ramsgate
Pugin, Edward Welby
  1860   St Augustine monastery, Ramsgate
  1865   St Catherine, Kingsdown
  1865   St Teresa of Avila, Ashford
  1865   SS Henry and Elizabeth, Sheerness
  1867   St Paul, Dover
  (St Augustine, Ramsgate, 1857)
Pugin and Pugin
  1881   Sacred Heart, Walmer
Purdie, A. E.
  1890   Our Lady Help of Christians,
          Blackheath
  1893   Virgin Mother, Hythe

Ranger, W., of London
  1878   Goudhurst, Wesleyan
Read, Thomas, of Deal
  1820   Dover General Baptist

Rebecca, J. B.
   (St John the Baptist, Penshurst, 1820)
Reeve, B. J.
   (St Peter, River, 1876)
Reeve, R. Dalby
   1896   Margate Wesleyan
Richie and Brandon
   1853   Blackheath Congregational
Rickman, Thomas, a Quaker
   1839   Holy Cross, Goodnestone
             (with Hussey)
Rickman and Hutchinson
   1831   St Mary, Lower Hardres
Rickwood, William, of Plumstead
   1858   St Margaret, Plumstead
   1873   College Park Baptist, Lewisham
Robson, E. R.
   1884   Christ church, Chatham
Rose, H. and E.
   1853   St Mark, Rosherville
Roumieu, R. L.
   1864   St Mark, Broadwater Down,
             Tunbridge Wells
Round, J. N.
   1864   St Philip, Sydenham
             (with Edwin Nash)
Rowland, John
   1893   Holy Trinity, Charlton
Rowse, A. G.
   1877   Bromley Common Primitive
             Methodist
Ruck, Son and Smith
   1882   Tonbridge Rd. Wesleyan, Maidstone
Rule, William T.
   1897   Bethel, Queenborough

St Aubyn, James Piers
   1864   St Mark, New Brompton
   1874   Christ church, Erith
   (St Michael, Harbledown, 1880; St Margaret,
   Halstead, 1897)
Salvin, Anthony
   1839   Christ church, Kilndown
   1853   St Mary, Betteshanger
Scholes, Jabez
   1845   Tunbridge Wells Congregational
Scott, George Gilbert
   1846   Christ church, Ramsgate
   1848   St Gregory, Canterbury
   1853   Christ church, Lee
   1857   Woolwich dockyard chapel
   1861   All Saints, Hawkhurst
   1862   St John, Higham (?)
   1862   All Saints, Langton Green
   1863   St Stephen, Lewisham
   1870   St Margaret, Underriver
   1871   Ramsgate cemetery chapels

Scott, George Gilbert (*continued*)
   (St Margaret, Canterbury, 1850; St Paul,
   Canterbury, 1856; St Mary Virgin, Hayes,
   1856; St Mary, Patrixbourne, 1857; St
   Mary of Charity, Faversham, 1858, 1873;
   St Peter, Bridge, 1859; St Mary Magdalene,
   Cobham, 1860; St Mary-in-Castro, Dover,
   1860; St John the Baptist, Penshurst, 1864;
   St Dunstan, Frinsted, 1870; Rochester
   cathedral, 1870; All Saints, Chillenden,
   1871; St Bartholomew hospital chapels,
   Chatham and Sandwich)
Scott, George Gilbert, Jnr.
   1870   St Mary Virgin, Speldhurst(?)
   (All Saints, Hollingbourne, 1876)
Scott, John Oldrid
   1870   St Mary Virgin, Speldhurst
             (says Pevsner)
   (St Mary Virgin, Hayes, 1878; St Nicholas,
   New Romney, 1880; St Bartholomew
   hospital chapel, Sandwich, 1887)
Scott, W. Gilbert
   1893   St George mission, Brockley
Scott and Moffatt
   1843   Christ church, Dover
Searle, C. G., of Bloomsbury
   1871   Tonbridge Baptist–Congregationalist
Seddon, John Pollard
   1869   Orphanage, St Peter's
Seth-Smith, William Howard
   1885   Congregational school chapel, Lee
   1896   St Luke, Maidstone
Seward, Thomas
   1878   Strode Crescent Baptist Sheerness
Shaw, Richard Norman
   1893   All Saints, Galley Hill
Sherwood, Major E. J., Salvation Army
   1885   Ramsgate Salvation Army
   1886   Tunbridge Wells Salvation Army
Slater, William
   (Christ church, Gravesend, 1856; St Mary,
   Stowting, 1857; St Laurence, Hawkhurst,
   1859; St Dunstan, Cranbrook, 1863; Christ
   church, Milton)
Smirke, Robert
   1821   St John the Divine, Chatham
Smirke, Sydney
   1850   Christ church, Folkestone
Smith, Albert William, of Maidstone
   1883   Sellindge Wesleyan
   1891   Wesleyan garrison chapel,
             Old Brompton
Smith, George
   1829   St Michael and All Angels,
             Blackheath Park
Smith, James Moffat
   1858   Erith Congregational

Smith, W.
    1865   St Saviour, Forest Hill
Smith, William Bassett
    1890   St Luke, Gravesend
    1901   St Paul, Plumstead
Smith, W. E., of London
    1873   St Catherine, Manston
    1875   St Luke, Ramsgate
Smith
    1879   Holy Trinity mission, Greenwich
Smith and Williams
    1872   St Paul, Beckenham
Stallwood, Spencer Slingsby, of Folkestone
    (St Peter, Folkestone, 1870; SS Mary and
    Eanswythe, Folkestone, 1872; St Nicholas,
    Rodmersham, 1875)
Stenning, A. R.
    1879   St James, Beckenham
Stenning, A. and Hall, H.
    1878, 1884   St Barnabas, Beckenham
Stenning and Jennings
    (Christ church, Dover, 1895)
Stephens, E. W., of Maidstone
    1846   St Peter, Pembury
    1862   St John, Higham(?)
    1872   St Faith, Maidstone
    1881   St Mary, Burham
    1873   Tunbridge Wells cemetery
    (St Philip, Maidstone, 1869, 1878; St Mary,
    St Mary's Hoo, 1881)
Stevens, H. J., of Derby
    1849   St Paul, Rusthall (with N. E. Stevens)
Stevens and Alexander, of London
    1844   Trinity, Ramsgate
Stokes, Leonard
    1889   Our Lady Help of Christians,
           Folkestone
Street, George Edmund
    1868   Holy Trinity, Eltham
    1870   St Andrew, Gravesend
    (St Mary Virgin, Stone, 1859; St Bartholo-
    mew, Otford, 1863; St Mary, High Halden,
    1868; St Mary, Chartham, 1873)
Strudwick, P. V.
    1894   St Luke cemetery, Bromley
Sulman, John, Congregationalist
    1873   Milton Congregational
    1873   Albion Rd. Congregational,
           Tunbridge Wells
    1874   Wycliffe Congregational, Gravesend
    1878   Congregational school chapel,
           Beckenham
    1881   Widmore Congregational,
           Bromley
    1882   Congregational school chapel,
           Dartford
    1883   Westgate-on-Sea Congregational

Sulman and Rhodes
    1873   Sutton Valence Congregational

Tarring, John
    1853   Vines Congregational, Rochester
    1865   St John's Congregational, Sevenoaks
    1866   Lewisham Congregational
Tarver, E. J.
    (St Peter, Fordcombe 1883)
Taylor, George Ledwell
    1828   St George, Sheerness
    1835   Holy Trinity, Sheerness
Taylor, Henry
    1887   St Paul's mission, Rusthall
Teulon, Samuel Saunders
    1849   St Paul, Sandgate
    1865   St Paul, Greenwich
    1866   St Peter, Greenwich
    (St Mary, Westerham, 1854; Ebony church
    to Reading Street, 1858)
Teulon, W. M.
    1880   St Margaret, Halstead
Theobalds, William
    1878   Providence chapel, Curtisden Green
    1882   Lee Bible Christian
Thorne, Francis Freeman, of Lee
    1873   Lee Cemetery
Tinkler and Morphew
    1857   Dartmouth Road Baptist,
           Forest Hill
Tolley and Son
    1899   St George school chapel, Catford
Townsend, P. L. Banks
    1884   Blackheath Congregational school
           and vestries
Tress, W.
    1835   Bromley chapel
Tress and Chambers
    1855   Christ church, Woolwich
Trimen, Matthew
    1850   Park chapel, Sydenham
Truefitt, George
    1876   Bromley cemetery
    1879   St John the Evangelist,
           Bromley
Tucker, of Dover
    1876   River Wesleyan

Vaughan, G. T.
    (Christ church, Herne Bay, 1868)
Vicars, Albert
    1890   Our Lady of the Sacred Heart,
           Herne Bay
Vulliamy, George and Johnson, John
    1855   St Mary, Greenhithe
Vulliamy, Lewis
    1827   St Bartholomew, Sydenham

Wadmore and Baker
    1859   Tonbridge school chapel
    (All Saints, Tudeley, 1885)
Wadmore, Wadmore and Mallett
    (St Mary, Plaistow, 1899)
Wallen, F.
    1868   St Mary Bredin, Canterbury
Waller, J. C., of Dartford
    1874   Dartford Primitive Methodist
Walters, Frederick Arthur, Roman Catholic
    1882   Our Lady and St Philip Neri,
             Sydenham
    1885   St Thomas, Deal
    1893   St Patrick, Plumstead
    1896   St Thomas, Sevenoaks
    1900   St Anselm, Dartford
    (St Michael, Chatham)
Wardell, William Wilkinson
    1851   Our Lady Star of the Sea,
             Greenwich
    1854   St Mary, Chislehurst
Waring and Blake
    1863   Bromley college chapel
    1863   St Mary, Plaistow
Waterhouse, Alfred
    (St Martin, Brasted, 1864)
Watson, T. H.
    1870   St Luke, Deptford
Weeks and Hughes
    1877   Primitive Methodist,
             Tunbridge Wells
Weir, James
    1884   Tenterden Wesleyan
    1887   Bromley Rd. Wesleyan,
             Beckenham
Wheeler, Robert, of Brenchley
    1869   All Saints, Horsmonden
    1872   St Paul, Sheerness
    1873   St Paul, Ramsgate
    1874   St Clement, Leysdown
    1875   St John the Baptist, Swalecliffe
    (St Nicholas, Otham, 1864; St Peter, Pem-
    bury, 1867; St George, Wrotham, 1876;
    St Paul, Margate)
Whichcord, John, Sen., of Maidstone
    1826   Holy Trinity, Maidstone
    1839   St Stephen, Tovil
    1840   Christ church, Dunkirk
Whichcord, John the Younger
    1867   Blessed Virgin Mary, Beckenham
Whichcord and Walker
    1841   St Mary Platt
    1842   Holy Trinity, East Peckham

Whichcord and Whichcord
    1856   St Philip, Maidstone
    (St John the Baptist, West Wickham 1847)
Whitaker, E. W.
    1884   Elmers End Congregational,
             Beckenham
White, William
    (St Clement, Knowlton, 1855; St Mildred,
    Preston, 1857; St Andrew, Deal, 1867;
    Holy Innocents, Adisham, 1869; St George,
    Ramsgate, 1884)
Wigginton, William
    1866   St Paul, Charlton
Wild, James William
    1838   Holy Trinity, Blackheath
Williams, Walter A.
    1887   Christ church, Bromley
Willis, A.
    1882   Belgrave St. Primitive Methodist,
             Dover
Wills, John, of Derby
    1881   Victoria Baptist, Deal
    1886   Brasted Baptist
    1886   Vine Baptist, Sevenoaks
    1887   Townend memorial chapel,
             Knockholt
    1889   New Brompton Baptist tabernacle
    1892   Yalding Baptist
    1897   St Lawrence Wesleyan
    1899   Cavendish Baptist schools, Ramsgate
Wilson, James, of Bath
    1838   Ramsgate Congregational
    1840   Cavendish Baptist, Ramsgate
    1844   Holy Trinity, Milton
    1863   Blackheath Wesleyan
Wimble and Molyneux
    1860   Sittingbourne cemetery chapels
Wimble and Taylor
    1867   Countess of Huntingdon,
             Tunbridge Wells
Wollaston
    1844   St John the Evangelist, Sidcup
    (St Nicholas, Chislehurst, 1857)
Woodroffe, W. H.
    1896   Woolwich Baptist tabernacle
    1900   Perry Rise Baptist lecture hall,
             Sydenham
Wray, C. G.
    1880   St Francis, Maidstone
Wyatt, Thomas Henry
    1863   St George, Woolwich
    (St Margaret, Horsmonden, 1867; SS Peter
    and Paul Shorne, 1874)

BIBLIOGRAPHY

Amery, Colin and Cruickshank, Dan (1975) *The Rape of Britain* (London: Elek)

Andrews, Jessie Forsyth (*c.* 1930) *In Newest Kent: a Congregational Reconnaissance*

Architect, The

Architectural Review

Ashford: a Record of 500 Years (1970) (Ashford)

Bailey, Lorna and Brian (1970) *A History of the Nonconformist Churches in Tunbridge Wells, Tonbridge and Southborough* Typescript in Tunbridge Wells reference library

Baker, L. A. J. (1961) *Churches in the Hundred of Blackheath* Greenwich and Lewisham Antiquarian Society

Baldock, Kay and Hales, Irene (1980) *Old Maidstone* (Rainham: Meresborough)

Baptist Handbook

Baptist Historical Society, *Transactions of*

Barr, John (1975) *Derelict Britain* (Harmondsworth: Penguin)

Batcheller, W. (1828) *A New History of Dover* (Dover: Kings Arms Library)

Beckenham Journal

Belsey, F. F. and Dunstall, W. (1899) *Centenary of Ebenezer Sunday School, Chatham 1799-1899* (Chatham: W. & J. Mackay)

Betjeman, John (1958) *Collins Guide to English Parish Churches* (London: Collins)

Betts, Maria (1888) *The Dickensons: or, God's Work in Pembury* (Tunbridge Wells: A. K. Baldwin)

Bible Christian Magazine

Binney, Marcus and Burman, Peter (1977) *Chapels and Churches: Who Cares?* (London: British Tourist Authority)

Bird, James E. (1974) *The Story of Broadstairs and St Peter's* (Broadstairs: Lanes)

Bishop, C. H. (1973) *Folkestone: the Story of a Town* (Ashford: Headley)

Blackwell, David (1965) *Salvation Army Corps Buildings* Unpublished thesis

Blunt, J. H. (1874) *Dictionary of Sects, Heresies, Ecclesiastical Parties and Schools of Religious Thought* (London: Rivingtons)

Boggis, R. J. E. (1907) *A History of St Augustine's College Canterbury* (Canterbury: Cross & Jackman)

Boorman, H. R. Pratt (1942) *Hell's Corner 1940* (Maidstone: *Kent Messenger*)

Booth, Charles (1902) *Life and Labour of the People of London* 3rd series. (London: Macmillan)

Borrowman, Robert (1910) *Beckenham, Past and Present* (Beckenham: Thornton)

Bourne, Frederick William (1905) *The Bible Christians: their Origin and History* (London)

Bourner, M., Hull, F. and Tate, R. (n.d.) *A History of Bearsted and Thurnham* (Bearsted and Thurnham History Book Committee)

Bradford, Gary (1972) *Dissent in Eden: the History of the Nonconformists in Edenbridge*

British Almanac and Companion (London: Charles Knight)

Broadstairs Congregational Church (1951) *Congregationalism in Broadstairs: a Brief History of 1601-1951*

Bromley, J. (1837) *History of Bromley Chapel*

Bromley Record

Bromley Times

Buckingham, Christopher (1967) *Lydden: a Parish History* (Lydden: Thomas Becket Books)

Buckingham, Christopher (1968) *Catholic Dover* (Lydden: Thomas Becket Books)

Builder, The

Bushell, T. A. (1976) *Barracuda Guide to County History, 1: Kent* (Chesham, Barracuda)

Cairns, John (1913) *John Hawkes and his Successors* (Woolwich: W. J. Squires)

Cantacuzino, Sherban; Halls, Hamish; Petrie, Flavia and Woodcock, David (1970) *Canterbury* (London: Studio Vista)

Canterburiensis (Pseud.) (1838) *The Life and Extraordinary Adventures of Sir William Courtenay* (Canterbury)

Cardozo, D. A. Jessurun and Goodman, Paul (1933) *Think and Thank: the Montefiore Synagogue and College 1833-1933* (London; Oxford University Press)

Carr, William (1951) *The Spot that is called Crayford* (Crayford Urban District Council)

Carstairs, Rowan (1979) 'The renaissance of Catholic Sheppey' *Kent Recusant History*, 2

Cass, Alex J. (1954) *The Congregational Church, Blackheath SE3: the First Hundred Years 1854-1954: a Record* (London: Blackheath Press)

Castells, F. de P. (1910) *Bexley Heath and Welling* (Bexley Heath: Thos. Jenkins)

Catholic Directory

Census of Great Britain (1851) *Returns*

Chamberlain, Frank (1964) *The First Hundred Years of Folkestone Methodism*

Chambers, Ralph F. (*c.* 1957) *The Strict Baptist Chapels of England, 3: Kent* (Thornton Heath: Chambers)

Chapman, F. (1976) *The Book of Tonbridge: the Story of the Town's Past* (Chesham: Barracuda)

Chatham News

Chatham Observer

Chowns, L. M. (1977) *Shadoxhurst: a Village History* (Shadoxhurst; the author)

Church, Derek (1976) *Cuxton: a Kentish Village* (Sheerness: Arthur J. Cassell)

Clark, W. Philip (1981) *Eythorne: Our Baptist Heritage*

Clarke, Basil F. L. (1938) *Church Builders of the Nineteenth Century* (London: S.P.C.K.)

Clarke, Basil F. L. (1966) *Parish Churches of London* (London: Batsford)

Clarke, Basil F. L. Manuscript records held by the Council for the Care of Churches, London Wall.

Clifton, Michael (1979) 'The early history of the Catholic church in Woolwich' *Kent Recusant History*, 1.

Coad, F. Roy (1968) *A History of the Brethren Movement* (Exeter: Paternoster)

Cohn-Sherbok, Dan (1981) 'Sir Moses Montefiore and the Canterbury Jewish community' *Bygone Kent*, 2

Cole, David (1980) *The Work of Gilbert Scott* (London: Architectural Press)

Congregational Historical Society, *Transactions of*

Congregational Yearbook

Cooke, S. H. (1942) *A History of Northfleet and its Parish Church* (Northfleet: Parochial Church Council)

Copeland, H. Rob (1970) *The Village of Old Beckenham*

Copus, Geoffrey (1970) *St Barnabas' Tunbridge Wells 1870-1970: Notes to accompany the Historical Exhibition*

Copus, Geoffrey (1981) *The Parish of St Barnabas Tunbridge Wells 1881-1981: a History*

Cousins, David (1981) 'Kent and the 1851 religious census' *Kent Recusant History*, 5

Cray, The

Crouch, Joseph and Butler, Edmund (1901) *Churches, Mission Halls and Schools for Nonconformists* (Birmingham: Buckler and Webb)

Daly, Augustus A. (1904) *The History of the Isle of Sheppey from the Roman Occupation to the Reign of His Most Gracious Majesty King Edward VII* (London; Simpkin, Marshall, Hamilton and Kent)

Dane, Herbert (n.d.) *The War Years 1939-1945 in Faversham and District* (Faversham: Austin)

Dane, Herbert (1954) *A Hundred Years of Faversham History 1854-1954* (Faversham: Faversham Historical Society)

Dane, Herbert (1975) *The Story of 1,000 Years* (The Faversham Society: *Faversham Papers*, 5)

Davies, C. Maurice (1873) *Unorthodox London or Phases of Religious Life in the Metropolis* (London: Tinsley)

Davies, W. S. (1967) *'In Pleasant Places' 1767-1967: the Story of Tenterden Baptist Church over Two Centuries*

Dews, Nathan (1884) *The History of Deptford* (Greenwich; republished by Conway Maritime Press 1971)

Dickens, Charles (edn. 1973) *Our English Watering Place* (Broadstairs: Dickens House Museum)

Douglass, D. Alexander (1975) *From Princes Street to Milton Mount 1662-1975*

Dover Express

Drummond, Andrew L. (1938) 'The architectural interest of the English meeting house' *RIBA Journal*, 45

Duncan, Leland L. (1908) *History of the Borough of Lewisham* (Blackheath: Charles North)

Eames, Geoffrey L. (1976) *Pastimes and Times Past in the Parish of Plaistow* Typescript in Bromley reference library

Eames, John (n.d.) *The Early Years of the Kent Congregational Association*

Earthen Vessel, The

East Kent Mercury

Eastlake, Charles L. (1872) *A History of the Gothic Revival in England* (London: Longmans Green. Reprinted by Leicester University Press 1970, edited by J. Mordaunt Crook)

Ecclesiologist, The

Elham Circuit (United Methodist) (1911–   ) *Circuit Messenger*

Elleray, D. Robert (1981) *The Victorian Churches of Sussex* (Chichester: Phillimore)

Elthamian, The

Evans, R. J. and Lee, W. L. [1930] *The Book of Church Extension in Greater London*

Evening Standard

F., A. W. (1960) *Brief Outline of the History of Deal Congregational Church*

F., C. W. (1906) 'A tour of the churches: impressionist sketches' *Lewisham Journal*

Farley, J. G. W. (1962) *Pull No More Poles: an Account of a Venture among Hop-pickers* (London: Faith Press)

Ferrey, Benjamin (1861) *Recollections of A. W. N. Pugin and his Father Augustus Pugin* (London: Scholar Press edn. 1978)

Ferriday, Peter (1964) *Victorian Architecture* (Philadelphia: Lippincott)

Folkestone Chronicle

Folkestone Herald

Funnell, K. J. (1980) *Snodland Paper Mill* (Snodland: C. Townsend Hook)

Gillham, Christopher (1968) *A History of the Independent Sect and Congregation in Dartford 1818–1968* Unpublished typescript in Dartford reference library

Gillingham Public Library *Local History Series, 6: Chronology of Gillingham 1860–1903*

Giraud, Francis F. and Donne, Charles E. (1876) *A Visitor's Guide to Faversham* (Faversham: Voile and Roberson)

Glynne, Stephen R. (1877) *Notes on the Churches of Kent* (London: John Murray)

Goodsall, Robert H. (1938) *Whitstable, Seasalter and Swalecliffe: the History of Three Kent Parishes* (Canterbury: Cross and Jackman)

Gordon, John (1898) *History of the Congregational Churches of Sheerness, Queenborough, Minster and the Isle of Grain from the Year 1725 to 1898* (Sheerness-on-Sea: the author)

Gospel Herald

Gospel Standard

Gowers, Edward and Church, Derek (1979) *Across the Low Meadow: a History of Halling in Kent* (Maidstone: Christine Swift)

Grayling, Francis (1913) *The Churches of Kent* (London: George Allen)

Green, I. W. (1955) *The Story of All Saints: a History of the Parish Church of All Saints, Whitstable*

Green, Ivan (1978) *The Book of Dover* (Chesham: Barracuda)

Green, Ivan (1980) *Yesterday's Town: Dover* (Buckingham: Barracuda)

Gregory, R. R. C. and Nunn, F. W. (1924) *The Story of Lee* (Lewisham: Lewisham Newspaper Co.)

Harland, Adrian (1981) 'Hop-picking in Kent' *Bygone Kent*, 2

Harris, John (1885) *The Parish of Erith in Ancient and Modern Times* (London: Mitchell and Hughes)

Hart, F. H. (1882) *History of Lee and its Neighbourhood* (Lee: the author)

Haslewood, Richard (1976) 'Neither time nor Hitler could destroy them' *East Kent Times*, 23 April

Herne Bay Press

Hewitt, G. (1964) *The Story of Emmanuel*

Hiscock, Robert (1976) *A History of Gravesend* (Chichester: Phillimore)

Hiscock, Robert H. (1977) 'The proprietary chapel of St John, Gravesend' *Archaeologia Cantiana*, 93

Hitchcock, Henry-Russell (1954)   *Early Victorian Architecture in Britain*   (London: Trewin: Copplestone)

Hobsbawm, E. J. and Rudé, George (1969) *Captain Swing* (London; Lawrence and Wishart)

Hodge, Sydney (1972) *The Methodist Church, East Street, Tonbridge*

Holmes, Mrs. Basil (1896) *The London Burial Grounds* (New York: Macmillan)

Holyoak, Walter (1914) *Dover Baptists: a Brief History* (Dover)

Homan, Roger (1970) 'Sunday observance and social class' In Martin, David and Hill, Michael. *A Sociological Yearbook of Religion in Britain*, 3 (London: SCM Press)

Honeysett, Reginald J. *et al.* (1969) *History of Jireh Chapel Tenterden 1841-1969*

Hook, Judith (post-1972) *Pratts Bottom: an English Village*

Hooper, Evangeline H. (1921). *A Short History of Wye* (Wye)

[Hope-Bell, E.] [1954]   *'Remembering the Way'. Brockley Congregational Church (formerly Lewisham High Road) 1854-1954*

Horsburgh, E. L. S. (1929) *Bromley, Kent from the Earliest Times to the Present Century* (S.R. Publishers, republished 1971)

Horton, W. D. (1979) *The Story of Methodism in Sevenoaks from 1746*

Howarth, W. (1885) *Greenwich: Past and Present* (London: Effingham Wilson)

Igglesden, Charles (1936) *A Saunter Through Kent with Pen and Pencil* 31 vols. (Ashford: *Kentish Express)*

Illustrated London News

Intellectual Repository, The (Monthly magazine of the New Jerusalem Church)

Jones, J. Bedworth (1910) *The History of Paradise Chapel, Milton, Kent* (Sittingbourne: W. J. Parrett)

Judd, Walter D. (1932) *The Record of Wesleyan Methodism in the Sevenoaks Circuit 1746-1932.* (Bedford: Rush and Warwick)

Judge, Roy (1973) 'Hither Green; St Swithun's parish and Corbett estate' *Transactions of the Lewisham Local History Society*

Kaehler, R. D. (1939) *Historical Records of St Andrew and St Mary Breadman, Canterbury* (MS in Canterbury reference library)

Kelly, Bernard (1907) *Historical Notes on English Catholic Missions* (London: Kegan Paul, Trench, and Trübner)

Kelly's Directory of Kent

Kelly's London Suburban Directory

Kent Advertiser

Kent and Sussex Courier

Kent Conservation Bulletin Kent Council

Kent Herald

Kentish Express

Kentish Gazette

Kentish Observer

Kent Messenger

Keyes, Sidney Kilworth (1933) *Dartford: Some Historical Notes Written and Collected* (Dartford: Perry)

Keyes, Sidney Kilworth (1938) *Dartford: Further Historical Notes Written and Collected* (Dartford: Perry)

Knight, H. T. and Duffield, F. H. (1926) *The Story of St Mary's, Shortlands* (Bromley: *Kentish District Times)*

Laker, John (1921) *History of Deal* (Deal: T. F. Pain)

Lapthorne, William H. (1971) *Historic Broadstairs*

Lawrence, Margaret (1979) *Remember East Peckham*

Lemmy, Raymond (1949) *The History of Hither Green Congregational Church, Torridon Road, Catford . . . 1899-1949* (London: Independent Press)

Lewis, Mary (1981) *Old Days in the Kent Hop Fields* (Maidstone: West Kent Federation of Women's Institutes)

Lewisham Journal

Lewisham Local History Society *Transactions*

Lidbetter, Hubert (1961) *The Friends Meeting House: an Historical Survey* (York: William Sessions)

Little, Bryan (1966) *Catholic Churches since 1623* (London: Robert Hale)

Local Government Act (1888)

London Gazette

MacDougall, Philip (1980) *The Hoo Peninsula* (Rochester: Hallewell)

Mace, J. Ellis (1902) *Notes on Old Tenterden* (Tenterden: W. Thomson)

McIntosh, Kinn H. (1972) *Sturry: the Changing Scene* (Ramsgate: the author)

McIntosh, Kinn H. (1979) *Chislet and Westbere: Villages on the Stour Lathe* (Ramsgate: the author)

Mackie, Samuel Joseph (1883) *A Descriptive and Historical Account of Folkestone and its Neighbourhood, with Gleanings from the Municipal Records* (Folkestone: J. English)

McLeod, Hugh (1974) *Class and Religion in the Late Victorian City* (London: Croom Helm)

McNay, Michael (1980) *Portrait of a Kentish Village: East Malling 827-1978* (London: Victor Gollancz)

Marsh, Ronald (1974) *Rochester: the Evolution of the City and its Government* (Rochester; City Council)

Mason, Ursula S. (1967) *St James, Kidbrooke: the Story of a Church* (Kidbrooke: Parochial Church Council)

Matkin, Robert B. (1982) *Maritime Thanet* (Thanet District Council)

Matthews, Brian (1971) *A History of Strood Rural District* (Strood: Rural District Council)

Mearns, Andrew (1882) *Guide to the Congregational Churches of London* (London: Hodder and Stoughton)

Meller, Hugh (1981) *London Cemeteries: an Illustrated Guide and Gazetteer* (Amersham: Avebury)

Methodist Church (1980) *Statistical Returns* (Manchester: Methodist Church Property Division)

Methodist Recorder

Miller, A. C. (1924) *Eythorne: the Story of a Village Baptist Church*

Montgomery, John (1962) *Abodes of Love* (London: Putnam)

Morrison, John (n.d.) *The Fathers and Founders of the London Missionary Society* (London: Fisher)

Mudie-Smith, Richard (1904) *The Religious Life of London* (London: Hodder)

Muthesius, Stefan (1972) *The High Victorian Movement in Architecture 1850-1870* (London: Routledge and Kegan Paul)

Nairn, Ian (1966) *Nairn's London* (Harmondsworth: Penguin)

Neve, Arthur H. (1933) *The Tonbridge of Yesterday* (Tonbridge: Free Press)

Newman, John (1969a) *The Buildings of England: North East and East Kent* (Harmondsworth: Penguin)

Newman, John (1969b) *The Buildings of England: West Kent and the Weald* (Harmondsworth: Penguin)

O'Rorke, L. E. (1917) *The Life and Friendships of Catherine Marsh* (London: Longmans)

Oyler, T. H. (1910) *The Parish Churches of the Diocese of Canterbury* (London: Hunter and Longhurst)

Parfitt, Andrew (1977) *Assembly of God, Brewer Street, Maidstone 1927-77 Jubilee*

Parsons, Maggy (1981) 'Hollingbourne Wesleyan chapel' *Bygone Kent*, 2

Paul, S. F. (1966) *Further History of the Gospel Standard Baptists, 5: Some Surrey and Kent Churches* (Brighton: S. F. Paul)

Pearce, Luke (1904) *Historical Associations of the Free Churches of Tunbridge Wells 1642-1904* (Tunbridge Wells: Pearce)

Pearce, Luke (1912) *Historical Associations of Pembury* (Tunbridge Wells: Pearce)

Pearce, Luke (1917) *Historical Associations of Particular Baptist Chapels* (Tunbridge Wells: Pearce)

Peculiar People

Pevsner, Nikolaus (1952) *The Buildings of England: London except the Cities of London and Westminster* (Harmondsworth: Penguin)

Philip, Alex J. (1954) *A History of Gravesend and its Surroundings from Prehistoric Times* (Wrasbury, Bucks.: the author)

Pile, C. C. R. (1980) *Cranbrook: a Wealden Town* (Cranbrook and District Local History Society)

Pitts, Hubert A. (1969) *Nineteenth Century Fragments of Methodist History* (Hythe: Methodist Church Trust)

Port, M. H. (1961) *Six Hundred New Churches: a Study of the Church Building Commission 1818-1856 and its Church Building Activities* (London: S.P.C.K.)

Porteus, Geoff (1979) *The Book of Dartford* (Buckingham: Barracuda)

Porteus, Geoff (1981) *Yesterday's Town Dartford* (Buckingham: Barracuda)

Presbyterian Church of England *Official Handbook*

Prichard, John A. (1974) *Belvedere and Bostall* (London Borough of Bexley: Libraries and Museums Department)

Pugin, Augustus Welby N. (1843) *An Apology for the Revival of Christian Architecture in England* (London: John Weale, republished Blackwell 1969)

Pugin, Augustus Welby N. (1853) *The True Principles of Pointed or Christian Architecture* (London: Henry G. Bohn)

Pullen, Doris E. (1974) *Sydenham* (Sydenham: the author)

Pullen, Doris E. (1979) *Forest Hill* (Sydenham: the author)

Punch, or the London Charivari

Redundant Churches Fund *Annual Report and Accounts*

Rhind, Neil (1976) *Blackheath Village and Environs 1790-1970* (Blackheath: Blackheath Bookshop)

Richardson, Christopher Thomas (1885?) *Fragments of History pertaining to . . . Ramsgate* (Typescript at Ramsgate reference library)

Richardson, Henry R. (1834) *Greenwich, its History, Antiquities, Improvements and Public Buildings* (London: Simpkin and Marshall)

[Ritchie, A. M.] (1948) *St George's Place Baptist Church, Canterbury: History and Manual*

Rivers, Elphinstone (1904) *Some Records of Eltham 1060-1903* (Eltham: Turner and Robinson)

Rochester Gazette

Rogers, Philip G. (1961) *Battle in Bossenden Wood: the Strange Story of Sir William Courtenay* (London: Oxford University Press)

Rogers, Philip G. (1963) *The Sixth Trumpeter: the Story of Jezreel and his Tower* (London: Oxford University Press)

Rootes, Andrew and Craig, Ian (1974) *A Mosaic History of Higham*

Roth, Cecil (1950) *The Rise of Provincial Jewry: the Early History of the Jewish Communities in the English Countryside, 1740-1840* (London: *Jewish Monthly*)

Rowberry, D. E. and Hunt, A. R. (c. 1960) *Welling Baptist Church: a Brief Record of the First 25 Years*

Royal Institute of British Architects (n.d.) *Tunbridge Wells Churches: a Short Architectural Appreciation* (RIBA: Tunbridge Wells District Branch)

Rule, William T. (1898) *History of the Congregational Churches of Sheerness, Queenborough, Minster and the Isle of Grain 1725-1898* (Sheerness: John Gordon)

Russell, J. M. (1881) *The History of Maidstone* (Rochester: Hallewell reprint 1978)

Sandall, Robert (1950) *The History of the Salvation Army, 3: 1878-86.* (London: Nelson)

Scott, George Gilbert (1879) *Personal and Professional Recollections* (London: Low)

Shaw, Thomas (1965) *The Bible Christians 1815-1907* (London: Epworth)

Sheen, Alfred L. (1980) *To God be the Glory: a History of the West Wickham and Shirley Baptist Church 1930-1980*

Shindler, R. (n.d.) *Mission Work among the Hop-pickers in the Weald of Kent* (London: Morgan and Scott);

A Short History of the Strict Baptists in the Isle of Thanet (1877) (London: Robert Banks)

Showler, Karl (1970) *A Review of the History of the Society of Friends in Kent 1655-1966* (Canterbury: Canterbury Preparative Meeting of the Society of Friends)

Smetham, Henry (1899) *History of Strood* (Rochester: Hallewell reprint 1978)

Sorrell, Mark (1979) *The Peculiar People* (Exeter: Paternoster)

Stallworthy, W. (1866) *Grateful Recollections or, a Brief History of the Planting of the Baptist Church, Meopham* (Gravesend: the author)

Standen, Hugh Wyatt (1958) *Kippington in Kent: its History and its Churches* (Sevenoaks: the author)

Stanton, Phoebe (1971) *Pugin* (New York: Viking Press)

Strange, Charles Hilbert (1930) *Mount Pleasant Congregational Church, Tunbridge Wells. A Sketch of its History 1830-1930* (Tunbridge Wells: Pelton)

Strange, Charles Hilbert (1949) *Nonconformity in Tunbridge Wells* (Tunbridge Wells: *Courier*)

Summerson, John (1948) 'Pugin at Ramsgate' *Architectural Review*, 103

Sussex Weekly Advertiser

Swaine, Anthony (1969) *Faversham: its History, its Present Role and the Pattern of its Future* (Kent County Council: Faversham Borough Council)

Sykes, David (1937) *Our Rural Deanery* (Greenwich) (Diocese of Southwark)

Taylor, Arthur F. (1926) *The Free Churches of Canterbury: a Sketch of Their History and of Their Relations to One Another*

Thornburgh, Roger (1978) *Exploring Loose Village*

Tiffin, Alfred W. (1935) *The Goudhurst Jubilee Book* (Tunbridge Wells: *Courier*)

Timpson, Thomas (1859) *Church History of Kent from the Earliest Period to the Year MDCCCLVIII* (London: Ward)

Tindall, Edwin, H. (1974) *The Wesleyan Methodist Atlas of England and Wales* (London: Bemrose)

Tomlinson, Norman (1979) *The Book of Gillingham* (Buckingham: Barracuda)

Tonbridge Free Press

Topping, K. M. (1980) *The Church of St Francis, Maidstone 1880-1980. From Mission to Parish* (Faversham: Carmelite Press)

Toy, Philip (1968) *Elham: a Village Study* (Committee for the Preservation of Rural Kent)

Trappes-Lomax, Michael (1932) *Pugin: a Medieval Victorian* (London: Sheed and Ward)

Tunbridge Wells Gazette

Turner, F. E. (1950) *The Early History of Ash Congregational Church* (Typescript in Dr William's Library)

Unitarian and Free Churches *Year Book of the General Assembly*

United Reformed Church *Year Book*

Vickers, John A. (1961) *The Story of Canterbury Methodism in 1750-1961* (Canterbury: St Peter's Methodist Church)

Vickers, John A. and Young, Betty (1980) *A Methodist Guide to London and the South-East* (Bognor Regis: World Methodist Historical Society)

Vincent, W. T. (1890) *The Records of the Woolwich District* (London: J. S. Virtue)

Wadmore, Beauchamp (1906) *Some Details of the History of the Parish of Tonbridge* (Tonbridge: M. Stonestreet)

Wakeley, R. M. (1902) *Gathered Fragments: a Memorial of Thomas Stanley Wakeley* (Oxford: J. C. Pembrey)

Wall, C. de Rockfort (1928) *Snodland and its History 55 B.C. to A.D. 1928* (Snodland: Hambrook)

Ward, W. R. (1972) *The Early Correspondence of Jabez Bunting 1820-29* (London: Royal Historical Society)

Watson, A. C. (1979) *A History of Religious Dissent and Non-conformity in Ashford, Kent* (Ashford: L. R. B. Historical Publications)

Watson, Ida L. (1959) *The History of West Wickham, Kent* (Sidcup: P. M. F. Erwood)

Watson, R. J. (1967) 'Presbyterian Canterbury' *Journal of the Presbyterian Historical Society of England*, 13

Webb, E. A., Miller, G. W. and Beckwith, J. (1899) *History of Chislehurst* (London: George Allen)

Weller, James (1844) *The Wonders of Free Grace* (Battle: Ticehurst)

Wesleyan Chapel Committee *Annual Report*

Whatmore, Leonard (1973) *Recusancy in Kent: Studies and Documents* (Hailsham: the author)

White, F. C. (1938) 'The Baptists of Greenwich' *Baptist Quarterly*, 9

White, James F. (1962) *The Cambridge Movement: the Ecclesiologists and the Gothic Revival* (Cambridge: Cambridge University Press)

Whitley, W. T. (1928) *The Baptists of London 1612–1928* (London: Kingsgate)

Whitley, W. T. (1934) 'Ashford in Kent' *Baptist Quarterly*, 7

Dr Williams's Trust (1973) *Nonconformist Congregations in Great Britain: a List of Histories and other Materials in Dr Williams's Library* (London)

Woodthorpe, T. J. (1951) *A History of the Isle of Sheppey, Kent* (Sheerness: Smiths)

Woolmer, J. (1894) *Historical Jottings of the Parish of Snodland* (Snodland: the author)

Yates, Nigel (1983) *Kentish Sources, 7: Kent and the Oxford Movement* (Maidstone: Kent Archives Office)

Young, Kenneth (1972) *Chapel* (London: Eyre Methuen)

Young, Malcolm (1968) *Tonbridge Baptist Church: 1868–1968* (Tonbridge: Tonbridge Baptist Church)

LIST OF SUBSCRIBERS

W. P. Anelay
The Marquess of Anglesey, DL, FSA, FRHistS, Hon. FRIBA, FRSL
R. A. Baldwin
Canon Colin Beswick
The Revd. Father Peter E. Blagdon-Gamlen
T. F. Blood
R. H. Bond
John Bowles
Geoffrey K. Brandwood
British Architectural Library
A. S. Brooks
Tim Tatton-Brown
F. Browne
Ivor Bulmer-Thomas
Donald R. Buttress, FSA
Ian Caldwell, BSc, BArch, RIBA
Canterbury College of Art Library
Revd. D. L. Cawley, FSA, AKC
Fred William Challenger
C. B. Chapman
Mrs. A. G. Christopherson, ARIBA

Dr. John M. Court
Revd. Dr. L. W. Cowie
Mrs. Jean Crisfield
Professor A. M. Everitt
Allen Grove
John Hammon
Dr. & Mrs. Anthony W. Henfrey
John Bernard Henman
Robert H. Hiscock
Hans-Juergen Hollerbaum
Stephen Charles Humphrey
Frank Jessup
Ronald Jessup
Denis Frederick Keeling
D. R. Kenrick
C. A. Anthony Kilmister
Revd. Brian R. Lay
Revd. Kenneth N. J. Loveless, FSA
Noel Mander
Desmond Mandeville
Colin Martin
S. G. A. Mead
John Newman
Ronald F. Newman
John Physick, FSA

N. M. Plumley
William Hugh Plummer
Ann Pym
Michael Robbins
Dr. N. A. Routledge
Roger W. Shambrook
Neil O. Skelton
Julian H. Small
Eric E. F. Smith
Revd. W. J. T. Smith
M. J. Stacey
J. J. Stanton
C. F. Stell, FSA
F. M. Strang
P. J. Tester, FSA
Roger F. S. Thorne
The Venerable G. B. Timms
Roy W. Tricker
Anthony Turner
John E. Vigar
D. Vinnels
Warwick University Library
Andrew Wells
Barbara I. Wilkinson
J. C. Wittich